People, Cultures and Societies: Exploring and Documenting Diversities

The series proposes to capture the diversities in people and their communities in India. It provides a unique and innovative resource for anthropological knowledge, philosophy, methods, and tools to understand, analyse and formulate sustainable, innovative solutions to address socio-cultural issues in India.

India is a repository of varied cultures and diversities. With the globalisation and development process, the cultural fabric is changing. Customs, traditions, beliefs, on one hand, food habits, art and craft, weaving, dyeing, and handloom artefacts, on the other, are undergoing a metamorphosis. It is imperative to explore, understand and document the process of changing diversity and relational inequalities. The series encompasses richness in art, craft, language, dance, music, folklore, food culture and beliefs, traditions and practices. It addresses the issues of development disparities, inequality, and segregation on the axes of caste, class, religion, region, ethnicity, and gender. The series publishes methodologically rigorous and theoretically sound, critical and comparative, empirical research peer-reviewed volumes related to non-codified healing practices, gender-based violence, migration induced vulnerabilities, child abuse, social identity-based work on a national, regional and local level, welcoming case studies, as well as comparative and applied research.

The series is of interest to the academicians and students in the discipline of sociology, anthropology, psychology, social work, history, philosophy, and public health, and to all of those interested in a wide-ranging overview of art, culture, and politics. It accepts monographs, edited volumes, and textbooks.

UMAKANT

Dalit Human Rights in India

State Accountability and the Crisis of Due Diligence

Springer

UMAKANT
Independent Scholar
Delhi, Delhi, India

ISSN 2662-6616 ISSN 2662-6624 (electronic)
People, Cultures and Societies: Exploring and Documenting Diversities
ISBN 978-981-95-5750-9 ISBN 978-981-95-5751-6 (eBook)
https://doi.org/10.1007/978-981-95-5751-6

This Springer imprint is published by the registered company Springer Nature Singapore Pte Ltd.
The registered company address is: 152 Beach Road, #21-01/04 Gateway East, Singapore 189721, Singapore

In memory of my father

Preface

Dalit rights are human rights. The logic for advancing Dalit human rights rests on the fact that Dalits have been facing untouchability, caste-based atrocities, discrimination, exclusion and violence for millennia. The stranglehold of the caste system remains intact, in a modified manner, to a large extent even now as it is verified by the incidents of Dalit human rights violations reported from almost everywhere in the country. In a situation wherein every day Dalits have to undergo a traumatic experience of facing caste-based abusive behaviours of the non-Dalit upper and even middle caste people, how could anyone say that there is no need to discuss Dalit human rights issues separately? The ground situations prevailing in Indian society is full of everyday ordeals of Dalits and Adivasis (Indigenous) indicating towards a life of misery and dehumanizing experiences. The lived experience of untouchability, atrocities along with discrimination and exclusion presents a dark chapter of Indian civilization's onward march.

The tentacles of the Brahmanical caste system cover almost every aspect of a human's life. In a hierarchically divided caste system, Dalits have been prescribed to do all kinds of menial and filthy jobs of cleaning society's dirt. This is, however, not to be confused with the division of labour. Ambedkar quite rightly explained that the caste system is not a division of labour; rather it is division of labourers. In this system of graded inequality there is an ascending order of reverence and a descending order of abhorrence, meaning thereby that discrimination and exclusion are inbuilt in the system itself (Ambedkar, 1979, p. 47). Commenting on Indian village, this is what Ambedkar observed. "The Indian village is not a single social unit. It consists of castes. But for our purposes, it is enough to say- I. The population in the village is divided into two sections- (*i*) Touchables and (*ii*) Untouchables. II. The Touchables form the major community and the Untouchables a minor community. III. The Touchables live inside the village and the Untouchables live outside the village in separate quarters. IV. Economically, the Touchables form a strong and powerful community, while the Untouchables are a poor and a dependent community. V. Socially, the Touchables occupy the position of a ruling race, while the Untouchables occupy the position of a subject race of hereditary bondsmen" (Ambedkar, 1989, pp. 20–21).

It is not that urban areas are different completely as far as human settlements are concerned. It is certainly not exactly like a village, but even in urban areas, traces of Brahmanical settlements/enclaves are very much present. The journey from base to the super structure of political and economic power is quite complex. Since caste system is sanctified by the religious codes, it has taken deep roots among its followers mainly the upper strata and even a certain section of the middle castes to such an extent that following the religious codes is part of duty to remain vigilant about any attempt to defy the already entrenched/internalized caste norms. Thus Ambedkar was of the view that "Psychologically, caste and untouchability are one integral system based on one and the same principle. If the caste Hindus observe untouchability it is because they believe in caste. Looked at from this point of view, the idea of hoping to remove untouchability without destroying the caste system is an utter futility which would not bear any result. The underlying idea that caste and untouchability are two different things is founded on a fallacy. The two are one and are inseparable. Untouchability is only an extension of the caste system. There can be no severance between the two. The two stand together and will fall together" (Ibid: 101).

It was for the first time in 1996 that a UN body, Committee for Elimination of All Forms of Racial Discrimination (CERD), quite emphatically asserted that the problems of Scheduled Caste and Scheduled Tribes would be covered under Article 1(1) of the International Convention for Elimination of Racial Discrimination which is basically about discrimination based on work and descent. Henceforth, several other human rights bodies in the UN have raised the concern and also given set of recommendations to the state party: India. These are Human Rights Committee, Committee for Elimination of Discrimination against Women (CEDAW), Committee for Rights of Child (CRC), Committee for Economic Social and Cultural Rights (CESCR), the erstwhile UN Commission on Human Rights and Sub-Commission on Protection and Promotion of Human Rights and several other UN human rights mechanism which are called special procedures, and also India's report has been examined at Human Rights Council as part of Universal Periodic Review (UPR) in recent years.

The year 1997 marked the golden jubilee of India's independence and also started the preparation for 50 years of adoption of the Universal Declaration on Human Rights (UDHR) of the UN to be held in 1998. These two important events inspired several Dalit civil society organizations in India to start a campaign with a call to "Cast out Caste" and "Dalit Rights are Human Rights". Thus was established the National Campaign on Dalit Human Rights (NCDHR). It started another campaign, "Stop Caste Discrimination", and collected millions of signatures from all over India which were finally submitted to the president and also the prime minister of India. NCDHR also prepared a campaign document—"Black Paper"—containing fact sheets on Dalit human rights violations and how national and international human rights standards and treaties were not being complied with. The World Conference against Racism, Racial Discrimination, Xenophobia and Related Intolerance (WCAR) was held at Durban in South Africa in 2001. As NCDHR and several other Dalit organizations decided to participate in the World Conference at Durban in 2001, it was a historic moment for Dalits at a global forum in a highly organized manner which helped them in creating global visibility and concern for Dalit human rights for the first time.

While Dalits were advocating for Dalit human rights at global level and in the process made some crucial progress at the UN and amidst denial by the Indian government delegation about the need for discussing Dalit issues at any international forum, Dalit human rights were being violated all across India in a big way. Bihar, the land of Buddha, had already become "Killing Fields" from the 1970s onwards. For more than three decades, Dalits faced all kinds of caste-based atrocities, untouchability and rape of Dalit women and were killed by private caste militias and groups of caste Hindu individuals and at times even by the state itself, which is a clear case of it being labelled as victimization of the Brahmanical Social Order's tyranny. It is certainly beyond any kind of sensibility and imagination that hundreds and thousands of innocent Dalits were killed in Bihar. Neither the state nor the society at large has been held accountable for these gross human rights violations of Dalits.

The subhuman or in other words the dehumanizing lived experiences of Dalits, which happens on a regular everyday basis, despite constitutional protections and subsequent legislations to prevent atrocities and untouchability practices in India and for the same reason Bihar is not an exception, presents a sad picture of human rights status. The human rights-based approach to governance includes three most important elements. They are Constitution and the subsequent set of legislations, due diligence and accountability. We do have a Constitution, and over the years several legislations have been passed by the government, but what about due diligence and accountability? These two elements are missing somehow. People in power and duty bearers do not even seem to be aware about the term due diligence. As it is in the governance, in policing and even in the judiciary, the human rights concepts have not taken any root. The concept of due diligence as developed by the UN human rights system in a layman's language would mean implementing the constitutional provisions and subsequent legislation in their true letter and spirit. In the UN terminology due diligence means the responsibility of the state to prevent human rights violations and protect and promote human rights in true letter and spirit, meaning thereby with proper due diligence. Holding the state and the non-state perpetrators who indulge in human rights violations accountable for their acts of omission and commission is actually part of the due diligence process. The Indian state is found to be completely negligent and non-serious about fixing the accountability and cracking the impunity which the state (duty bearers) and non-state perpetrators enjoy.

The chapters on Fundamental Rights and Directive Principles of State Policy are a brilliant example of incorporating human rights, dignity, justice and accountability into the Constitution. This is where the question of constitutional morality as was raised by Ambedkar, while the Constitution was being adopted in the Constituent Assembly of India, needs to be raised again in the context of gross injustices meted out to Dalits over the years in Bihar and elsewhere in the country. Whatever happened in the 1970s, 1980s and 1990s and whatever is still happening since 2000 onwards are clearly a reflection of the past and present testimony of inhuman nature of the state and society at large. Could they run away from their failure of not being sincere enough to honour the Constitution of India and legislations which have remained largely on paper? Non-implementation of the legislations and development schemes are a big problem in this country, and sadly enough the issues are not being sincerely addressed even by now. Constitutional bodies like the National Commission for Scheduled Castes and the National Commission for Scheduled Tribes and even statutory bodies like the National Human Rights Commission and National Commission for Women, etc., in their annual reports which are submitted to the government of India, carry a set of recommendations to be followed by the government at the centre and in the states, which are not at all sincerely complied with at both levels.

India has signed and ratified several international human rights treaties and in some cases has not signed, whereas in some other cases, it has signed but also not ratified. As part of its obligations for protection and promotion of human rights for all, it is required for the state party, India, to submit periodic reports to UN human rights treaty monitoring bodies. The experience so far has been delayed submission of periodic reports by India and complete non-compliance of the committee's recommendations for ways and means through which human rights for all could be protected and promoted. Some of UN bodies' concerns and recommendations after examining India's periodic reports have been compiled as appendix in this volume to signify their importance and the need for Indian and state governments to honour its national and international obligations on human rights.

The human rights violations of Dalits do not happen in isolation. As a matter of fact, they operate in socio-religious and cultural universe which is highly discriminatory and violent. This also holds true for non-implementation of legislations and development schemes. It is also true that violations do not happen once in a while; it is a recurrent feature, meaning thereby that state and its agencies are to be squarely blamed for their failure to prevent all such breakdown of the rule of law. The government statistics on cases of untouchability, caste-based atrocities, rapes, killings and other cognizable crimes keeps on increasing year after year, and no efforts are being made to rectify their shortcomings. This is also to say that any sincere attempts are not being made to check the ever-growing cases of caste-based discrimination, exclusion and violence against Dalits in the country. The government—both central and state—has been found to be flouting the guidelines for budgetary allocations as per proportion to Dalit's population, and whatever is allocated is diverted for other purposes, thereby violating its own guidelines on bar to diversion of allocated funds, and most of the time, the allocated funds are allowed to lapse without being used. In this way, the central government and all the state governments in India have been found to be guilty of not making allocations of funds to the tune of thousands and lakhs of crores of rupees under Scheduled Caste Sub-Plan (SCSP) and Tribal Sub-Plan (TSP).

In the post-Millennium Development Goals (MDGs) period, Agenda 2030 of the Sustainable Development Goals (SDGs) was adopted by 195 countries at the UN in 2015 to accelerate the process of an inclusive development which could cover both growth and justice. The call for leaving no one behind is a novel and very good strategic goal to fight global poverty along with discrimination and exclusion that is faced by several social, cultural, ethnic, minority and indigenous groups in different parts of the world. An intersectional approach for dealing with the question of poverty, discrimination and exclusion, thereby not enabling the economic, social and cultural rights a reality for a large number of people, could help us understand how caste-based sociocultural and religious customs and practices prevalent in societies across the world prevent the integration of a large section of these societies into the national and global mainstream. It is from this understanding about the significance of SDGs as a model for an inclusive and equitable development model which could help us in tackling the caste-based discrimination, exclusion and poverty in the most judicious manner. But in the case of India on the whole and Bihar in particular, there does not seem much progress that has been achieved as far as Dalits and Adivasis are concerned. The data that has been cited in this book reflects very clearly how communities like Dalits and Adivasis have remained on the margins in every sense of the term up to a large extent. This kind of lopsided growth model warrants a serious as well as a sincere response from the government both at the centre and in the states.

It has also been observed that the criminal justice system that we have in the country has not lived up to deliver justice to the victims and survivor's families of caste-based discrimination and violence-related cases. It is quite common to see most of the cases that are filed up in the police stations end up not delivering justice to Dalits. There seem to be problems with prosecution and chargesheeting of the investigated cases, and finally, when they reach the courts, the overwhelming majority of cases turn into acquittals, and the conviction rate is pathetically low. The judges on their part justify lower conviction and thereby higher rate of acquittals on the ground saying that the prosecution did not do its jobs in the proper manner and also the witnesses are found to be non-reliable. The lower court may give one kind of judgement which generally gets overturned by the higher courts completely. Neither the police/prosecution nor the judges pay much attention to the provisions of the special legislations like the Protection of Civil Rights Act and the Prevention of Atrocities Act and their Rules while dealing with the cases.

This is how the predicament of Dalits and Adivasis in their day-to-day life prepares the ground situations for the harrowing lived experiences in multiple forms. Instead of applying the provisions of special legislation, the police officials either do not file the first information report (FIR) or they are more interested in arranging peace meetings between Dalits and the alleged accused individuals. At times under pressure from the dominant caste people, the police have been found to threaten Dalits from filing up cases of atrocities. The crime data as revealed in the annual report like Crime in India reveals the high pendency rate of cases both for investigation by the police and also for trials by the courts. Neither the government nor the judiciary seems to be bothered much on this matter. The government in power may lack the required political will, whereas the judiciary may harp on insufficient judicial infrastructure to deal with pending cases which already run in to crores across the country. The representation of Dalits and Adivasis in the judicial services and subsequently in judges' appointment is abysmally low, which in all practical sense means nothing. This is a truth despite the fact that judges as part of their training (from acquiring law degree to regular practice or even after being appointed as a judge) do not receive any caste sensitization special training. Neither the Supreme Court nor the High Courts have taken any initiative in this regard. In such a hostile and insensitive atmosphere, is there any hope or even a scope for Dalits to secure justice? This is an issue that must be addressed by all the stakeholders, or else the claim for delivering justice would always remain hollow and partial.

Looking at the figures of right to education, literacy rates, right to health and representation of deprived community people in government services and in overall governance structure in society, economy and polity could make us question why the government has not paid the required attention to human development, poverty eradication programmes, educational empowerment programmes, right to health and other state interventions which are a must for overall development in their true sense of the term. Last but not the least, what needs to be emphasized here is the fact that this present volume seeks to not only compile and analyse cases of Dalit human rights violations from the contemporary past and also the present times, but at the same time it seeks to make it a repository for future references as far as the question of Dalit human rights is concerned. It also goes without saying that Dalit lives matter. It is indeed a long way to go for the constitutional goal of establishing an egalitarian society based on principles of liberty, equality and fraternity to be realized.

Delhi, India UMAKANT

References

Ambedkar, B. R. (1979), Babasaheb Ambedkar Writings and Speeches, Vol. 1, Bombay, Government of Maharashtra, 47.

Ambedkar, B. R. (1989), Babasaheb Ambedkar Writings and Speeches, Vol. 5, Bombay, Government of Maharashtra, 20-21 & 101.

Book Endorsements by Four Well-Known Scholars

"This volume expands the existing anthropological discourse on Dalits and their struggle for full citizenship and the realization of fundamental rights."

—**Rosa Maria Perez,** *Professor and Senior Researcher in Anthropology, Lisbon, Portugal.*

"A must-read for scholars, social and economic policy makers, and indeed, any member of the public wishing to understand how the human rights of Dalits are violated in India."

—**Rupa Viswanath**, *Professor, CeMIS, University of Göttingen, Germany.*

This will be an enriching resource book for scholars and activists interested in knowing about caste discrimination and the struggle against it.

—**Eva-Maria Hardtmann**, *Associate Professor, Department of Social Anthropology, Stockholm University, Sweden.*

"This meticulously researched book redefines our understanding of Dalit human rights and would certainly change the way one thinks about human rights."

—**Aakash Singh Rathore**, author of *Ambedkar's Preamble* and *Becoming Babasaheb.*

Acknowledgements

I have received substantial help from many people in completing this work. Prof. Aswini K. Ray shared his guidance, scholarship, and experience with me. His critical as well as constructive help was crucial in shaping this work. I express my sincere gratitude to him.

I am indebted to my parents, Munna Bhaiya, Chunnu Bhaiya, Bhabhi, Bablu, Pinki, Nishu, Rajeev, Sabuj, Harshit, and Shaurya for their much-needed support and inspiration.

My special thanks are also due to Prof. S. K. Thorat, for his encouragement at every stage in the preparation of this work. His help in terms of giving conceptual clarity and providing important data, books, and articles is duly acknowledged. Frankly speaking, I have no words to express my gratitude for all the help provided by him.

I thank Mr. Deeplal Rajak (IPS), Mr. Ram Nandan Prasad (IPS), and Mr. Amitabh Kumar Das (IPS) for their assistance during the course of data collection in Patna. P.D. Singh has been of help right from the beginning till the end of this work. My association with National Campaign on Dalit Human Rights (NCDHR), the International Dalit Solidarity Network (IDSN), and Dalit Solidarity Networks helped me in understanding the Dalit human rights issues from a broader perspective. My special thanks are also due to them. Friends are always there when I need them the most. I shall remain grateful to them. Jayant Jigyasu's kind support is warmly acknowledged.

I express my heartfelt thanks to the staff of A. N. Sinha Institute of Social Studies, Patna, the JNU Library, and Nehru Memorial Library, New Delhi, for their necessary assistance in getting access to relevant materials.

I am quite overwhelmed and express my gratitude to Prof. Rosa Maria Perez, Prof. Rupa Viswanath, Dr. Eva-Maria Hardtmann, and Dr. Aakash Singh Rathore for endorsing this book. Their insightful comments matter a lot and I shall remain grateful to them for reading the manuscript and send the endorsement despite their busy work schedule.

Thanks are also due to the blind reviewer/s and series editors of *People, Culture and Societies: Exploring and Documenting Diversities*, along with Senior Editor Books, Human Sciences, and her editorial team at Springer Nature. I shall remain indebted to them for all their kind help.

Finally, I take sole responsibility for all acts of omission and commission.

UMAKANT

New Delhi

Competing Interests The author has no competing interests to declare that are relevant to the content of this manuscript.

Contents

List of Tables

Role of the State, Political Parties, Judiciary and Media

Conclusion

Introduction

Abstract This introductory chapter examines the situation of Dalits within the Indian social structure and how it has been impacting Dalit human rights for millennia. It also attempts to understand the overall situation of Dalit human rights in India before shifting its focus to Bihar, which is the main concern of this book. This chapter highlights violations of civil, political, economic, social and cultural rights, along with caste-based untouchability and atrocities, and provides an overall situational analysis of Dalit human rights.

Keywords Dalit human rights in India · Due diligence and state accountability · Dalit human rights in Bihar · Civil and political rights of Dalits · Economic, social and cultural rights of Dalits · Caste-based untouchability and atrocities · National Crime Records Bureau (NCRB)-Crime in India · Caste and criminal justice system · Caste of convicts in Indian prisons · Caste of undertrial prisoners · Caste of detenues · Literacy rates among Dalits in India · Gross enrolment ratio (GER) among Dalits · All India Survey on Higher Education (AISHE) · Pre-Matric Scholarship for SC and ST students · Post-Matric Scholarship for SC and ST students · Dalit and Adivasi students' suicides · Dalit's economic deprivation · Dalit's access to agricultural lands · Caste and labour market · The Scheduled Caste Sub Plan (SCSP) · Dalit Adivasi budget analysis (DABA) · Dalit's right to health · National Family Health Survey (NFHS) · Life expectancy of Dalits · Constitutional and legal safeguards for Scheduled Castes and Scheduled Tribes · Bihar Caste Survey 2022–2023 · Social demographic profile of Bihar

UMAKANT, *Dalit Human Rights in India*, People, Cultures and Societies: Exploring and Documenting Diversities,
https://doi.org/10.1007/978-981-95-5751-6_1

1 Status of Dalits in Indian Society

The evolution of society and its people as per the norms of purity, pollution and the need for hierarchical ordering along with control over life and various work that each caste was supposed to do, the brahmanical caste system thus emerged long ago which still remains fully operationalized. Ambedkar was of the view that 'The basic conception of social organisation which prevails among the Hindus starts with the rise of four groups or Varnas into which Hindu Society is believed to have become divided. These four classes were named: (1) Brahmins, the priestly and the educated class, (2) Kshatriyas the military class, (3) Vaishyas the trading class, and (4) Shudras the servant class. For a time these were merely groups. After a time what were only groups (Varnas) became Castes (Jatis) and the four castes multiplied into several sub-castes. In this way, the modern caste system was only the evolution of the ancient Varna System' (Ambedkar, 1987, pp. 141–142). The Brahmanical social order thus created a strongly knit social, religious, economic and political order, where, on the one side, transgressions of rights and privileges existed and, on the other side, a set of duties were to be strictly performed, or else provisions for punishments would be prescribed.

In a hierarchically divided caste society, there were strict norms to be followed. The sanctity derived from religion had also affirmed that each varna has a specific role to play. Ambedkar further commented: 'The four-fold varna system was like a tight knit compartment where caste fluidity and caste intermingling was not allowed. According to Manu, the Hindu Law giver, there were originally four Varnas and four they must remain. He was not going to admit the untouchables who were supposed to be outside the four fold division of the caste system. That the untouchables were to remain out of the Hindu social structure is clear from the name, with which he describes the untouchables. Manu speaks of them as *Varna-Bahyas* (those outside the Varna system). They must remain separate and segregated without being a part of the Hindu Society. And if they a part they are a part but not of the whole' (Ambedkar, 1989, p. 169).

The Brahmanical social order thus created a society wherein the ascending order of reverence and the descending order of abhorrence was a normal practice. It was a clearly defined code system that had to be followed quite strictly. By implication, those who were/are below the pollution line have been called *Panchamas*, the fifth one. Legitimised by the theory of karma and reincarnation, the *Panchamas* deserved to be *untouchables* (Oommen, 1994). These kinds of segregation may not have been in practice since time immemorial, but they may have developed at a later stage in history, when orthodoxy started looming large on the horizon of Indian society. Untouchability, with its manifold manifestations, is rooted in the notions of purity and pollution, which are believed to have developed in the later Vedic period, when *Brahmanic* literature emerged in the form of *Smritis*, *Samhitas* and the *Upanishads*. In these later Vedic period texts, the *Chandala* and the *Poulkasa* are manifested as objects of spite and abhorrence. They existed at the lowest ritual and social level (Jha, 1975, pp. 28–31).

Naming and shaming is a major and unique feature of caste system segregation practices. Thus, we see nomenclature also playing an important role in deciding who stood where and what rights, privileges and duties they have. Segregation became a natural corollary to the ardently preached and widely shared belief in pollution, which in turn gave rise to several terms in the Hindu shastras, such as *Antya*, *Antyaja* and *Antyavasin*. The word *Antya* means not the end of creation but rather the end of the village. It referred to those people who lived on the outskirts of the village, i.e. on its *Antya*, who were called *Antyaja* or *Antyavasin* and were regarded as *untouchables* (Ambedkar, 1990, pp. 278–279).

The homogeneity in terms of the rules and regulations to be followed and the heterogeneity of everyday life situations may appear contradictory to each other, but both have remained essential features of the caste system. The very fact that the caste system is a well-knit social set-up makes it difficult to disentangle it from the clutches of casteism and other caste-related codes of behaviour and interactions. In this design, it was necessary to follow religious norms quite sincerely. Ambedkar further commented that 'Psychologically, caste and untouchability are one integral system based on one and the same principle. If the caste Hindus observes untouchability it is because they believe in caste. Untouchability is only an extension of the caste system. There can be no severance between the two. The two stand together and will fall together' (Ambedkar, 1989, p. 101).

Discussing how romanticisation played a role in explaining life in villages under Brahmanical rule, Ambedkar very clearly stated: 'The Indian village is an idealized world for most of Caste Hindus. The situations on the ground tell a different story altogether. The Indian village is the very negation of a republic. If it is a republic, it is a republic of the touchables, by the touchables and for the touchables. It is a kind of colonialism of Hindus designed to exploit the untouchables. The untouchables have no rights. They are there only to wait, serve and submit. They are there to do or to die. They have no rights because they are outside of village republics; they are outside of the Hindu fold. This is the vicious circle. But this is the fact, which cannot be gainsaid' (Ambedkar, 1989, p. 26).

These practices have been carefully designed and religiously put into practice and have been passed on from generation to generation. Over the millennia, their influence could be seen in varying degrees and forms in society, the economy and polity in this part of the world. Ambedkar affirmed: 'The society is highly divided internally as well as externally. The Indian village is not a single social unit. It consists of castes. But for our purposes, it is enough to say that the population in villages is divided into two sections: the touchables and the untouchables. It is also necessary to point out here that the touchables have a code, which the untouchables are required to follow. The following is a list of offences that arise from non-compliance with such codes: 'The untouchables must live in separate quarters away from the habitation of Hindus; the quarters of the untouchables must be located towards the South, since the south is the most inauspicious of the four directions; it is an offence for a member of the untouchable community to acquire wealth, such as land or cattle; it is an offence for the member of the untouchable community to put on a clean dress, wear shoes, and put on watch or gold ornaments; it is an offence for a member of the untouchable community to sit on a chair in the presence of a Hindu; it is an offence for a member of the untouchable community to ride on a horse or a palanquin through the village; and it is also an offence for the member of the untouchable community to speak a cultured language" (Ambedkar, 1990, pp. 20–22).

A caste-segregated society provides rights and privileges for a few, who are placed higher in the social hierarchy, and imposes multiple sets of duties on the larger number of people, standing at different levels in a hierarchically divided society. Ambedkar further highlighted that there are also other rules, and a contravention of any of those rules is considered an offence. Next in line come the duties, which the code requires members of the untouchable community to perform for the touchables. Under this category, the following examples may be mentioned: (a) a member of an untouchable community must carry messages regarding any event in the house of a Hindu, such as death or marriage, to his relatives living in other villages; (b) when the whole village community is engaged in the celebration of a general festivity, such as Holi or Dussehra, the untouchables are required to perform all menial works; and (c) on certain festivities, the untouchables must submit their women to members of the village community, to be made the subject of indecent fun. The list of duties to be performed by the untouchables is certainly not limited to a few tasks, and they are required to perform several other mandatory works assigned/prescribed to them without any complaint.

These and other duties have to be performed without any remuneration. Another important thing to note is that the punishment for these offences is always collective. The whole community of untouchables is subject to punishment, even though a single individual may have committed the offence. The question that needs to be asked at this point in time is this: how had it been possible for caste system and its several inhuman practices with regard to untouchable community people to have survived for so long? It may not be difficult to find the answer, and it has been clearly explained by Ambedkar in the following words: 'Of the forces which sustain the system the most important is the determination of the Hindus to maintain it at all cost. The Hindus are prepared to use every means to suppress the untouchables whenever the untouchables try to upset it even in the slightest degree' (Ambedkar, 1989, p. 35).

Even with a modern constitution and subsequent legislation according equal rights, dignity and justice to all, the pernicious characteristic feature of the caste system has remained unscathed to a large extent even now. This continuing persistence and application of caste norms, rules and regulations have been further explained by Ambedkar thus: 'There is another reason why untouchability cannot disappear by a stratagem, legal or rational. As has already been pointed out, the Hindu social order is based on the principle of graded inequality. It may not be an exaggeration to say that not many people understand the significance of this principle. The social system based on inequality stands on a different footing from a social system based on graded inequality. The former is a weak system which is not capable of self-preservation. The latter on the other hand, is capable of self-preservation. In a social system based on inequality, the low orders can combine to overthrow the system. None of them have any interest to preserve it. In a social system based on graded inequality the possibility of a general common attack by the aggrieved parties is nonexistent. In a system of graded inequality, the aggrieved parties are not on a common level' (Ambedkar, 1989, pp. 101–102).

2 Dalits and the Nomenclature

As time passed by and lower-caste groups became more assertive in their efforts to reclaim their humanhood, the demand for a better nomenclature also gained prominence. By the 1920s, a new *Adi* movement, asserting an ideological claim to being heirs of a *non-Aryan* or original Indian equalitarian tradition, began to take off in many regions of India. Movements such as *Ad-Dharm* in Punjab, *Adi-Hindu* in Uttar Pradesh (UP) and Hyderabad, *Adi Dravida* and *Adi-Andhra* in Madras Presidency and *Adi-Karnataka* all indicated a common claim of being the original inhabitants (Omvedt, 1995, pp. 35–38).

Vithal Ramji Shinde, a Maratha social reformer, coined the term *depressed classes* and established the '*Depressed Class* Mission' in Bombay as early as 1906 (Guru, 1998, p. 16). Later, the British government introduced the terms *depressed classes* and *exterior castes* for administrative purposes. In 1930, the Indian Statutory Commission noted that, in origin, these castes appeared to be functional, comprising those engaged in occupations regarded as unclean or degrading, such as scavenging and leather work, and partly tribal groups, i.e. *aboriginal tribes* absorbed into Hindu fold and transformed into imposed castes (Indian Statutory Commission, 1930, p. 37). The term *exterior castes* appeared for the first time in the Census of India, 1931. This designation for Hindu castes, previously known as *depressed classes*, was originally suggested by C.S. Mullan, the Census superintendent for Assam. It was subsequently adopted in the Census of 1931 as a more satisfactory alternative to the unfortunate and disparaging label 'depressed class' (Report, Census of India 1931, p. 471).

The British Government of India prepared an exhaustive list of untouchable communities in 1935 and attached it to the Order-in-Council issued under the *Government of India Act of 1935*. To this Order-in-Council, there was a *Schedule* attached. The *Schedule* was divided into nine parts. Each part corresponded to a province and enumerated the castes, races or tribes that were deemed *untouchables* within that province, either in its entirety or in specific parts thereof (Ambedkar, 1990, p. 259). After independence, the framers of the Indian Constitution retained the term Scheduled Caste (SC), which came to be used for castes described earlier as *untouchables* (Ahuja, 1993, p. 364). This term has been used as an official category and hence considered a legal term to date. But the term has proceeded without a single connotative definition. The selection has proceeded on the basis of untouchability measured by the incidence of social disabilities but at the same time this criterion has been combined in varying degrees with economic, occupational, educational, residential and religious tests (Galanter, 1984, p. 134).

Further, the resulting list then designates all those groups that, in view of the Parliament, require the special protection provided by the Constitution. It specifies who may stand for reserved seats and who may enjoy the benefits and reservations provided for the Scheduled Castes. However, it does not necessarily include every person or group that might be considered untouchable under any conceivable definition. It omits some groups, like communities that historically suffered disabilities (e.g. Ezhavas) or those considered untouchables under the 1931 Census tests. It also excludes non-Hindus (other than *Sikhs*) even when they would clearly qualify as untouchables under judicial tests of 'origin' in groups considered beyond the pale of the caste system (Galanter, 1984).

Harijan is another term coined by Narsinh Mehta, a Gujarati poet of the Bhakti movement, to refer to the illegitimate children of Devadasis—the female temple dancers—as the children of god. M.K. Gandhi later adopted and popularised the term as a designation for the untouchables. Gandhi's purpose in using the term Harijan for the untouchables was to confer dignity upon them and also to persuade caste Hindus to admit these unfortunates into their (Hindu) fold (Issac, 1965, p. 39). But educated and conscious untouchables have not taken this patronising nomenclature kindly as they think that to single them out as children of god merely sought to make their condition tolerable rather than to destroy a system that bred inequality (Burman, 1977, p. 84). As a result of protests from members of Scheduled Castes, the use of the word Harijan was banned by the central government in 1991. It was removed from the official lexicon in 1994, with the argument that it has to be discarded because it undermines human dignity (Jiloha, 1995, p. 114).

The Marathi word Dalit, like the word Black, was chosen by the untouchable community itself and is used proudly by this group. The term Dalit signifies those who have been broken or ground down by those above them in a deliberate and active way. There is in the word itself an inherent denial of pollution, karma and caste hierarchy (Zelliot, 1996, p. 267). Jotiba Phule, who began the Satya Shodhak (truth-seeking) movement in an attempt to reduce Brahmanical influence on lower castes, appears to have been the first to use the word Dalit in a caste-related context, in the expression 'Dalitodhar'—uplift of the depressed (Zelliot, 1996, p. 271). But according to Gopal Guru, the category Dalit was first used by Ambedkar himself in his fortnightly Bahiskrit Bharat, where he defined it comprehensively: 'Dalithood is a kind of life condition which characterises the exploitation, suppression and marginalisation of Dalits by the social, economic, cultural and political domination of the upper caste brahmanical order' (Guru, 1998).

The clearest definition of the term Dalit in its contemporary usage was given by Gangadhar Pantawane: 'To me, Dalit is not a caste. He is a man exploited by the social and economic traditions of this country. He does not believe in God, Rebirth, Soul, Holy Books teaching separatism, Fate and Heaven because they have made him a slave. He does believe in humanism. Dalit is a symbol of change and revolution' (Omvedt, 1995).

In the post-Ambedkar era, the Dalit literary movement and the Dalit Panther movement popularised and used the term comprehensively in Maharashtra. It was frequently used in the 1960s in writings emerging chiefly from *ex-untouchables*—many of whom are now Buddhists in Maharashtra—or other oppressed groups. In the 1970s, the term acquired a broader connotation and included women, lower castes, untouchables, tribes, the working class, the landless, poor peasants and all the suppressed, depressed, exploited, harassed and degraded groups in society (Chitre, 1982, pp. 93–95).

It is important to highlight here that in the struggle to rename a group of people who have hitherto been denied dignity, equal status and equal rights, the community's lived experiences play quite a significant role. Neither through any patronage from the well off dominant castes nor through any religious sanction, in this case the Brahmanical Hindu caste system, the term Dalit has acquired a life-long craving for being identified as a human being worthy of dignity. The term Dalit is not a metaphysical construct. Rather, it derives its epistemic and political strength from the material social experiences of the community. It is this social construction of *Dalithood* that makes it authentic and dynamic rather than passive and rigid (Guru, 1998). Hence, the designation Dalit provides a militant alternative to the Gandhian term Harijan (Omvedt, 1995). Dalit, unlike Harijan or other designations, does not derive its substance from the politics of patronage or rhetorical concessions that liberal politics tend to offer to Dalits and other toiling masses.

The term did not emerge from a mechanical movement along the highways of politics. Instead, it arose from the bylanes of critical cultural traditions, such as the Buddhist, Warkari and Kabir movements. It interrogates the structures of social and material hierarchies that sustain a particular cultural ethos (Guru, 1997).

3 Human Rights Violations of Dalits

In any part of the civilised world, one would expect that with a modern constitution and a set of legislation, primordial forms of social violence would cease to operate. But strangely enough, in a country like India, caste-based violence against Dalits has seen an upsurge over the years. It is clearly reflected in the 'Crime in India', an annual report of the National Crime Records Bureau. A comparison of annual crime data reported against Dalits from the first two decades up to the year 2022 of the current millennium would be good enough to understand how the rising cases of reported crimes against Dalits have been a recurrent feature in Indian society. Caste-based atrocities and violence simply refuse to go away (Table 1).

It is clear from the above-mentioned figures on cognizable crimes against Dalits recorded at police stations across India that on average, 29,000–30,000 cases were reported every year during this 11-year time period (Table 2).

In the time period from 2011 to 2022, the total number of cognizable crimes committed against Dalits from across the country was around 517,384 (five lakh seventeen thousand three hundred eighty-four). On average, 43,115 (forty-three thousand one hundred fifteen) cases of cognizable crimes against Scheduled Castes were reported per year at police stations across the country.

Table 1 Reported cases of cognizable crimes against Dalits in India (2000–2010)

Year	Reported cases
2000	25,455
2001	33,501
2002	33,507
2003	26,252
2004	26,887
2005	26,127
2006	27,070
2007	30,031
2008	33,615
2009	33,594
2010	32,712
Total	328,751

Source: Crime in India (2000–2010), National Crime Records Bureau, New Delhi, Government of India

Table 2 Reported cases of cognizable crimes against Dalits in India (2011–2022)

Year	Reported cases
2011	33,719
2012	33,655
2013	39,408
2014	40,401
2015	38,670
2016	40,801
2017	43,203
2018	42,793
2019	45,961
2020	50,291
2021	50,900
2022	57,582
Total	517,384

Source: Crime in India (2011–2022), National Crime Records Bureau, New Delhi, Government of India

The total number of cases pending police investigation at the end of the year 2022 was 19,090; the chargesheeting rate was 79.9. The total number of cases pending trial at the end of 2022 was 283,589; the conviction rate was 34.0, and the pendency percentage was 94.4.

There was not much of a difference the year before. The total number of cases pending investigation by the police at the end of 2021 was 18,569; chargesheeting rate: 80.0. The total number of cases pending trial at the end of 2021 was 254,475; conviction rate: 36.0, pendency percentage: 96.1.

As per the Crime in India 2022 report, at the end of that year, the top 12 states where cognizable crimes against Dalits were registered with the police were as follows: Uttar Pradesh (15,368 cases), Rajasthan (8752 cases), Madhya Pradesh (7733 cases), Bihar (6509 cases), Odisha (2902 cases), Maharashtra (2743 cases), Andhra Pradesh (2315 cases), Karnataka (1977 cases), Telangana (1787 cases), Tamil Nadu (1761 cases), Haryana (1633 cases) and Gujarat (1279 cases).

With slight variation, the situation was almost similar in the year 2021. As per the Crime in India 2021 report, the top 12 states where cognizable crimes against Dalits were registered with the police in that year were as follows: Uttar Pradesh (13,146 cases), Rajasthan (7524 cases), Madhya Pradesh (7214 cases), Bihar (5842 cases), Maharashtra (2503 cases), Odisha (2327 cases), Andhra Pradesh (2014 cases), Telangana (1772 cases), Karnataka (1673 cases), Haryana (1628 cases), Tamil Nadu (1377 cases) and Gujarat (1201 cases).

In such situations where the number of cases being registered at police stations and pending trial is so high, it becomes impossible to deliver justice to survivors' families. The high number of cases pending trial in courts at all levels of the judiciary, be it district or higher, clearly reflects an ill-equipped judicial system in the country. A court in Uttar Pradesh's Mainpuri district sentenced to death three men for the cold-blooded murder of 24 Dalits, including women and children, 44 years ago, in what came to be known as the Dehuli massacre. 'They targeted and killed as many Jatavs as they could find', recorded the court as it pronounced its judgment on March 18, 2025. While sentencing the three surviving accused persons, special judge (dacoity and affected areas) Indira Singh said that the crime brought shame to humanity as well as to the legal system. 'It is a crime which falls in the category of destroying the social structure', said judge Singh, noting that the murders were committed 'as a result of deep rooted caste prejudice' by the dominant Thakurs against the Dalit Jatavs. She also stressed that none of the convicted persons displayed any form of remorse for their acts. Notably, after committing the massacre against the Dalits, which went on for more than 2 h, the accused persons did not try to flee from the village. Instead, they leisurely ate their meals at the homes of some local Thakurs (Rashid, 2025).

In another case, a 42-year delay in delivering judgment for the killing of ten Dalits in the state of Uttar Pradesh is certainly an example of 'justice delayed is justice denied'. A 90-year-old man was sentenced to life imprisonment by the Firozabad district and sessions court for his role in the killing of ten people belonging to the Dalit community 42 years ago. The court in UP also imposed a fine of Rs 55,000 on the lone surviving accused, Ganga Dayal (The Times of India, 2023b).

It is also a sad reality that the manner in which the criminal justice system operates in the country turns heavily against survivors' attempts to get justice. Non-implementation of legislative provisions is a common ailment that afflicts the Indian system at every level, be it local administration or police. In the same way, non-registration of cases or failure to register them under the appropriate sections of the PoA Act results in reduced punishment for perpetrators by diluting the seriousness of the offence. This has been the case so far, which is significantly documented in a report by the National Dalit Movement for Justice (NDMJ) of the National Campaign on Dalit Human Rights (NCDHR). Victims lose the chance to receive higher compensation if cases are registered under less serious sections. This practice encourages the police to neglect their duties in successive cases. Also, it encourages police collusion with dominant caste perpetrators of atrocities in future. Undue delays in investigation and failure to file charge sheets promptly result in the slow disposal of cases, which, in turn, causes prolonged delays for victims in accessing justice. This delay in chargesheeting can also affect the direction of court cases to a large extent, with courts letting off the accused on the sole ground of delay in filing the charge sheet (Report, 2020, p. 81).

Judgments in atrocity cases generally come only after long and protracted legal, administrative and police dilatory tactics. It is no surprise then that a recent judgment by a Special Court for Scheduled Castes and Scheduled Tribes at Alwar in Rajasthan has been delivered only after 31 years. A news report describes this delay in justice: a special court for SC/ST cases awarded life sentences on September 30, 2023, to nine people involved in the sensational 'Kumher Kaand' case of Bharatpur district, in which 16 Dalits were killed and over 44 others were injured in 1992. The court acquitted 41 others who were accused in the case. A dispute between two communities—Jatavs, a Scheduled Caste, and Jats—in the Kumher area led to the massacre of 16 people on June 6, 1992, in what remains the largest carnage of Dalits in the state. The investigation was handed over to the Central Bureau of Investigation (CBI), which filed a charge sheet against 83 accused after recording the statements of 283 people. During the prolonged trial of the case in the SC/ST court, 32 accused died, while one remains absconding (The Times of India, 2023a).

A division bench comprising Justice Inderjeet Singh and Justice Ashutosh Kumar of the Jaipur High Court suspended, on March 20, 2024, the life imprisonment sentences of nine persons awarded by a special court for SC/ST cases in Bharatpur in the Kumher massacre case. The defence lawyers contended that none of the convicts were named in the First Information Report (FIR) registered by the Kumher police at the time of the incident. Also, they argued that during the investigation, the police failed to recover arms from the nine convicts. Furthermore, the police did not conduct an identification parade on these nine individuals, which means that the police, too, had doubts about their involvement in the incident. On these grounds, the court ordered the suspension of the sentences (The Times of India, 2024).

4 Caste and the Criminal Justice System

Caste-based discriminatory attitudes could be easily seen affecting officials in the performance of their duties. It is but a common experience for people belonging to the lowest strata of society to face a whole lot of disturbing actions at the hands of the police and other local officials. It has been found through media reports and also through official sources as cited in the next paragraph that many Dalit and Adivasi groups have been seen and are being treated as habitual offenders for indulging in criminal activities. Detention and arrests of persons belonging to the Dalit and Adivasi communities following reports of any criminal activity are quite frequently resorted to by the local police almost everywhere in the country. This practice also leads to the foisting of false cases and imminent torture in police lock-ups. Once alleged criminals are produced before a magistrate within 24 h of their arrest, they are placed in either police or judicial custody. The entire process of the criminal justice system is so lengthy and complicated that life becomes hell for Dalit and Adivasi prisoners. Long years of incarceration as undertrial prisoners and even after conviction as well as precarious living conditions inside prisons, where they are compelled to perform cleaning and menial jobs, are a clear reflection of discriminatory practices by the state and its agencies. This is where society's religious-cultural biases and discriminatory behaviours are found to be in full operation without any hindrances.

A special report on atrocities against the Kuravan community in Tamil Nadu, conducted in 2016 by the National Commission for Scheduled Castes (NCSC), revealed that even after six decades of political independence in India, the community continued to be subjected to physical torture by the Tamil Nadu police under the guise of them being 'habitual offenders'. Members of the community, including women, men and children, are subjected to systematic atrocities at the hands of the police. It has become convenient for the police to catch hold of the 'Kuravans' and foist false cases against them; the Kuravans are kept under illegal detention and are subjected to torture to extract 'false confessional statements' for crimes they had not committed. For these reasons, the entire community lives in fear of detention and arrest. There are allegations that the police compile pending unsolved theft cases, charge the people from the community to show these cases as solved and protect and defend actual perpetrators and anti-social elements in order to keep their rackets going. The Kuravans in districts like Thanjavur, Ariyalur, Thiruvarur, Salem, Trichy and Villupuram experience high levels of false criminal charges, illegal detention, torture while in custody, sexual abuse and custodial deaths (Report, Special, 2016, pp. 7–8).

Most of the states in India have more or less been continuing with prison manuals and only little changes have been made from the British time. Caste has always played a big role in assigning work inside the prisons. Sukanya Shantha, writing for *The Wire*, noted: 'In several states, prison manuals still dictate that labour within the prison should be assigned on the basis of caste. Across states, prison manuals and rules stipulate the labour that needs to be carried out on a daily basis. The division of labour is roughly determined on the dichotomous "purity-impurity" scale, with the higher castes handling only work that is considered "pure" and those lower in the caste grid being left to carry out the "impure" jobs. The National Crime Records Bureau data has consistently pointed to the over-representation of Scheduled Castes, Scheduled Tribes and OBCs in Indian jails' (Shantha, 2020).

It is quite interesting to note in this connection that the Supreme Court, on January 3, 2024, said that the caste-based discrimination of prisoners, the segregation of manual work among them according to caste hierarchy and the treatment of inmates from de-notified tribes as 'habitual offenders' within the four walls of Indian prisons constitute a 'very important issue' that needs to be addressed. A three-judge bench headed by Chief Justice of India D.Y. Chandrachud found that prison manuals in more than ten states, including Uttar Pradesh, West Bengal, Odisha, Maharashtra, Tamil Nadu and Kerala, still contain provisions that sanction discrimination and forced labour on the ground of caste in prisons. The court ordered the states and the union to respond to a petition filed by journalist Sukanya Shantha, represented by senior advocate S. Muralidhar and advocate Prasanna S, within 4 weeks. In the petition, Mr. Muralidhar argued that centuries of caste discrimination continue unabated inside prisons. Labour is segregated on the basis of caste. Modern manuals promoting reforms in prisons do not seem to have entered the prison walls. 'Dalits even have a separate ward in prisons … Despite changes in the prison manuals, caste discrimination continues. These provisions in the prison manuals of the States should be repealed', the senior lawyer submitted (The Hindu, 2024a).

Subsequently, the central government directed the states and union territories to remove discriminatory provisions in prison manuals. The union government took serious note of some states discriminating against prisoners on the basis of their caste and religion and assigning them work accordingly. Saying it was unconstitutional, the Ministry of Home Affairs (MHA) wrote to chief secretaries of all states/union territories, urging them to ensure that their jail manuals did not contain any discriminatory provisions. In case any such discriminatory provision exists, immediate steps must be taken to amend/remove such provision from the manual/Act. It is reiterated that there should be no caste-based assignment of duties or work in the prisons, the MHA said (The Hindu, 2024b).

Finally, the Supreme Court, on October 3, 2024, declared that caste-based discrimination of prisoners, the segregation of manual work among them according to caste hierarchy and the treatment of inmates from de-notified tribes as 'habitual offenders' within the four walls of Indian prisons are oppressive to fundamental human dignity and personality. A three-judge bench headed by Chief Justice of India D.Y. Chandrachud emphasised, 'everyone is born equal' and cannot suffer the lifelong stigma attached to their caste. The judgment struck down caste-based discrimination within prison walls as unconstitutional and directed the immediate rewriting of prison manuals.

Chief Justice Chandrachud said that members of de-notified tribes should not be subject to arbitrary arrest and detention. The court warned that states would be held accountable for discriminatory practices committed within prison walls. According to the court, prison manuals institutionalising the caste-based distribution of work to prisoners blatantly disregard the constitutional ethos. These manuals and practices reflect inherent biases against members of marginalised communities. The judgment authored by the chief justice observed that caste cannot be used as a tool for discrimination against the oppressed classes. The segregation of prisoners on the basis of their caste and assigning them stereotypical work affect their rehabilitation and 'reduces individual persons to a group identity' (The Hindu, 2024c). While this is a remarkable judgment passed by the Supreme Court, it remains to be seen how the situation will turn out in future.

It is worth noting here that the deliberate physical and psychological mistreatment of inmates by prison officials remains a persistent and pervasive issue of concern. Dalits and Adivasis are particularly vulnerable to deliberate mistreatment. Research shows how caste-based prejudice leads to the presence of a high number of vulnerable communities inside prisons and how often these prisoners are denied minimum legal protections and due process guarantees during their arrest, detention or imprisonment. Findings also reveal how barriers are enforced on incarcerated Dalits inside jails and how their legitimate rights are being infringed, such as their right to food, wages, employment, accommodation, medical care, bail, parole and similar other important rights related to trial and appeals (Singh, 2018, p. 106).

Following this remarkable verdict from the Supreme Court, the central government amended the prison manual rules. In a communication to the chief secretaries of all states and union territories, the Union Home Ministry highlighted that to address the issue of any caste-based discrimination of prisoners, the 'Model Prison Manual, 2016' and the 'Model Prisons and Correctional Services Act, 2023' have been amended. The changes have been made in the wake of the October 3, 2024, order of the Supreme Court on the caste-based discrimination of prisoners. According to the new provision in the manual, prison authorities will have to strictly ensure that there is no discrimination, classification and segregation of prisoners on the basis of their caste. 'It shall be strictly ensured that there is no discrimination of prisoners in allotment of any duty or work in prisons on the basis of their caste', it stated. The Home Ministry also clarified that the provisions of 'The Prohibition of Employment as Manual Scavengers and Their Rehabilitation Act, 2013' shall have a binding effect even in prisons and correctional institutions. 'Manual scavenging or hazardous cleaning of a sewer or a septic tank inside a prison shall not be permitted' (The Hindu, 2025).

Dalits, Adivasis and people belonging to Other Backward Castes (OBCs) are found to be in large numbers in Indian prisons. This finding is verified by the Government of India's own report, Prison Statistics India (PSI), published by the National Crime Records Bureau (NCRB). The vulnerabilities that these communities face in society, the economy and polity also get reflected in the criminal justice system in the country. The tables mentioned below, which provide figures on caste-affected communities in Indian prisons across the country from 2014 to 2022, reveal the ever-growing nature of discriminatory practices within prisons (Table 3).

What is clear from the above table is that from 2014 onwards, convicts belonging to the Scheduled Caste (SC), Scheduled Tribe (ST) and Other Backward Caste (OBC) communities outnumber all other convicts. In 2014, the figure was 66.60%; in 2015, 65.86%; in 2017, 68.14%; in 2018, 69.40%; in 2019, 70.37%; in 2020, 72.0%; in 2021, 73.09%; and in 2022, 69.0%.

Strangely enough, the 2016 report did not contain any data related to the caste and religion of convicts. Prison Statistics India 2016, published in April after a long and unexplained delay, omits details about the caste and religious identities of the prison population (Gokhale, 2019) (Table 4).

Even in the case of undertrial prisoners, the overwhelming majority belong to the Scheduled Caste (SC), Scheduled Tribe and Other Backward Caste (OBC) communities. In 2014, the figure was 62.62%; in 2015, 65.56%; in 2017, 62.27%; in 2018, 70.66%; in 2019, 71.67%; in 2020, 70.72%; in 2021, 71.70%; and in 2022, 66.0% (Table 5).

Similar trends have been observed as far as the caste of detenues is concerned. In 2014, the combined figure for Scheduled Caste (SC), Scheduled Tribe (ST) and Other Backward Caste (OBC) detenues was 81.24%. In 2015, it was 75.21%; in

Table 3 Caste of convicts

Year	Scheduled Caste (SC)	Scheduled Tribes (ST)	Other Backward Caste (OBC)	Others	Total
2014	27,997	15,598	44,008	43,914	131,517
2015	28,033	18,403	41,931	45,801	134,168
2016 [a]					
2017	29,580	17,415	47,823	44,331	139,149
2018	29,370	18,814	48,643	42,681	139,508
2019	31,342	19,698	50,394	42,691	144,125
2020	23,948	15,613	41,860	31,628	113,049
2021	26,643	17,310	45,849	33,050	122,852
2022	26,952	17,910	47,226	33,329	133,415

Source: Report (2014–2022)
[a] Caste and religion data not available in the 2016 report

Table 4 Caste of undertrial prisoners

Year	Scheduled Caste (SC)	Scheduled Tribe (ST)	Other Backward Caste (OBC)	Others	Total
2014	57,045	31,648	88,448	105,738	282,879
2015	61,139	34,999	88,809	97,129	282,076
2016 [a]					
2017	61,744	33,390	97,113	116,471	308,718
2018	67,050	35,102	107,477	87,010	296,639
2019	69,302	34,756	113,062	85,810	302,930
2020	77,716	39,031	127,736	101,194	345,677
2021	90,037	42,211	151,287	111,878	395,413
2022	90,951	40,221	155,864	114,383	434,302

Source: Report (2014–2022)
[a] Caste and religion data not available in the 2016 report

Table 5 Caste of detenues

Year	Scheduled Caste (SC)	Scheduled Tribes (ST)	Other Backward Caste (OBC)	Others	Total
2014	1232	165	1233	607	3237
2015	628	192	1107	635	2562
2016 [a]					
2017	422	153	884	677	2136
2018	476	167	997	666	2306
2019	585	183	1444	866	3078
2020	808	249	1634	795	3486
2021	800	195	1283	952	3230
2022	970	220	1881	1064	4324

Source: Report (2014–2022)
[a] Caste and religion data not available in the 2016 report

2017, 68.30%; in 2018, 71.11%; in 2019, 71.86%; in 2020, 77.19%; in 2021, 70.52%; and in 2022, 71.02%.

How ironic it is that even after 75 years of independent governance and 75 years since the passing of the Universal Declaration of Human Rights, Dalits are still struggling for freedom, dignity and justice. Day in and day out, Dalits are humiliated and killed, and Dalit women are raped, discriminated against and subjected to various other human rights violations. Stringent laws have been passed, but the law takes its own course in imparting justice and, at times, has proven ineffective in dealing with such monstrous attacks on Dalits' dignity and human rights.

5 Need for a Re-Look at Dalit Human Rights in Contemporary Times

There is a need to examine earlier reports to understand the magnitude of caste-based human rights violations in their entirety. Between 1992 and 1997, a total of 176,183 cases nationwide were registered with the police as cognisable crimes against Scheduled Castes (Report, 1994–1997). Given that Dalits are both reluctant and unable (for lack of police cooperation) to report crimes committed against them, the actual number of abuses they experience is presumably higher. Cases related to the practice of *untouchability* and attempts to defy social order, cases involving land disputes and demands for minimum wages and cases of atrocities by the police generally remain unreported (Narula, 1999, pp. 8–9).

The hierarchical structure of society, with its inbuilt system of graded inequality, in which Dalits are placed at the lowest level, is reflected in their social and economic status as well. The social, religious and cultural codes of interactions and everyday conduct within the Brahmanical social order prevent Dalits from living a life of dignity and equal opportunity. These kinds of discriminatory and exclusionary practices are reflected in multiple forms in the educational and economic fields, too.

The National Commission for Scheduled Castes, in its annual report, highlights that the social status of Dalits/Scheduled Castes in the country remains in a precarious condition. It states very emphatically: 'the Scheduled Caste constitutes about 16.6 *per cent* (20.14 crore (CR)) of the total population of India as per 2011 census. These communities are still subjected to social discrimination by other sections of society. This has resulted into denial of educational, economical, social, political and cultural development to these communities' (Report, 2018–2020, p. 113).

The sad reality of Dalit human rights in the country is reflected not just in the denial of civil and political rights but at the same time in the curtailment of economic, social and cultural rights. It is quite instructive to highlight how the Sustainable Development Goals (SDGs), with their slogan of not leaving anyone behind, have not been sincerely adopted to tackle caste-based discrimination, exclusion and violence, which deny equal status to Dalits and Adivasis, placing them in the margins in every sense of the term. When we view the SDGs vis-à-vis Dalits and Adivasis, what we come to know is quite shocking. The recurrent untouchability and atrocities that Dalits have to face on an almost everyday basis keep them excluded from much of the development process. The data presented here in the previous and the following sections clearly reveals the failure on part of the central as well as state governments by not implementing several policies and programmes properly thereby resulting in to non-incorporation of SDGs as part of an all inclusive national framework for development.

6 Educational Development Still a Mirage

Education is considered an enlightening process that helps individuals and communities bound in slavery-like situations to break free and lead a life of dignity and acquire enough consciousness and wisdom to challenge conservative and traditional belief systems. Socio-educational backwardness still bears testimony to the prevalence and hegemony of the social system, which prevents lower-caste people from acquiring knowledge through education. What is being described here throws enough light on the precarious life conditions that Dalits and other similarly disadvantaged communities in the hierarchically organised Brahmanical social order have to face in their day-to-day lives. Government data may claim higher literacy rates over the years and even higher percentages of gross enrolment rates as a sign of progress, but these narratives fail to highlight higher dropout rates among students belonging to the Dalit, Adivasi and Other Backward Caste (OBC) communities (Table 6).

It is clear from the above-mentioned table that literacy rate among the Scheduled Castes has improved slightly from 2001 to 2011. But it still lags behind others as far as the overall literacy rate is concerned (Table 7).

Table 6 Literacy rate of Scheduled Castes vs total literacy rate

Indicator	Effective literacy rate (2001)	Effective literacy rate (2011)
Total population		
Total	64.8	73.0
Rural	58.7	67.8
Urban	79.9	84.1
Scheduled castes		
Total	54.7	66.1
Rural	51.2	62.8
Urban	68.1	76.2

Source: Census 2011, cited in Annual Report (2018–2019 and 2019–2020), National Commission for Scheduled Castes, New Delhi, Government of India

Table 7 Literacy rate gender wise

Indicator	Literacy rate (males) 2001	Literacy rate (males) 2011	Literacy rate (females) 2001	Literacy rate (females) 2011	Gender gap 2001	Gender gap 2011
Total population						
Total	75.3	80.9	53.7	64.6	21.6	16.3
Rural	70.7	77.2	46.1	57.9	24.6	19.3
Urban	86.3	88.8	72.9	79.1	13.4	9.7
Scheduled castes						
Total	66.6	75.2	41.9	56.5	24.7	18.7
Rural	63.7	72.6	37.8	52.6	25.9	20.0
Urban	77.9	83.3	57.5	68.6	20.4	14.7

Source: Census 2011, cited in Annual Report (2018–2019 and 2019–2020), National Commission for Scheduled Castes, New Delhi, Government of India

The literacy rate gender gap among Scheduled Castes and other communities remains a matter of serious concern. These figures also reveal how the state and its agencies have failed miserably in empowering disadvantaged communities. The discriminatory practices prevalent in society also creep into the educational system, resulting in a large chunk of people, especially Dalits and, more particularly, Dalit women, remaining uneducated and illiterate.

The situation is not so rosy even in the sphere of higher education as far as Dalits are concerned. Across India, the situation remains quite bad and should be a matter of concern for policymakers and implementers. According to National Sample Survey (NSS 71st Round data), the percentage of Scheduled Castes with graduate and above educational attainment is highly uneven throughout the country. States with the highest percentages of Scheduled Castes that have attained graduate and above educational levels are Arunachal Pradesh (21.6%), Manipur (18.9%), Himachal Pradesh (17.4%) and Tamil Nadu (17.2%). Union territories with the highest percentages of Scheduled Castes that have attained graduate and above degrees are Puducherry (46.5%) and Delhi (13.9%). States with the lowest percentages of Scheduled Castes attaining graduate and above levels are Bihar (1.6%), Tripura (2.9%), Haryana (4.4%), Nagaland (4.6%) and Sikkim (5.0%). States with a high percentage of Scheduled Caste populations, such as Uttar Pradesh, Madhya Pradesh and Haryana, show percentages of 8.0%, 6.6% and 4.4%, respectively. As far as the total population is concerned, the percentage attaining graduate and above educational levels is far more than that of the Scheduled Castes—that is, almost 50% (Acharya & Sahoo, 2019, pp. 399–400).

States with the highest percentage of graduate and above degrees are Nagaland (27.6%), Tamil Nadu (27.3%), Kerala (27.0%) and Goa (26.1%). Union territories with the highest percentages of graduate and above levels are Puducherry (38.2%),

Table 8 Gross enrolment ratio of Scheduled Caste students

Level/year	2013–2014	2014–2015
Primary level (I–V) 6–10 years	113.0	111.9
Upper primary (VI–VIII) 11–13 years	98.3	101.0
Elementary (I–VIII) 6–13 years	107.7	108.0
Secondary (IX–X) 14–15 years	78.7	82.7
Senior secondary (XI–XII) 16–17 years	50.5	54.3
Higher education 18–23 years	17.1	19.1

Source: Report (2016), pp. 28–29

Chandigarh (32.2%), Delhi (31.9%) and Dadra and Nagar Haveli (25.4%). States with the lowest percentages of graduate and above educational attainment are Tripura (5.2%), Bihar (6.3%), Assam (6.4%) and Chhattisgarh (8.6%). Among the union territories, the Lakshadweep Islands have the lowest percentage of Scheduled Castes with graduate or above educational levels—only 11.7% (Ibid) (Table 8).

Dalit students participation in higher studies right from the school days keeps decreasing substantially. As revealed in the above table, this kind of situation persists. Is there any hope for a better future? This question would perhaps remain unanswered in the years to come.

The average annual dropout rate for Scheduled Caste students for the year 2013–2014 stood as follows: primary level: 4.14, upper primary level: 4.38, secondary level: 18.66 and senior secondary level: 1.81 (Report, 2016, p. 37).

The gross enrolment ratio (GER) of Scheduled Caste students for the year 2015–2016 stood as follows: primary level: 110.9, upper primary level: 102.4, elementary level: 107.9, secondary level: 85.3, senior secondary level: 56.8, IX–XII level: 71.4 and higher education level: 19.9 (Report, 2018, pp. 31–32).

What is clear from the above-mentioned data is the fact that the gross enrolment ratio of Scheduled Caste students at the school level is quite impressive. But at the same time, the dropout rate becomes quite high by the time students reach higher studies in schools, colleges and universities. This also shows, in other words, that due to several factors, the retention rate for students belonging to deprived caste and communities at different levels of education warrants urgent intervention by the government to initiate corrective measures.

7 All India Survey on Higher Education (AISHE)

The All India Survey on Higher Education (AISHE) was initiated in 2011, with data collection conducted for the period 2010–2011. The survey was necessitated as none of the existing sources of data provided a complete picture of higher education in the country. And in view of its immense utility in providing comprehensive data, AISHE continued to be conducted on an annual basis over the years.

Presented here is a snapshot of data on the representation of Scheduled Castes and Scheduled Tribes in higher education in the country from the period 2014–2015 to the period 2020–2022, years for which the latest report is available.

7.1 AISHE 2014–2015

The gross enrolment ratio (GER) for the age group 18–23 years for the period 2014–2015 was as follows: all categories—24.3%, Scheduled Castes—19.1% and Scheduled Tribes—13.7% (AISHE 2014–2015, p. 25).

The total enrolment for Scheduled Castes is 13.5% and for Scheduled Tribes, 4.8% (Ibid, p. 18).

Representation in teaching positions at the all-India level stood as follows: others—67%, Scheduled Castes—7.1% and Scheduled Tribes—2.1% (Ibid, p. 26).

7.2 AISHE 2015–2016

Gross enrolment ratio (GER): all categories—24.5%, Scheduled Castes—19.9% and Scheduled Tribes—14.2% (AISHE 2015–2016, p. 24).

Total enrolment: Scheduled Castes—13.9% and Scheduled Tribes—4.9% (Ibid, p. 17).

Representation in teaching positions at the all-India level: others—65%, Scheduled Castes—7.5% and Scheduled Tribes—2.1% (Ibid, p. 25).

7.3 AISHE 2016–2017

Gross enrolment ratio (GER): all categories—25.2%, Scheduled Castes—21.1% and Scheduled Tribes—15.4% (AISHE 2016–2017, p. 24).

Total enrolment: Scheduled Castes—14.3% and Scheduled Tribes—5.2% (Ibid, p. 17).

Representation in teaching positions at the all-India level: others—58.2%, Scheduled Castes—8.3% and Scheduled Tribes—2.2% (Ibid, p. 25).

7.4 *AISHE 2017–2018*

Gross enrolment ratio: all categories—25.8%, Scheduled Castes—21.8% and Scheduled Tribes—15.9% (AISHE 2017–2018, p. 19).

Total enrolment: Scheduled Castes—14.4% and Scheduled Tribes—5.2% (Ibid, p. 14).

Representation in teaching positions at the all-India level: others—56.8%, Scheduled Castes—8.6% and Scheduled Tribes—2.3% (Ibid, p. 20).

7.5 *AISHE 2018–2019*

Gross enrolment ratio: all categories—26.3%, Scheduled Castes—23.0% and Scheduled Tribes—17.2% (AISHE 2018–2019, p. 18).

Total enrolment: Scheduled Castes—14.89% and Scheduled Tribes—5.53% (Ibid, pp. 13–14).

Representation in teaching positions at the all-India level: others—56.8%, Scheduled Castes—8.8% and Scheduled Tribes—2.4% (Ibid, p. 19).

7.6 *AISHE 2019–2020*

Gross enrolment ratio (GER): all categories—27.1%, Scheduled Castes—23.4% and Scheduled Tribes—18.0% (AISHE 2019–2020, p. 25).

Total enrolment: Scheduled Castes—14.7% and Scheduled Tribes—5.6% (Ibid, p. 19).

Representation in teaching positions at the all-India level: others—56.5%, Scheduled Castes—9.0% and Scheduled Tribes—2.4% (Ibid, p. 26).

7.7 *AISHE 2020–2021*

Gross enrolment ratio (GER): all categories—27.3%, Scheduled Castes—23.1% and Scheduled Tribes—18.9% (AISHE 2020–2021, p. 26).

Total enrolment: Scheduled Castes—14.2% and Scheduled Tribes—5.8% (Ibid, p. 14).

Representation in teaching positions at the all-India level: others—56.1%, Scheduled Castes—9.1% and Scheduled Tribes—2.5% (27).

7.8 AISHE 2021–2022

Gross enrolment ratio (GER): all categories—28.4%, Scheduled Castes—25.9% and Scheduled Tribes—21.2% (AISHE 2021–2022, p. 32).

Total enrolment: Scheduled Castes—15.3% and Scheduled Tribes—6.3% (Ibid, p. 17).

Representation in teaching positions: others—55.8%, Scheduled Castes—9.3% and Scheduled Tribes—2.6% (Ibid, p. 36).

Over the years, the educational development of Dalits and Adivasis has shown little improvement. Successive governments, both at the centre and in the states, have failed to create an enabling environment that would allow Dalits and Adivasis to acquire education to liberate themselves from the bondage of ignorance. Why is data on backlog vacancies in teaching and other government jobs reserved for SCs, STs and OBCs not made available by the government in the public domain?

Reports presented here in snapshots above have no data on dropouts at different levels of education of different social category. So it is not clear exactly how many students belonging to Dalit and Adivasi community are actually dropping out at schools, colleges and universities across the country due to several reasons. However, the government has shared information on dropout rates in the Parliament as a reply to questions raised by members. A news report thus claimed: 'As per the Ministry of Education, over 19,000 students belonging to OBC, SC, and ST categories dropped out from various courses at central universities, IITs, and IIMs during the period of 2018 to 2023. Union Minister of State for Education, Subhas Sarkar, shared this information in response to a written question in Rajya Sabha. The available records reveal that a total of 19,256 students dropped out from Central Universities (CUs), Indian Institutes of Technology (IITs), and Indian Institutes of Management (IIMs) from 2018 to 2023. Out of the total dropouts, 14,446 were from central universities, 4444 from IITs, and 366 from IIMs' (India Today, 2023).

On another occasion, the Union Minister of State for Education, Mr. Subhash Sarkar, while replying to a question in the Lok Sabha on December 04, 2023, reported that as many as 13,626 Scheduled Caste (SC), Scheduled Tribe (ST) and Other Backward Class (OBC) students have dropped out of central universities, Indian Institutes of Technology (IITs) and Indian Institutes of Management (IIMs) in the last 5 years. In total, 4596 OBC candidates, 2424 SC students and 2622 ST students dropped out of central universities in the past 5 years. As many as 2066 OBC candidates, 1068 SC students and 408 ST students dropped out of IITs, while 163 OBC, 188 SC and 91 ST candidates have dropped out of IIMs (Indian Express, 2023).

8 Pre-Matric Scholarship Stopped by the Government

The union government has stopped Pre-Matric Scholarships for students from class 1 to 8 belonging to Scheduled Caste (SC), Scheduled Tribe (ST), Other Backward Community (OBC) and minority communities from the academic year 2022–2023. The government explained that these students are covered by the Right to Education (RTE) Act, 2009, which makes it obligatory for the government to provide free and compulsory elementary education (classes 1–8) to each and every child (The Hindu, 2022).

'Only students in classes 9 and 10 are now covered under the pre-metric scholarship scheme', the government stated. Under the Pre-Matric Scholarship scheme, the centre and state governments share the financial burden in the ratio of 75:25. A student is eligible if his parental income from all sources does not exceed ₹2.50 lakh per annum. Earlier, the scheme covered class 1–10 students from SC and OBC communities under the Ministry of Social Justice and Empowerment, ST students under the Ministry of Tribal Affairs and minority communities under the Ministry of Minority Affairs. The scholarship amount was ₹225 per month for day scholars and ₹525 per month for hostel residents, given for a period of 10 months per year. Books and ad hoc grants for day scholars were ₹750 and ₹1000 for hostel residents (Ibid).

A parliamentary panel has reiterated its recommendation to raise the ceiling for parental income eligibility under the Pre-Matric and Post-Matric Scholarship schemes for Scheduled Caste and Scheduled Tribe students, objecting to the government's earlier rejection of the proposal. The Committee on Welfare of SCs and STs has, in a report tabled in late March of 2023, cited inflation and income rise as reasons why the current income cut-off of Rs 2.5 lakh per year, set 6 years ago, deprives many deserving students of the scholarships. In an earlier report, the committee had recommended that the figure be raised to Rs 8 lakh to align it with the income ceiling used in determining eligibility for reservation benefits of Other Backward Class (OBC) and Economically Weaker Section (EWS) students (The Telegraph, 2023b).

In its reply, the social justice and empowerment ministry said that the ceiling for Pre-Matric and Post-Matric Scholarship schemes for OBC and EWS students was Rs 2.5 lakh, too, implying that raising it only for SC and ST scholarships would be discriminatory. It added that the union cabinet had decided in 2021 to continue with the current income ceiling until the period 2025–2026. In response to this, the parliamentary panel, in its latest report, asked the ministry not to be rigid about the 2025–2026 timetable. 'This would prove detrimental and would make numerous students lose out on scholarship', it said. 'The committee would once again stress that keeping in mind the current inflation and miscellaneous educational expenses, the ceiling of parents' income should be suitably enhanced so that more and more students can reap the benefits of the scheme' (Ibid).

The government has also quietly discontinued a scheme designed to incentivise the education of backward class girl students, which was conceptualised and introduced during the tenure of the first United Progressive Alliance (UPA) government. The scheme was announced by then Finance Minister P. Chidambaram and was called the National Scheme of Incentive to Girls for Secondary Education (NSIGSE). Also, in the Union Budget 2022–2023, there was a 30% drop in allocations for scholarships for Scheduled Caste (SC), Scheduled Tribe (ST) and Other Backward Class (OBC) students compared to the previous financial year (NewsClick, 2022).

The incentive scheme, launched in May 2008 but now discontinued, was an extension of the Kasturba Gandhi Balika Vidyalaya scheme, under which 1000 residential schools were opened for SC, ST and OBC girl students in 2006–2007, for which Rs 128 crore was initially allocated. Later, an additional commitment of Rs 172 crore was made. The objective was to encourage girl students who had passed class VIII to complete their education up to secondary school level to address the problem of high dropout rates driven by compelling socio-economic circumstances. Reference to several documents clarifies that the discontinuation of the incentive had been on the centre government's agenda for the past 3 years or so. However, due to pressure groups, the Department of School Education and Literacy, which administered the scheme, delayed its withdrawal until an opportune moment. Nonetheless, allocations to the scheme were gradually reduced, dropping in 4 years to a nominal Rs 01 crore from as high as Rs 320 crore (Ibid).

9 Dalit and Adivasi Students' Suicide at Elite Institutions of Higher Education

Students belonging to Dalit, Adivasis and Bahujan communities continue to face quite a hostile atmosphere in elite institutions of higher education. This has led to a spurt in suicide cases reported on a regular basis by several institutions, such as the Indian Institute of Technology (IITs), central universities, the National Law University, the National Institute of Technology (NITs), medical colleges and others. Institutions of higher education in India take pride in merit and efficiency as the principles that govern them. The logic of merit and efficiency is actually a euphemism to hide the discriminatory practices that persist against Scheduled Caste (SCs), Scheduled Tribe (STs) and Other Backward Caste (OBCs) students. Caste Hindu faculty and students who have maintained a stranglehold over these higher education institutions regularly humiliate and practice discrimination against SC, ST and OBC students. So far, these institutions have not set up any institutional mechanism to tackle caste discrimination and exclusion. Some of these institutions may claim to have started psychological counselling facilities for SC, ST and OBC students to address academic loads and stresses, but they operate without the required support system. Why is there no policy against discrimination and exclusion for educational institutions? Also, why are there no sensitisation programmes organised for all faculty members and students despite the fact that caste-based hostility is commonly found and practised in almost all institutions of higher education in the country? These questions have so far remained unanswered, mainly because these institutions have persistently denied the existence of such problems and instead continued to question the merit and efficiency of SC, ST and OBC students and their inability to adjust in a competitive environment.

Passing comments on ‘quota students’, as a pretext for SC, ST and OBC students who get admission through reservation quota, meaning thereby that they are non-deserving students, have been a regular practice in most of these institutions of higher education. The former chairman of the University Grants Commission (UGC), Sukhadeo Thorat, who in 2007 led the first-ever government-appointed panel to study caste discrimination in higher education, said that the high incidence of suicide among Dalit student points to a continuing practice of discrimination, exclusion and humiliation. ‘Caste discrimination in higher education is unquestionably a problem’, Thorat told *Article 14*, adding that this could be reflected in practices among students, between teachers and students and by the administration (Article 14, 2023).

Every 2 months, a student at an Indian Institute of Technology (IIT) commits suicide, as shown by official data. Thirty-three IIT students, unable to cope with the academic pressure despite having cracked some of India’s toughest entrance exams, had ended their lives in the 63 months since the start of 2018. The National Institutes of Technology (NIT) witnessed 24 student suicides during the same period, while the Indian Institute of Management (IIM) witnessed four (The Telegraph, 2023a).

Junior Union Education Minister Subhas Sarkar provided suicide data in the Rajya Sabha on March 15, 2023, in response to questions from Congress member L. Hanumanthaiah. ‘Academic stress, family reasons, personal reasons, mental health issues, etc, are some of the reasons for such suicide cases’, Sarkar said. Data provided on December 20, 2021, by Education Minister Dharmendra Pradhan showed 37 student suicides at central universities and nine at the Indian Institute of Science, Bangalore, between 2014 and 2021 (Ibid).

The recent death of Anil Kumar, a 21-year-old student at the Indian Institute of Technology, Delhi (IIT-D), who committed suicide, has once again sparked a conversation regarding the institution’s mode of education. Anil Kumar, a resident of Banda district in Uttar Pradesh, belonged to the Dalit community. A student of Bachelor of Technology (B. Tech.) in Mathematics and Computing at the institute, his death on September 1, comes after a series of suicides in India’s prestigious colleges, including that of Ayush Ashna, a 4th-year Dalit student in the same department of IIT-Delhi (The Citizen, 2023).

10 Economic Deprivation Still a Reality

The National Commission for Scheduled Castes (NCSC), in its annual report for the year 2018–2019 and 2019–2020, makes a reference to Article 46 of the Constitution of India, aimed at the social and economic empowerment of Scheduled Castes and Scheduled Tribes. The article states: 'The State shall promote with special care the educational and economic interests of the weaker sections of the people, and in particular, of the Scheduled Castes and the Scheduled Tribes and shall protect them from social injustice and all forms of exploitation.' At the time of independence, about 95% of the Scheduled Caste population was below the poverty line.

How much progress has been made for the economic empowerment of Dalits in the country is still a question that warrants an urgent intervention by all stakeholders. Over the years, intervention by both the central and state governments has certainly brought some changes when it comes to the economic empowerment of Dalits and Adivasis, but a large chunk of the Dalit and Adivasi populations are still excluded from the development process at multiple levels. The discrimination and exclusion that these community members face in society are also reflected in the economic sphere.

The Planning Commission data on percentage of population below poverty line by social group for 2011–2012 stated that 31.5% in rural areas and 21.7% in urban areas belonged to Scheduled Castes. Whereas for all categories taken together the figure stood at 25.7% in rural areas and 13.7% in urban areas (Report, 2019–2020, p. 321). The government of India has currently no data on the actual percentage or the total number of people living below poverty line by social groups in the country. This was made clear in a response given by the Minister of Statistics and Programme Implementation in Rajya Sabha on March 27, 2023, wherein he made reference to the Planning Commission data released in 2013, which estimated 27 million people living below the poverty line (The Hindu, 2023).

According to the Global Multidimensional Poverty Index (MPI) 2021, in India, the Scheduled Tribe group accounts for 9.4% of the population and is the poorest; more than half (65 million of 129 million people) live in multidimensional poverty. This group accounts for about one-sixth of all people living in multidimensional poverty in India and records the highest incidence (50.6%) and intensity (45.9%). The Scheduled Caste group follows, with 33.3% (94 million of 283 million people) living in multidimensional poverty. On the other hand, 27.2% of the Other Backward Class group (160 million of 588 million people) lives in multidimensional poverty, showing a lower incidence but a similar intensity compared with the Scheduled Caste group, which is a little less than 45%. Overall, five out of six multidimensionally poor people in India live in households whose head is from a Scheduled Tribe, a Scheduled Caste or Other Backward Classes (Report, 2021, pp. 15–16).

How much progress has taken place over the years and Dalits' economic situation now need to be probed further. Even in government statistics, the situation is not something to be proud of. The National Sample Survey (NSS) 77th Round Report, 2019 reveals major gaps between Dalits and others vis-à-vis the land question in rural India (Table 9).

The average area (in hectares) owned per household across social groups is as follows: among agricultural households, SCs account for 0.520; STs, 0.862; OBCs, 0.912; and others, 1.054. Among non-agricultural households, the figure stands as follows: SCs, 0.059; STs, 0.127; OBCs, 0.80; and others, 0.118 (Report, 2019, p. 54). In such a complex scenario, it is the Dalit community that owns less land in comparison to other groups in rural areas (Table 10).

Both among agricultural and non-agricultural households the size class of land possessed as mentioned above is a matter of concern. Having land which is certainly not in large/medium range amounts to being in a landless situation. This kind of situation also forces Dalits to work as agricultural labour on other community's land (Table 11).

Table 9 The percentage distribution of agricultural and non-agricultural households in rural areas by social group

Social group	Agricultural households	Non-agricultural households
SC	15.9	28.4
ST	14.2	10.0
OBC	45.8	42.8
Others	24.1	18.8

Source: Report (2019), p. 46

Table 10 The percentage distribution of agricultural and non-agricultural households by size class of land possessed (per hectare) for Scheduled Castes

Size class of land	Agricultural households	Non-agricultural households
Less than 0.01	1.4	28.7
0.01–0.40	47.9	68.9
0.41–1.00	33.4	1.7
1.01–2.00	11.7	0.2
2.01–4.00	4.6	0.4
4.01–10.00	1.0	0.0

Source: Report (2019), p. 46

Table 11 Percentage distribution of rural households and percentage distribution of area owned by size category of ownership holdings for each household social group

Size category of ownership holdings (in hectares)	Agricultural households				Non-agricultural households			
	SC	ST	OBC	Others	SC	ST	OBC	Others
Landless	3.8	3.0	2.3	1.9	12.4	18.9	16.3	13.0
Marginal	81.7	68.6	70.3	64.2	86.9	77.4	82.5	84.9
Small	10.1	19.6	16.3	18.8	0.3	3.4	0.9	1.5
Semi-medium	3.7	7.0	7.9	11.2	0.4	0.4	0.3	0.5
Medium	0.7	1.7	2.8	3.6	0.0	0.0	0.0	0.1
Large	0.0	0.2	0.3	0.3	0.0	0.0	0.0	0.0

Source: Report (2019), p. 52

Here, again, we see the higher share of Dalits in the landless and marginal categories in comparison to others and also OBCs and STs. This also proves that landlessness and marginality are common features in rural India among Dalits. Despite all attempts at land reforms in various states in India, governments have failed to distribute land fairly and proportionately.

11 Caste and Labour Market Discrimination

The India Employment Report by the International Labour Organization (ILO) and the Institute for Human Development has highlighted the wide disparity in the labour market, wherein labourers belonging to Dalit and Adivasi communities face all kinds of problems that reflect the labour scenario in the country in a sorry state of affairs. The report goes on to observe that despite affirmative action and targeted policies, Scheduled Castes (SCs) and Scheduled Tribes (STs) still lag in terms of access to better jobs. SCs and STs have greater participation in work due to economic necessity but are engaged more in low-paid, temporary casual wage work and informal employment. They are also involved in low-skill and no-skill jobs and have low levels of educational attainment. These factors contribute to their overall lack of access to decent employment opportunities in the labour market (Report, 2024, p. 32) (Table 12).

From the above table, the actual situation in the labour market for different social groups is very clear. Why Dalits and Adivasis fare so poorly has remained a question that demands urgent intervention from different stakeholders, be it from the government or international organisations like the ILO. Whether the situation will improve in near future or not remains to be seen. But what is also clear is the fact that the discrimination and exclusion that Dalits and Adivasis face in society extends into the economy, with labour market discrimination perhaps being the first indicator in that sense. Why has Dalit and Adivasi representation remained the highest in the unorganised and informal sector? Why are Dalits and Adivasis found in large numbers in low-skill and no-skill jobs? On top of all these, they are found to have

Table 12 Employment characteristics (UPSS, aged 15+), by social groups, 2022, in %

Work category	Scheduled Tribes (STs)	Scheduled Castes (SCs)	Other Backward Classes (OBCs)	General category
Worker population in ratio	66.8	54.2	52.5	47.6
Unemployment rate	2.3	4.4	3.9	4.9
Self-employed	58.6	42.0	59.9	58.2
Regular	12.4	19.8	20.1	30.6
Casual	29.0	38.2	20.1	11.2
Unorganised	85.5	81.3	83.0	74.9
Formal	5.1	7.3	8.7	16.2
Informal	94.9	92.7	91.3	83.8
High- and medium-skill jobs	4.0	6.6	9.7	19.9
Low-skill jobs	65.5	53.1	69.3	66.7
No-skill jobs	30.5	40.4	20.9	13.4
Education (secondary +)	24.4	31.0	38.9	51.2
Population (%)	9.4	19.4	45.5	25.7

Source: Compiled from Periodic Labour Force Data 2022, cited in Report (2024), p. 231

lower levels of education as well. High- and medium-skill jobs are beyond their reach. In fact, whatever is presented here may actually be much worse as far as actual ground realities are concerned.

The situation we find in the government sector is also quite worrisome. Representations of Scheduled Castes in Groups A, B and C of the Central Government Services as of January 01, 2018, were as follows: Group A—13.66%, Group B—17.16%, Group C (excluding sanitation workers)—16.98% and sanitation workers—39.64%. The total representation for Scheduled Castes was 17.41%; for Scheduled Tribes, 7.42%; and for Other Backward Castes, 19.94% (Report, 2019–2020, p. 376).

It is pertinent to ask here where Dalits stand vis-à-vis representation in the labour market and employment in the government sector. The answer provided, as made available by government data, fails to substantially explain the poor representation of Dalits. Another fact that also does not get reflected in government reports is the brute reality of discrimination faced by Dalits in the labour market and government jobs. In postings to different positions and also regular promotions, Dalits have faced innumerable problems, and these issues have remained unaddressed to a large extent even now.

12 The Scheduled Caste Sub Plan (SCSP)

The Scheduled Caste Sub Plan (SCSP) along with Tribal Sub Plan (TSP) are two important initiative of the government both at central and state levels which is aimed at targeted intervention by the government for an overall development initiative through budget allocations and specific nature of schemes and other programmes. The guidelines for SCSP and TSP were spelt out by the erstwhile Planning Commission and which have been upheld by the National Institution for Transforming India (NITI) Aayog, include three most important elements:

1. The budget allocation must be in proportion to the population of SCs and STs.
2. The funds that have been allocated under the SCSP and TSP cannot be diverted for any programmes/schemes/purposes.
3. And the funds that have been allocated must not be allowed to lapse or remain unspent.

Not only the Government of India but also all state governments across the board violate these three important guidelines for the SCSP and TSP.

In the Union Budget for the financial year 2025–2026, the allocation is only Rs 168,478.38 Cr for Scheduled Castes (SCs) and Rs 129,249.75 for Scheduled Tribes (STs). However, as per the NITI Aayog notification, the due allocation for SCs should have been Rs 230,132 Cr and for STs, Rs 132,501 Cr. Non-allocation of the proportionate funds in the Union Budget clearly reflects non-sincere attitude of the government at Centre about the overall inclusive development of the deprived communities. The Dalit Adivasi Budget Analysis (DABA) further revealed that out of the total allocations for SC welfare, only Rs 62,150 Cr, and for ST welfare, only Rs 51,491.59 Cr, are directed towards targeted schemes, accounting for 3.9% and 3.3% of the total central sector (CS) and centrally sponsored scheme (CSS) funds, respectively. The majority of the schemes are either general or non-targeted, which do not directly benefit the targeted beneficiaries but rather cover broader sections of society. It has also been highlighted that out of 236 schemes under the SC budget, only 30 are targeted, and out of 244 schemes under the ST budget, only 31 are targeted schemes. A deeper analysis indicates that 30 schemes for SCs and 31 schemes for STs have their output and outcome indicators in their respective outcome budget documents. Thus, the total budgetary gap for SC and ST communities amounts to Rs 248,991 Cr, with only Rs 113,642 Cr allocated towards targeted schemes. Many effective and targeted schemes, like National Safai Karamchari Finance and Development Corporation, National Scheduled Caste Finance and Development Corporation, and Venture Capital Fund for SCs and OBCs, are systematically underfunded in this budget cycle (Dalit Adivasi Budget Analysis, 2025–2026, pp. 2–3).

Why should non-targeted schemes be a part of the budgetary allocation meant for SCs and STs? Is it not an example of diversion of SC and ST funds for general purposes? The funds allocated for SCs and STs cannot and should not be used for any other purpose under any circumstance, but the central government and the respective state governments have been found to be flouting important guidelines/notifications from the erstwhile Planning Commission and NITI Aayog. Could there be any explanation for the inclusion of non-targeted schemes under budgetary allocations for SCs and STs?

The following non-targeted schemes reveal that in the Union Budget for 2025–2026 for SCs and STs, the allocation also includes schemes that are not relevant for SC and ST development at all: (1) Urea Subsidy Payment for Indigenous Urea and Import of Urea—Rs 10,113 Cr under SC budget and Rs 5239 Cr under ST budget; (2) Nutrient-Based Subsidy Payment for Indigenous P and K Fertilizers and Imported P and K Fertilizers—Rs 4067 Cr under SC budget and Rs 2107 Cr under ST budget; (3) Modified Interest Subvention Scheme (MISS)—Rs 3993 Cr under SC budget; (4) Compensation to Service Providers for Creation and Compensation to Telecom Service Providers—Rs 2324 Cr under SC budget and Rs 979 Cr under ST budget; and (5) Reform Linked Distribution Scheme—Rs 3577 Cr under SC budget and Rs 1703 Cr under ST budget.

The following general schemes have large allocations within SCSP and TSP, which could otherwise address the development gap between SCs and STs and the rest of the population but are not specific and targeted as stated in the outcome budget of the union government: (1) Jal Jeevan Mission (JJM)—Rs 8800 Cr under SC budget and Rs 4000 Cr under ST budget; (2) Road Works under Roads Wing—Rs 15,430 Cr under ST budget; (3) Pradhan Mantri Kisan Samman Nidhi (PM-KISAN)—Rs (11,708 Cr under SC budget and Rs 5658 Cr under ST budget; (4) Flexible Pool for RCH and Health System Strengthening—Rs 6098 Cr under SC budget and Rs 2933 Cr under ST budget; and (5) Crop Insurance Scheme Pradhan Mantri Fasal Bima Yojana—Rs 2048 Cr (Ibid, p. 11).

The data further indicates that a substantial portion of the SC and ST budgets is allocated to general and obsolete schemes rather than to those specifically targeted at bridging the development gaps for these communities. This suggests that SC and ST communities are unlikely to benefit from these large fund allocations. The subsidy for these three programmes are meant for every one and not specific to SCs and STs. There is no reason to make allocation for such subisidy under SCSP and STP. There are general schemes which are meant for every one and there are specific schemes meant for SCs and STs. Under SCSP and TSP the budgetary allocations for schemes needs to be specific and targetted for SCs and STs. This could exacerbate existing poverty and other development indices if not balanced with targeted interventions. The 'National Means cum Merit Scholarship Scheme' for SC communities has also seen a minimal allocation of merely Rs 70 Cr. This is a new initiative which has started functioning in recent years. This is to promote entreprenuerships among SC, ST and OBC community. The 'National Scheduled Caste/Scheduled Tribe Hub Centre' scheme has received Rs 62.5 Cr for SC communities and Rs 60.49 Cr for ST communities. Even the 'Free Coaching for SCs and OBCs' scheme has been allocated a modest sum of Rs 20 Cr (Ibid, pp. 11–12).

It is evident from the above facts that only small amounts of funds are being earmarked for targeted and effective schemes. The most effective and targeted programmes are not given what should have been properly due. For instance, critical schemes such as 'Top-Class Education for SCs' have received a negligible allocation of only Rs 110 Cr. Similarly, the 'National Overseas Scholarship for SCs' under the SC budget has been allocated a mere Rs 130 Cr, benefiting only 120 students across the country. The situation is even more dire under the ST budget, where this same National Overseas Scholarship scheme has been allocated a paltry Rs 0.01 Cr, highlighting a grave concern for tribal communities (Ibid., p. 12).

The allocation in the Union Budget 2024–2025 for Scheduled Castes stands at Rs 165,493 crores and for Scheduled Tribes, Rs 124,909 crores. For the first time, 275 schemes have been included under the Allocation for the Welfare of Scheduled Castes (AWSC) and 281 schemes under the Allocation for the Welfare of Scheduled Tribes (AWST). However, if we place these figures against the background of large-scale poverty among SC and ST communities, as well as against the guidelines issued by the Ministry of Finance, these schemes will not go far to address the purpose of reducing the development gap between SCs/STs and the rest of the population. The proportion of targeted schemes is 83 for both SC and ST budgets, with Rs 87,921.86 Cr (30%) allocated for targeted schemes. A total of Rs 202,479.35 Cr (70%) is allocated for non-targeted schemes, which are diverted away from SCs and STs right at the inception itself. These are de facto general schemes masked as SC or ST budget schemes. They do not qualify as SC or ST schemes that benefit the communities they are intended to serve. This year's budget saw a systemic depreciation of dozens of critical schemes by starving them of necessary funds. For example, schemes like Post-Matric Scholarship, University Grants Commission (UGC), rehabilitation of bonded labour, self-employment of Safai Karamcharis, national fellowship for SCs, Kendriya Vidyalaya Sangathan, Navodaya Vidyalaya Samiti, Indira Gandhi National Open University (IGNOU), grants to voluntary organisations, and land records modernisation—few of the direct-benefiting schemes—are denied necessary funds for SC and ST development. The trend of non-targeted allocations in both statements 10A and 10B continues unabated. Good schemes are being starved, while allocations to irrelevant schemes keep increasing. This year, out of 275 schemes for SCs, 237 schemes are non-targeted and without any strategy to provide benefits to the community. Similarly, only 45 out of 281 schemes for Scheduled Tribes have the potential to provide direct benefits, while the rest of them are general in nature. Moreover, their outcomes do not spell out any clear roadmap for the sustainable development of SC and ST communities. The percentage-wise allocation for Scheduled Castes stood at 11.3%, whereas for Scheduled Tribes, 8.5% (Dalit Adivasi Budget Analysis, 2024–2025, pp. 1–2 & 4).

The allocation for Scheduled Castes in the fiscal year 2023–2024 was Rs 159,126 Cr and for Scheduled Tribes, Rs 119,510 Cr, which was a marginal increase of 0.4% for SCs and 1.1% for STs from the previous fiscal year. Targeted schemes that directly impact the welfare of SCs amounted to Rs 30,475 Cr (2.1%) of the total SC allocation, while for STs, it was Rs 24,384 Cr (1.7%) of the total ST allocation. The remaining plans in the Dalit and Adivasi budgets were de facto general plans disguised as SC or ST plans. A large portion of the schemes—73.30%, amounting to Rs 116,632 Cr for SCs, and 70.16%, amounting to Rs 83,851 Cr for STs—cannot be considered community-beneficial SC/ST schemes as per the guidelines given by the NITI Aayog. Out of the total allocation to SC and ST schemes, the Ministry of

Social Justice and Empowerment was allocated Rs 10,160.94 Cr (6.39%) and the Ministry of Tribal Affairs, Rs 12,386 Cr (10.36%). These are high-quality schemes that directly benefit SCs and STs. However, the schemes allocated to the departments/ministries of Road Transportation (Rs 23,375 Cr—8.39%), Rural Development (Rs 49,792 Cr—17.87%), Fertilizer (Rs 22,562 Cr—8.10%) and Agriculture and Farmers Welfare (Rs 28,706 Cr—10.30%) were either obsolete schemes or merely notional general schemes that did not have physical targets for the welfare of SCs and STs (Dalit Adivasi Budget Analysis, 2023–2024, p. 2).

Also in the fiscal year 2023–2024, out of the total allocation of Rs 2064.19 Cr for SCs under the Ministry of Labour and Employment, Rs 1522 Cr was allocated to the Employees' Pension Scheme 1995, which is a general scheme having no benefits for the community. Atmanirbhar Bharat Rojgar Yojana received Rs 384.24 Cr, which again is not a scheme targeted for Dalits. Likewise, out of the total allocation of Rs 1069.42 Cr for STs under the Ministry of Labour and Employment, Rs 788 Cr was allocated for the Employees Pension Scheme 1995 and Rs 201.70 Cr for Atmanirbhar Bharat Rojgar Yojana. This is a violation of the SCSP/TSP guidelines. In total, Rs 2895.94 Cr from Dalit and Adivasi budgets under the Ministry of Labour and Employment were diverted towards general schemes. Specifically, Rs 1906.24 Cr were diverted from the SC budget and Rs 989.7 Cr from the ST budget under the Ministry of Labour and Employment (Ibid, p. 4).

In the Union Budget 2023–2024, Rs 22,766.98 Cr from the SC budget and Rs 13,260.21 Cr from the ST budget were allocated to livelihood and skill development programmes. The allocation of Rs 3532.29 Cr for Dalits and Rs 2472.6 Cr for Adivasis was made under the National Rural Livelihood Mission, which is a general scheme. The Pradhan Mantri Anusuchit Jaati Abhyuday Yojana (PM AJAY) scheme was allocated Rs 2050 Cr for SCs, which is a targeted scheme. However, the allocation for the Crop Insurance Scheme was Rs 2666.94 Cr for SCs and Rs 1381.26 Cr for STs, which does not have any direct benefit for them. In total, Rs 9470.39 Cr was allocated to targeted schemes and Rs 26,556.8 Cr to non-targeted schemes, which is a huge amount (Ibid, p. 7).

The percentage allocation under the Union Budget has never made proportionate allocations under the SCSP. Figures from the last five fiscal years reveal the exact percentage of allocation to central sector schemes and centrally sponsored schemes: for 2019–2020, 8.6%; 2020–2021, 9.3%; 2021–2022, 11.7%; 2022–2023, 11.6%; and 2023–2024, 11.2% (Ibid, p. 5).

Thus, it is clear from the above-mentioned Dalit Adivasi Budget Analysis (DABA) that every year, the Government of India fails to allocate funds under the Union Budget to the tune of thousands of crores, thereby showing its insensitivity to the issue of Dalit development and empowerment. There is complete disregard for the NITI Aayog guidelines, as ministries and departments have been allocated funds of a general nature under the SCSP and TSP budgets. The diversion of funds thus also runs into crores of rupees. The unutilised funds are also a big problem for both the central and state governments. Is anyone listening?

13 Right to Health

Dalits and Adivasis face health-related problems which impacts their overall standing vis-à-vis the health condition. It is not only life expectancy that is low but on every indicator of being a healthy person, they lag behind mainly due to wretchedness that is part of their life. The society at large treats them as unworthy of being an equal citizen, it is no wonder that hunger, malnutrition, infant mortality, maternal mortality, anaemia, tuberculosis, cholera, malaria and host of many other diseases are found to be quite common amongst them.

14 National Family and Health Survey (NFHS-5) 2019–2021

The National Family Health Survey 2019–2021 (NFHS-5), the fifth in the NFHS series, provides information on population, health and nutrition for India, each state/union territory (UT), and 707 districts as of March 31, 2017. The main objective of each successive round of NFHS has been to provide high-quality data on health and family welfare and on emerging issues in these areas. NFHS-5 data will be useful in setting benchmarks and examining the progress that the health sector has made over time. An attempt has been made here to present snapshots of NFHS-5 data to throw light on the right to health of Dalits and other communities.

The overall basic sanitation services available during this time period was 69%. On the other hand limited sanitation service was found to be 8.4%. The open defecation figure stood at 19.4%. Access to toilet facility by different social category was like this: SC—76.9%; ST—68.5%; OBC—82.3% and for Others—92.5%. Bihar (38.1%), Jharkhand (32.9%) and Odisha (33.3%) are the worst performing states as far as the question of unimproved sanitation facilities are concerned.

On the question of infant and child mortality, the under-five mortality rate was higher in rural areas than in urban areas (46 deaths per 1000 live births versus 32 deaths per 1000 live births). The under-five mortality rate was highest in Uttar Pradesh (60 deaths per 1000 live births) and lowest in Kerala and Puducherry (five and four deaths per 1000 live births, respectively). Other worst-performing states included Bihar (56), Chhattisgarh (50), Madhya Pradesh (49), Uttarakhand (46), Jharkhand (45), Tripura (43), Odisha (41) and Meghalaya (40).

The under-five mortality rate was highest among Scheduled Tribes (50 deaths per 1000 live births), followed by Scheduled Castes (49 deaths per 1000 live births), Other Backward Castes (41 deaths per 1000 live births) and others (33 deaths per 1000 live births).

Prevalence of anaemia (with less than 11.0 g/dl) has been found to be highest among Scheduled Tribes (72.4%), followed by Scheduled Castes (69.5%), Other Backward Castes (65.2%) and others (65.8%).

15 Life Expectancy at Birth

Life expectancy at birth varies largely across castes, religions and regions in India. Life expectancy at birth is lowest among SCs (63.13), followed by STs (64.02), OBCs (65.06) and others (67.94). The caste system, with its societal stratification and social restrictions, continues to have a major impact in India. Poor socio-economic status is significantly associated with poor health outcomes and lower access to healthcare facilities. The benefits of caste-based employment, education and health schemes are largely availed by the better-off within deprived caste groups. As a result, the average remain low and the poor are getting poorer. Similarly, gender variations in health condition are found to be persistent, cutting across caste and religion (Kumari & Mohanty, 2020, pp. 3–8).

16 Deprivation and Discrimination Faced by Dalits

There is a long history of deprivation and discrimination that Dalits have been facing. In 1993–1994, as per the poverty estimates prepared by the erstwhile Planning Commission, about 48.11% of Scheduled Caste households were below the poverty line in rural areas and 49.48% in urban areas, as compared to 37.27% for the general population in rural areas and 32.36% in urban areas (Report, 1996–1998, p. 82). About three-fourths of them lived in rural areas. Of the total households, nearly 63% of them earned their living as wage labourers, and the remaining were engaged in self-employed economic activities of various kinds. Despite the implementation of wage employment programmes targeted at poor and vulnerable sections during the last several years, they were not able to provide a minimum livelihood to a large number of Scheduled Castes. Nearly 60% of agricultural labour households and a little more than 40% of wage labourers in the rural non-farm sector were below the poverty line and were unable to achieve a minimum level of income. Thus, a vast majority of Scheduled Caste wage labour households remained without the security of a minimum income and living standard (Thorat, 1999a, p. 19).

Most Dalits continue to live in extreme poverty, without land or opportunities for better employment or education. With the exception of a minority that has benefited from reservation quotas in education and government jobs, Dalits are relegated to the most menial of tasks, such as manual scavenging, removal of human wastes and dead animals, leather work, street sweeping, cobbling and similar occupations. The plight of India's 'untouchables' elicits only sporadic attention within the country. Public outrage over large-scale incidents of violence or, particularly, egregious examples of discrimination fades quickly, and the state is under little pressure to undertake more meaningful reforms (Narula, 1999, pp. 2–3).

Due to centuries of oppression, the Scheduled Castes have remained backwards in all respects and have come to occupy the lowest places in society. Poverty, illiteracy and unemployment have been the major problems facing the Dalit communities. According to the 1991 Census, Bihar had a Scheduled Caste population of 125.72 lakhs, which accounted for 14.55% of the state's total population of 863.74 lakhs. Of this, 92% of the Scheduled Castes in Bihar lived in rural areas, which was higher than the all-India average of 84%. Most of them earned their livelihood as agricultural labourers, nearly 73% compared to the all-India figure of only 48%. In Bihar, the Scheduled Castes did not receive year-round employment at reasonable wage levels. Thus, most of them manage to get only seasonal, low-paid employment, and very few own land as small and marginal farmers (Rath, 1996, p. 22).

The general condition of education among the Scheduled Castes has been quite disturbing. The literacy rate among Scheduled Castes, according to the 1991 Census, was only 37.41% as against the all-India average of 52.71% for general communities. It has been alarming to note that the literacy rate among the Scheduled Castes in Bihar was only 15.1%, which is the lowest in India. The overarching reach of the caste system, with its several conduct rules, affects the lives of the lowest-caste people in many ways and also has a deep impact on overall socio-economic and human development.

A report issued by the National Commission for Scheduled Castes and Scheduled Tribes underscored that 'untouchability' was practised in many forms throughout the country. The report described a number of social manifestations of caste-based discrimination in the 1990s: Scheduled Caste bridegrooms were not permitted to ride mares in villages, Scheduled Castes could not sit on their charpoys when persons of other castes passed by, Scheduled Castes were not permitted to draw water from common wells and hand pumps, and in many tea shops and dhabas, separate crockery and cutlery were used to serve Scheduled Castes (Report, 1994–1996, p. IV).

Most Dalit victims of abuse are landless agricultural labourers. Land is the prime asset in rural areas, determining an individual's standard of living and social status. The lack of access to land makes Dalits economically vulnerable; their dependency is exploited by upper- and middle-caste landlords, allowing many abuses to go unpunished. Whenever Dalits have tried to organise themselves or assert their rights, there has been a backlash from feudal lords, resulting in mass killings, gang rapes, looting, arson, etc. in Dalit bastis (Report, 1994–1996: Ibid).

Whether caste clashes are social, economic or political in nature, they are premised on the same basic principle: any attempt to alter village customs or to demand land, wage increase or the exercise of political rights leads to violence and economic retaliation on the part of those most threatened by changes in the status quo.

17 Constitutional and Legal Safeguards: An Overview

The Indian Constitution has provions for the rights of iys citizens in a very elaborate manner. It's Preamble, Part-III on Fundamental Rights containing Articles 12–39 and Part-IV on Directive Principles of State Policy comprising Articles 36–51 are considered as the great charter of freedoms for Indian citizens.

The Constitution of India contains an impressive array of provisions for the removal of disabilities and discrimination against Dalits. These provisions are related to prohibition of restrictions on access to public places (Article 15.2); reservation of appointments or posts in favour of backward classes of citizens not adequately represented in state services (Article 16.4); abolition of *untouchability* (Article 17); prohibition of traffic in human beings and forced labour (Article 23); guarantee of the right to profess, practice and propagate religion (Article 25); protection of the right to admission to educational institutions (Article 29.2); special care for the promotion of educational and economic interests of Scheduled Castes and Scheduled Tribes (Article 46); reservation of seats and special representation in Parliament and State Legislatures (Article 334); reservation in services for Scheduled Castes and Scheduled Tribes (Article 335); and appointment of a special officer for Scheduled Castes and Scheduled Tribes (Article 338) (Report, 1990, pp. 1–8).

These Constitutional safeguards are further buttressed by special enactments relating to Dalits, such as the *Untouchability Offence Act 1955*, which was renamed and amended (in 1976) as the *Protection of Civil Rights Act (PCRA) 1955*. This Act provides penalties for offences committed against Dalits, such as refusing their admission to hospitals, educational institutions or hostels; refusing to sell them goods or offer them services; preventing their exercise of the rights granted under Article 17; and demanding them to perform unlawful compulsory labour relating to *untouchability*, like scavenging, sweeping, the removal of carcasses, flaying animals, removing umbilical cords or any job similar to these in nature. The violation of these provisions under this Act invites imprisonment of not less than 2 years and a fine. The Act also provides for the cancellation and suspension of licences, the resumption or suspension of grants and the imposition of collective fines. Subsequent convictions carry higher penalties. Every offence punishable under the Act shall be cognisable. Every such offence, except where punishable by imprisonment for a minimum term exceeding 3 months, may be tried summarily (Report, 1994–1996).

Despite various measures to improve the socio-economic conditions of Scheduled Castes and Scheduled Tribes, they remain vulnerable. They are denied a number of civil rights. They are subjected to various offences, indignities, humiliations and harassments. They have, in several brutal incidents, been deprived of their life and property. Serious crimes have been committed against them for various historical, social and economic reasons. Under the circumstances, existing laws, such as PCRA 1955 and the normal provisions of the Indian Penal Code, have been found ineffective in checking and deterring crimes committed by non-Scheduled castes and Tribes against them. The need for new special legislation became necessary, and that is how the *Scheduled Castes and Scheduled Tribes (Prevention of Atrocities) Act 1989* was passed and put into force in 1990.

The Scheduled Castes and Scheduled Tribes (Prevention of Atrocities) Act 1989 specified the atrocities that are punishable under the Act. These are forcing the eating of noxious substances, dumping waste matter on land, denudation, wrongful occupation of land, dispossession, bonded labour, intimidation during voting, mischievous litigation, furnishing false information, public humiliation, outrage of modesty, sexual exploitation, fouling of water sources, obstruction of entry to a place of public resort, eviction from habitation, mischief with explosives, destruction of buildings and suppression of evidence. These offences under the Prevention of Atrocities Act carry heavier penalties than similar offences under the Indian Penal Code. For example, the offences of custodial rape, highway robbery and house breaking by night, which carry a minimum punishment of 10 years under the Indian Penal Code, are punishable under the Prevention of Atrocities Act by life imprisonment and a fine (Report, 1994–1996).

The Act casts specific responsibility on the police to promptly register cases under the provisions of the Act, investigate them speedily and have them submitted before the courts for speedy disposal. A public servant who is not an SC/ST and who wilfully neglects duties under the Act can be imprisoned for 6 months to a year. The Act provides for the appointment of special public prosecutors and the setting up of special courts to ensure speedy trials. Persons arrested under the Act do not have the right to seek anticipatory bail. And it is the responsibility of the central government to present an annual report before Parliament on the progress of the Act's implementation (Report, 1994–1996).

In addition to special enactments meant exclusively for Scheduled Castes and Scheduled Tribes, there are other enactments of general applicability that are also of relevance in the context of Scheduled Castes and Scheduled Tribes as they are meant to benefit them to a large extent. They are as follows.

18 The Bonded Labour System (Abolition) Act, 1976

This Act abolished bonded labour in all its forms, and every bonded labourer was freed and discharged from any obligation to render labour under compulsion. Every obligation to repay any bonded debt was also extinguished. Compelling a person to render any bonded labour, advancing any loan under an agreement that provides for bonded labour, failure to restore to a bonded labourer possession of any property seised from him or recovery of bonded debt are some of the offences under the Act (Report, 1994–1996).

The very definition of the term 'bonded labour' restricts its scope so much that it excludes many who are virtually compelled but may not be forced to work as bonded labourers. It is particularly difficult to establish the element of force applied by the creditors, with the result that many labourers are excluded from the meaning of the term, though their condition is by no means better than that of others. Because of the apparent loophole in the law, in states like Bihar, systems like *attached labour* cannot be brought under the purview of the Bonded Labour System (Abolition) Act, 1976. Terms like *attached labour* are, however, nothing but a euphemism for bonded labour. It is also an undisputed fact that about 80% of the bonded labourers identified so far belong to the Scheduled Caste and Scheduled Tribe categories (Report, 1982–1983, p. 112).

19 The Minimum Wage Act 1948

This Act provides for the fixation of minimum rates of wages in employment where labour is vulnerable to exploitation. The Act provides the machinery for fixing wages and makes other provisions relating to hours of work, overtime payments and rest day (Report, 1990, pp. 1–2).

Mere notification of minimum wages is not enough. The actual payment of minimum wages to agricultural workers who are not organised should be ensured, and instances are not wanting where agricultural landless labourers, most of whom happen to be Scheduled Castes, have to face inhuman atrocities when they dare to demand the wages prescribed by the government. As a matter of fact, next to land disputes, the issue of minimum wage payments figures prominently, and this has constituted about 12% of the cases in which members of the Scheduled Castes were victims (Report, 1982–1983).

20 The Child Labour (Prohibition and Regulation) Act 1986

This Act bans the employment of children below the age of 14 years in any factories, mines and other hazardous occupations and regulates the conditions of work for children engaged in non-hazardous jobs (Report, 1990, op. cit).

Children's participation in work is influenced by extra-economic factors emanating from social and economic relations based on the caste system in the tradional society. The 'low caste untouchables' are often obliged to work under elements of social compulsion and force. These relations are traditionally governed by caste considerations.

Evidence on the magnitude, patterns and causes of child labour during the 1990s disclosed that, overall, about 7% of children (in the age group 5–14) were engaged in employment. But compared to 'others', the level was two to three times higher among the discriminated against and the isolated groups of Scheduled Castes and Tribes. In fact, together, Scheduled Castes and Tribes accounted for about 40% of the country's child labourers, which was higher than their share in the total child population in the country (Thorat, 1999b, p. 173).

21 Social Profile of Bihar: Bihar Caste-Based Enumeration/ Survey 2022–2023

Bihar is located in the eastern part of the country (between 83°30′ and 88°00′ longitude). It lies midway between humid West Bengal in the east and sub-humid Uttar Pradesh in the west, giving it a transitional position in terms of climate, economy and culture. It is bounded by Nepal in the north and by Jharkhand in the south. The

Bihar plain is divided into two unequal halves by the river Ganga, which flows through the middle from west to east. It has nine administrative divisions and 38 districts (Bihar State Profile, n.d.).

The rationale for conducting a caste-based enumeration/survey by the Bihar government is rooted in its commitment to ensuring justice alongside growth. A need was felt to collect the social, economic and educational data of people belonging to different castes, communities, religions and work for the overall comprehensive development of the state. Thus, a consensus resolution was adopted in the Bihar Legislative Assembly and the Bihar Legislative Council on February 18, 2019, recommending to the central government the conduct of a caste-based census in 2021. A letter dated April 08, 2019 with a demand for caste census was thereafter sent to the Union Home Ministry. Subsequently, an all-party delegation from Bihar also met with the Prime Minister on August 03, 2021, putting forward the demand for a caste census in 2021. But there was no initiative from the central government in this regard. In the absence of any response from the central government on this matter, a meeting of all nine political parties in the Bihar Legislative Assembly was held on June 01, 2022, wherein a consensus decision to conduct caste-based enumeration in Bihar was reached. The State Council of Ministers on June 02, 2022, decided to conduct caste based enumeration in two phases by the month of February 2023 (Report, 2023, pp. 11–12).

Along with the need for a total headcount of people belonging to different castes, communities and religions in Bihar, there also emerged a demand for a social, economic and educational survey to enable the government to undertake proper policy interventions for all-inclusive development in the state. The following seven indicators were identified for data collection: I—income; II—employment; III—education; IV—housing; V—migration; VI—vehicle ownership; and VII—laptop/computer access. On the orders of the Council of Ministers, it was decided to entrust to the General Administration Department the conduct of caste-based enumeration/survey work. Accordingly, district magistrates and other officers in the district as well as administrative block-level officials, along with three lakh employees (primary school teachers, municipality corporation staff, etc.), were given training to conduct this massive exercise. The first phase of the caste-based enumeration/survey was conducted from January 07, 2023, to January 21, 2023. In this phase, about 1 crore, 76 lakh, 93 thousand and 038 (17,693,038) households were identified. In between, some writ petitions challenging the caste-based survey were filed before the High Court and the Supreme Court, which stalled their work for some time. By the time the Patna High Court issued its injunction to halt the survey on May 04, 2023, most of the work had already been done (Ibid, pp. 12–14).

Upon receiving clearance from the High Court and the Supreme Court, the second phase of the survey was completed, during which data was collected for 2 crore, 76 lakh, 68 thousand and 930 (27,668,930) households. Cross-checking of data was also undertaken at the panchayat, block and municipal corporation levels to clear all possible margins of errors. Finally, after verifying the collected data, the survey report was released on October 02, 2023. Subsequently, the report was shared with representatives of nine political parties on October 03, 2023 (Ibid, p. 15). The

Table 13 Social demographic profile

Social-caste category	Population in percentage
Other Backward Caste (OBC)	27.12%
Extremely Backward Caste (EBC)	36.01%
Scheduled Caste (SC)	19.65%
Scheduled Tribe (ST)	1.68%
General [a]	15.52%

Source: Report (2023), p. 23
[a]This includes upper castes among Hindus and Muslims, along with 12 unlisted castes

detailed results of Bihar's caste survey were made public on November 07, 2023, during the winter session of the state assembly.

According to the caste-based enumeration/survey of 2022–2023, the total number of people residing in Bihar stood at 12 crore, 53 lakh, 53 thousand and 288 (125,353,288). The total number of migrants living outside the state was found to be 53 lakh, 72 thousand and 022 (5,372,022). The male population in Bihar stands at 6 crore, 41 lakh, 31 thousand and 992 (64,131,992), whereas the female population stood at 6 crore, 11 lakh, 38 thousand and 460 (61,138,460). The transgender population has been found to be 82 thousand and 836 (82,836). The sex ratio in Bihar is 953 women per 1000 men (Ibid, pp. 16–17) (Table 13).

Brahmins account for 3.65%; Bhumihar, 2.86%; Rajput, 3.45%; Kayastha, 0.60%; Sheikh (Muslim), 3.83%; Pathan (Muslim), 0.75%; Saiyad (Muslim), 0.22%; and 12 unlisted castes, 0.1396% (Ibid, p. 24).

Among Other Backward Castes (OBCs), the most dominant castes are as follows: Yadav—14.26%, Kushwaha (Koiri)—4.21%, Kurmi—2.87% and Bania—2.31% (Ibid, p. 25).

Among Extremely Backward Castes (EBCs), the most dominant are Teli—2.81%, Mallah—2.60%, Kanu—2.21%, Dhanuk—2.13% and Momin/Julaha (Ansari/Muslim)—3.54% (Ibid, p. 28).

Among Scheduled Castes (SCs), the most populous are Dusadh—5.31%, Chamar—5.25%, Musahar—3.08%, Pan/Sawasi/Panar—1.70%, Pasi—0.98%, Bhuiyan—0.89% and Dhobi (Washer-man)—0.83% (Ibid, p. 36).

In Bihar, there are 22 castes listed under the Scheduled Caste category: (1) Dusadh, (2) Chamar, (3) Musahar, (4) Pan/Sawasi/Panar, (5) Pasi, (6) Bhuiyan, (7) Dhobi, (8) Chaupal, (9) Rajwar, (10) Dom, (11) Hari/Mehtar/Bhangi, (12) Bantar, (13) Nat, (14) Turi, (15) Bhogta, (16) Kurariar, (17) Dabgar, (18) Halalkhor, (19) Kanjar, (20) Bauri, (21) Lalbegi and (22) Ghasi (Ibid, pp. 36–37).

22 Nature of Problem

The perpetration of atrocities against Dalits has been closely linked to the persistence of untouchability. Dalits have been increasingly showing resentment against the social indignities emanating from the practice of untouchability in different forms. These include denial of entry into public places of worship, discrimination and differential treatment in hotels and tea stalls, as well as restrictions on movement in certain localities, wearing good clothes, riding horses and leading marriage processions through certain caste-Hindu localities.

Other major factors listed in reports of the SC/ST commission included envy of the dominant and well off communities for the welfare measures adopted by the government to ameliorate the socio-economic conditions of Dalits, the wide economic disparities arising out of landlessness, wage labour bondage, non-payment of fair share of agricultural produce to Dalit share croppers, forced harvesting of crops, forced eviction of Dalits from their land and house sites, dispute over non-payment of minimum wages prescribed by the state and land disputes especially as a result of land reforms and redistribution of surplus lands.

In the districts of erstwhile central Bihar, money lending, bonded labour, sexual assault on Dalit women and abuse of landless labourers by landowners have all contributed to violent clashes between various castes. From the mid-1970s onwards, sharp clashes were reported between Dalit agricultural workers and landlords. Much of the tension in the area could be directly traced to the rise of caste-based senas of the upper castes, as well as some backward castes, like Yadavs and Kurmis (and various left organisations). Every major carnage was accompanied by brutality, horror and savagery. Whether at Belchi, Pipra, Parasbigha or other places of carnage, Dalit agricultural labourers were targeted to be exterminated from the face of this earth. The ten districts that come under the erstwhile central Bihar have been the worst site of caste carnage during the 1970s, 1980s and 1990s. At times, even the local police inflicted heavy casualties on Dalits in these areas. The Arwal massacre was a classic example in this regard. Ranveer Sena, a private army of upper-caste landlords, has been in the news in recent years for the brutal massacres of Dalits. The worst-ever mass killing of Dalits at Laxmanpur Bathe, Jehanabad, on December 1/2, 1997, is an example of upper-caste barbarism.

23 Objectives

The main concern of this analysis is to analyse the menace of caste carnage and other human rights violations against Dalits in the erstwhile central Bihar from 1977 to 1997. In other words, the large number of human rights violations suffered by Dalits over two decades in the ten districts of erstwhile central Bihar is the main focus of this study. The objectives of this analysis are as follows:

1. To examine the factors responsible for the growing menace of caste carnage and other human rights violations against Dalits in India and the erstwhile central Bihar from 1977 to 1997.
2. To assess the role of radical groups and voluntary organisations in creating awareness among Dalits and the far-reaching consequences of the awareness programmes launched by these groups in relation to a large number of reported conflicts.

3. To evaluate the role of the state and its agencies in checking the growing violence and human rights violations against Dalits, including the role of the judiciary in the speedy trial of cases and in imparting justice, as well as the contributions of the media and political parties.
4. To compile data and information from several sources to analyse the human rights situations of Dalits in the post-Laxmanpur Bathe massacre phase within the districts of erstwhile central Bihar.

24 Methods and Sources of Data Collection

The methods used in this work are historical and analytical. At the micro level, information was collected through unstructured interviews, informal talks and non-participant observation. At the macro level, primary sources comprised data collected from the reports of the Welfare and Police departments in Patna. Secondary sources include books, journals, magazines, newspapers and reports prepared by various human rights organisations like the People's Union for Democratic Rights (PUDR). Various reports from the National Commission for Scheduled Castes and Scheduled Tribes and the Ministry of Home Affairs and other reports from the central government and the state government of Bihar have been taken into consideration for a wide and meaningful analysis.

25 The Scheme of Chapters

All in all, there are six chapters in this study, including introductory and concluding parts. The first chapter, which is the introduction, provides a general overview of the human rights situation of Dalits in India and the erstwhile central Bihar. It also discusses the constitutional and legal safeguards available to Dalits, the socio-economic profile of the region, the nature of the problem, the objectives of the study, the methods employed and the structure of the work.

The second chapter is about theoretical framework which focuses on the essence of human rights, several theories of human rights, the Universal Declaration of Human Rights, UN Human Rights mechanisms, human rights and Indian Constitution and also human rights from the Dalit perspective.

The third chapter focuses on the human rights situation of Dalits in Bihar, with special reference to the erstwhile central Bihar. Some of the major incidents of caste carnage, from Belchi in 1977 to Laxmanpur Bathe in 1997, have been highlighted in this chapter. The socio-economic and political factors responsible for the growing violations of human rights against Dalits have also been explored.

The fourth chapter deals with radical groups and voluntary organisations, highlighting their role in creating awareness against exploitation and assessing their fallouts.

The fifth chapter talks about the role of the state, its agencies and political parties in worsening the human rights situation of Dalits. The role of the judiciary in delivering speedy and fair justice and that of the media in the correct portrayal of the prevailing socio-economic and political order responsible for human rights abuses have been examined.

The sixth chapter serves as the conclusion, which aims to provide an overall assessment of Dalit human rights in India and in the state of Bihar.

References

Acharya, S., & Sahoo, H. (2019). Harihar, education among scheduled caste population in India. *Indonesian Journal of Geography, 51*(3), 399–400.

Ahuja, R. (1993). *Indian social system* (p. 364). Rawat Publication.

Ambedkar, B. R. (1987). *Symbols of Hinduism* (Vol. 3, pp. 141–142). Writings and Speeches, Education Department, Bombay, Government of Maharashtra.

Ambedkar, B. R. (1989). *The House the Hindu have built* (Vol. 5, pp. 169, 101, 26, 35, 101-02). Writings and Speeches, Education Department, Bombay, Government of Maharashtra.

Ambedkar, B. R. (1990). *Who were the untouchables* (Vol. 7, pp. 278-79, 20-22, & 259). Writings and Speeches, Education Department, Bombay, Government of Maharashtra.

Article 14. (2023, April 04). *Caste on campus: Dalit students face exclusion, alienation in India's higher educational institutions.* https://article-14.com/post/-caste-on-campus-dalit-students-face-exclusion-alienation-in-india-s-higher-education-institutions%2D%2D642b88a7149fe

Bihar State Profile. (n.d.) *Government of Bihar Website.* https://state.bihar.gov.in/main/Content.html?links&page=Bihar%20State%20Profile

Burman, B. K. R. (1977). The problems of untouchables. In R. Thapar's (Ed.), *Tribe, caste and religion in India* (p. 84). Macmillan India Limited.

Chitre, D. (1982). The architecture of anger: On Namdeo Dhasal's Golpitha. *Journal of South Asian Literature, 17*, 93–95.

Dalit Adivasi Budget Analysis. (2023–2024). *New Delhi, Dalit Aarthik Adhikar Andolan - National Campaign on Dalit Human Rights (NCDHR)* (pp. 2, 4, 5 & 7). http://www.ncdhr.org.in/wp-content/uploads/2023/02/NCDHR-Budget-2023_9-Feb-With-cutmark_pages-to-jpg-0001.jpg

Dalit Adivasi Budget Analysis. (2024–2025). *New Delhi, Dalit Aarthik Adhikar Andolan - National Campaign on Dalit Human Rights (NCDHR)* (pp. 1–2 & 4). https://www.ncdhr.org.in/wp-content/uploads/2024/07/Dalit-Adivasi-Budget-Analysi-2024-25_page-0001.jpg

Dalit Adivasi Budget Analysis. (2025–2026). *New Delhi, Dalit Arthik Adhikar Andolan - National Campaign on Dalit Human Rights (NCDHR)* (pp. 2–3 & 11–12). http://www.ncdhr.org.in/wp-content/uploads/2025/02/Screenshot-43.png

Galanter, M. (1984). *Competing equalities, law and the backward classes in India* (p. 134). Oxford University Press.

Gokhale, N. (2019, May 21). What the Crime Records Bureau's data says about conditions in India's prisons (and what it doesn't). *Scroll.* https://scroll.in/article/922655/what-the-crime-records-bureaus-data-says-about-conditions-in-indias-prisons-and-what-it-doesnt

Guru, G. (1997, November 1998). *Dalit cultural movement and the dialectics of Dalit politics in Maharashtra, Mumbai, Vikas Adhyan Kendra*, cited in seminar 471 (p. 18).

Guru, G. (1998). The politics of naming. *Seminar, 471*, 16.

India Today. (2023, March 30). *19,000+ SC, ST, and OBC dropouts in higher education within 5 years.* https://www.indiatoday.in/education-today/news/story/19000-sc-st-and-obc-dropouts-in-higher-education-within-5-years-2353661-2023-03-30

Indian Express. (2023, December 04). *Over 13,000 SC, ST, OBC students dropped out of central varsities, IITs, IIMs in 5 years.*

Issac, H. R. (1965). *India's ex-untouchables* (p. 39). Asia Publishing House.

Jha, V. (1975). Stages in history of untouchability. *Indian Historical Review, II*(1), 28–31.

Jiloha, R. C. (1995). *The native Indians: In search of identity* (p. 114). New Delhi, Blue Moon Books.

Kumari, M., & Mohanty, S. K. (2020). Caste, religion and regional differentials in life expectancy at birth India: Cross-sectional estimates from recent National Family Health Survey. *BMJ Open*. https://bmjopen.bmj.com/content/bmjopen/10/8/e035392.full.pdf

Narula, S. (1999). Broken people: Caste violence against India's "untouchables". *Human Rights Watch* (pp. 8-9 & 2-3).

NewsClick. (2022, February 11). Budget '23 - Scheme for SC/ST girl students dropped, misguided focus on E-learning. *NewsClick*

Omvedt, G. (1995). *Dalit visions* (pp. 35–38). Orient Longman.

Oommen, T. K. (1994, May 11). *Panchamas to Dalits: The context and content of identity*. The Times of India.

Rashid, O. (2025, March 19). 'No remorse': 44 years after 24 Dalits were killed in UP massacre, three get death penalty. *The Wire*. https://thewire.in/caste/no-remorse-44-years-after-24-dalits-were-killed-in-up-massacre-three-get-death-penalty

Rath, R. L. (1996). *Reservation and social transformation among SCs and STs* (p. 22). Inter India Publications.

Report. (1930). Indian Statutory Commission (Vol. I, p. 37).

Report. (1933). Census of India 1931 (Vol. I, p. 471).

Report. (1982–1983). Scheduled Castes and Scheduled Tribes Commission, New Delhi, Government of India (p. 112).

Report. (1990). National Commission for Scheduled Castes and Scheduled Tribes, New Delhi, Government of India (pp. 1–8).

Report. (1994–1996). National Commission for Scheduled Castes and Scheduled Tribes, New Delhi, Government of India (p. IV).

Report. (1994–1997). *Crime in India.* National Crime Record Bureau, Ministry of Home Affairs, New Delhi, Government of India.

Report. (1996–1998). National Commission for Scheduled Castes and Scheduled Tribes, New Delhi, Government of India (p. 82).

Report. (2014–2022). *All India Survey on Higher Education (AISHE).* Ministry of Education, New Delhi, Government of India.

Report. (2014–2022). *Prison Statistics India (PSI).* National Crime Record Bureau, New Delhi, Government of India.

Report. (2016). *Educational statistics at a glance* (pp. 28, 29 & 37). Ministry of Education, New Delhi, Government of India.

Report. (2018). *Educational statistics at a glance* (pp. 31–32). Ministry of Education, New Delhi, Government of India.

Report. (2018–2020). National Commission for Scheduled Castes, New Delhi, Government of India (p. 113).

Report. (2019). *National Sample Survey, 77th Round* (pp. 46 & 52). Ministry of Statistics and Programme Implementation, New Delhi, Government of India.

Report. (2019–2020). Ministry of Personnel, Public Grievances and Pensions. New Delhi, Government of India, cited in Handbook on Social Welfare Statistics 2021, Ministry of Social Justice and Empowerment, New Delhi, Government of India, 376.

Report. (2020). *Quest for Justice* (p. 81). National Dalit Movement for Justice - NCDHR, New Delhi.

Report. (2021). *Global multidimensional poverty index 2021, unmasking disparities by ethnicity, caste and gender* (pp. 15–16). Oxford Poverty and Human Development Initiative (OPHI) and United Nation Development Programme (UNDP).

Report. (2023). *Bihar Caste Based Enumeration 2022–23* (pp. 11-12, 12-14, 15, 16, 17, 23, 24, 25, 28, 36 & 37). Department of General Administration, Patna, Government of Bihar.

Report. (2024). *India employment: Youth employment, education and skills* (pp. 32 and 231). International Labour Organization (ILO), Geneva.

Report, Special. (2016). *Atrocities against Kuravan Community in Tamil Nadu.* National Commission for Scheduled Castes, New Delhi, Government of India (pp. 7–8). https://ncsc.nic.in/files/review%20proforma/REPORT%20_NCSC_kuruvan.pdf

Shantha, S. (2020, December 10). From segregation to labour, Manu's caste law governs the Indian prison system. *The Wire.* https://thewire.in/caste/india-prisons-caste-labour-segregation

Singh, R. (2018). *Criminal justice in the shadow of caste* (p. 106). National Dalit Movement for Justice (NDMJ) - National Campaign on Dalit Human Rights (NCDHR).

The Citizen. (2023, September 07). What's forced Dalit IITian to end his life? There is an emerging pattern in IIT, another student dies by suicide. https://www.thecitizen.in/india/whats-forced-dalit-iitian-to-end-his-life-959949

The Hindu. (2022, November 29). Union Government stops pre-matric scholarship for SC, ST, OBC and minority students of Class 1 to 8, and explains why.

The Hindu. (2023, March 28). When asked for data on poverty reduction, Government of India gives 10 year old data.

The Hindu. (2024a, January 03). Supreme Court seeks response from Centre, States on caste discrimination in prisons.

The Hindu. (2024b, February 29). End caste, religion-based discrimination in prisons: Centre.

The Hindu. (2024c, October 03). Segregation of work in prisons on the basis of caste unconstitutional: Supreme Court.

The Hindu. (2025, January 01). Centre amends prison manual rules, asks States to address issue of caste-based discrimination.

The Telegraph. (2023a, March 17). Grim data on suicides at IITs.

The Telegraph. (2023b, April 09). Tussle over pre-matric and post-matric scholarships for SC-ST students.

The Times of India. (2023a, October 01). Kumher Dalit massacre: 31 years on, 9 get life term for killing 16 Dalits in Rajasthan.

The Times of India. (2023b, June 03). UP: 42 years after Dalit killing, life term for 90 year old.

The Times of India. (2024, March 21). HC suspends sentence of all 9 convicts of Kumher massacre.

Thorat, S. K. (1999a). Social security in unorganised sector in India: How secured are the scheduled castes? *Indian Journal of Labour Economics, 19.*

Thorat, S. K. (1999b). Poverty, caste and child labour in India. In K. Voll (Ed.), *Against child labour* (p. 173). Mosaic Books and Third Millennium Transparency.

Zelliot, E. (1996). *From untouchable to Dalit.* (pp. 267 & 271). Manohar Publishers.

Theoretical Framework: Human Rights from the Dalit Perspective

Abstract This chapter explains the essence of human rights and how the conceptual understanding of human rights evolved over a long period of time. Along with this theoretical journey, it examines how the United Nations took up the issues and problems centred on massive human rights violations reported from all over the world, highlighting the role of the state and its constitutional and legislative measures in the promotion and protection of human rights, as well as the principles of due diligence and accountability of the state. The chapter then proceeds to discuss how the concept of Dalit human rights emerged and what it entails.

Keywords Theoretical framework on human rights · Natural law and natural rights · Utilitarian theory · Theory of justice · Neo-negative liberalism theory · Social welfare theory · Theory of dignity: Marxian theory on rights · New generation of rights · Third generation of solidarity rights · The World Conference on Human Rights 1993 · United Nations and caste discrimination · Discrimination based on work and descent · RKW Goonesekere · Asbjorn Eide and Yozo Yokota · Yozo Yokota and Chin Sung Chung · Dalit perspective on human rights

1 The Essence of Human Rights

Every human being is entitled to human rights, dignity and equality under each and every kind of situation. This cannot be compromised under any circumstances. Thus, we see Article 1 of the Universal Declaration of Human Rights (UDHR) of 1948 emphasising the following principle: 'All human beings are born free and equal in dignity and rights. They are endowed with reason and conscience and should act towards one another in a spirit of brotherhood.' As a matter of fact, the idea of human and citizenship rights began to take legal form as early as the seventeenth and eighteenth centuries in Europe and America (Madsen, 1996, p. 3).

The codification of human rights can be summarised as follows (Ibid):

UMAKANT, *Dalit Human Rights in India*, People, Cultures and Societies: Exploring and Documenting Diversities,
https://doi.org/10.1007/978-981-95-5751-6_2

1689: Bill of Rights (England)
1776: Virginia Declaration of Rights
1789: Declaration of the Rights of Man and of the Citizen of France
1791: US Federal Bill of Rights

Many other conventions have been enacted over the last two/three centuries, which further strengthened the resolve of the enlightened global community to protect and honour human rights in their totality. The enactment of Universal Declaration of Human Rights (UDHR) by the United Nations (UN) General Assembly on December 10, 1948, very aptly asserted the recognition of the inherent dignity and equal inalienable rights of all the members of the human family as the foundation of freedom, justice and peace in the world. And this is how the world prepared itself to embark on a new journey to ensure human rights for all without any kind of discrimination.

Human rights and their necessity have been widely acknowledged across the globe, yet there is no one definition of human rights. What is important to note here is that, as understood today, they are rights that apply to everyone solely from the fact of being human, irrespective of nationality, caste, creed, sex or any other particular social or cultural traits. Conditions have to be created by the government to make it available to its citizens as well as non-citizens. Working judiciously, practising due diligence as an important tool of governance and fixing the accountability of state and non-state actors are significant elements of human rights.

Generally speaking, we can define human rights as those conditions that are inherent to nature and without which one cannot live as a human being. These rights and fundamental freedoms allow one to develop fully and use one's human qualities, intelligence, talents and conscience to satisfy one's spiritual, physical, social and other needs. They are based on humankind's increasing demand for a life in which the inherent dignity and worth of each human being are respected and protected. Constitutional protections and subsequent legislation could remain only on paper if there is no attempt or if there is a mere half-hearted effort to make human rights available to each and every person.

2 Theories of Human Rights

Although there is no universally endorsed definition of human rights, the United Nations defines the term as those rights that are inherent in our nature and without which we cannot live as human beings. They are rights that enable people to fully develop and utilise their innate qualities, such as intelligence and talent, and to satisfy deeper needs. They provide the foundation for a quality of life in which every individual's inherent dignity and worth receive due respect and protection. What is also important to note here is the fact that human rights are inalienable because human life is not possible or not worth living when rights, justice, due diligence and accountability are absent or not put into practice.

Human rights are generally identified as those rights that are important, moral and universal. Two very broad categories of enquiry on human rights have often been extensively discussed and debated. The first one, often referred to as analytical jurisprudence, raises questions about the nature and origin of rights and how it is possible to know if we possess any rights at all. The second category of enquiry, which is sometimes called normative jurisprudence, poses questions about the specificities of rights that individuals are acknowledged to possess and how such rights stand in relation to each other (Davidson, 1990, p. 26). A clear and uncomplicated understanding of theorisation thus helps us in further broad basing the overall gambit of rights which individuals possess and how the state has to play a facilitating role to make them happen in real sense of the term.

3 Natural Law and Natural Rights

The American Declaration of Independence and the French Declaration of the Rights of Man and of the Citizen both had their origin in natural rights theory. Natural imbalances need to be rectified so as to create a reordering of society, religion, economy and polity in such a manner that emphasis shifts to an equal and level playing field for natural justice. The Saint Thomas was of the view that natural law was that part of God's perfect law which could be divined through the application of human reason. Faith in religion and its dictates played an important role in deciding what could be part of natural law and natural rights. Thus, from a faith-based understanding of human life and the need for the legitimisation of the governing principles and structures of governance, it was felt necessary to place religion as a guiding principle for ensuring natural rights and natural justice. The next stage in the development of natural law, however, involved severing it from its theistic origins and making it a product of enlightened secular and rational thoughts. Grotius argued that it was possible to rationalise the existence of natural law, which was the basis of all positive or written law, on a non-empirical basis by examining the axioms of geometry (Ibid, p. 27).

Throughout the seventeenth century, the Grotian view of natural law was refined and, eventually, transmuted into natural rights theory, as a result of which subjective, individual rights came to be recognised. Changes in the way perceptions and also practices in society and religion were happening, which were also visible in the economy and polity, necessitated a non-theistic approach to ensure equal treatment and the conferral of equal rights to all.

Thomas Hobbes' *Leviathan* questioned the theistic interpretation of natural law and emphasised that in the state of nature, God did not seem to play any role. John Locke argued that all individuals were endowed by nature with inherent rights to life, liberty and property, which were their own and could not be removed or abrogated by the state. The language of both American and French Revolutions, and the writings of French philosopher Jean-Jacques Rousseau and German moral philosopher Immanuel Kant, demonstrated the philosophical pedigree of natural law and natural rights (Ibid, p. 28).

The global/western countries journey for democratisation evolved through constitutional exercise made it amply clear that for human rights be incorporated in to any society or polity, it is not only important to give them eminence in the governance set up that was forthcoming, but also make these safe from any political or religious interference which could transform human rights as null and void. The journey also broadened the scope for granting human rights not only to the privileged sections but almost to every living beings over a long period of time.

Several other debates started and continued before a much more nuanced understanding of human rights concepts came to be accepted. The emphasis shifted more towards the role of the state in ensuring rights for all so that everyone could claim, as a matter of right, principles that govern the equalising affairs of the state, society, the economy and polity on the whole. Immanuel Kant argued that congregation of humans into a state-structured society resulted from a rational need for protection from each other's violence that would be found in a state of nature. However, the fundamental requirements of morality demanded that each person treat others according to universal principles. Kant's political doctrine, which was derived from his moral philosophy, argued that a state must be organised through the imposition of, and obedience to, laws that apply universally; moreover, these laws should respect the equality, freedom and autonomy of citizens (Reiss, 1991, p. 125).

4 Utilitarian Theory

How could life conditions be made more comfortable, and what role could the state play in ensuring that miseries are avoided and a life of happiness becomes a reality? From these questions, a new way of looking at the necessities of life gained prominence. The central thesis of utilitarianism, as propounded by Jeremy Bentham, was that human existence was dominated by pleasure and pain and that by increasing the former and diminishing the latter, a lot of mankind would be improved. The aim of utility, therefore, was to increase the overall stock of human pleasure, which could be calculated on a mathematical basis. The ultimate test of utility, therefore, was the implementation of rules that gave the greatest happiness to the greatest number of people—the maximisation of felicity (Gauba, 1985, p. 285). The utilitarian theory emphasised that avoiding pain and pursuing pleasure and happiness are identical to living a life grounded in principles of equality, where the state, society and the economy treat everyone on an equal footing.

Rights cannot be seen as an outcome of some fanciful ideas or even religious dictates. It needs to be firmly grounded in the material conditions that people face in their day-to-day lives. Rationalism, instead of theistic interpretation, had taken centre stage by now. According to Bentham, rights are the fruits of law and law alone. There are no rights without law, no rights that are contrary to law and no rights that are anterior to law. Rights are not natural but in the form of demands made by society and the individuals living in society, which gain recognition only through laws. Real laws give birth to real rights. The right is the guarantee. Bentham condemned natural rights as an invention of fanatics, which are dogmatic, unintelligible and devoid of reasoning (Ibid, p. 176). This heralded a new era in which human rights issues are approached in a much more rational and secular way.

5 Theory of Justice

In the discourse on human rights, the concept of justice is an important element as the idea of human rights cannot even be conceived in its absence. Without creating enabling conditions that could ensure that justice prevails, the concept of human rights cannot seem to exist or operate in any civilised society. According to John Rawls, justice is the first virtue of social institutions, just as truth is the first virtue of systems of thought. Human rights, of course, are an end of justice; consequently, the role of justice is crucial for understanding human rights. Principles of justice provide a way for assigning rights and duties within the basic institutions of society. Those principles define the appropriate distribution of the benefits and burdens of social cooperation. Every person possesses an inviolability founded on justice that even the welfare of society as a whole cannot override (Chandra, 1990, p. XXV). Fairness thus becomes the cornerstone of a rational approach to justice to embark on a path leading to the creation of conditions that could ensure the realisation of all human rights for all.

A general consensus among different stakeholders becomes important for incorporating human rights concerns into the governance structure. But at the same time, it is necessary to take into consideration the need for fairness and equality and the larger sense of the very notions of a just society, which in turn could provide it the much-needed legitimacy. A well-ordered society, according to Rawls, is effectively regulated by public conceptions of justice. It is a society in which everyone accepts and knows that others accept the same principles of justice, and the basic social institutions satisfy these principles. The justice of a social scheme depends essentially on how fundamental rights and duties are assigned and on the economic opportunities and social conditions in the various sectors of society. The guiding idea for Rawls was that the principles of justice for the basic structures of society are the object of 'the original agreement' (Asirvatham & Mishra, 1997, pp. 353–354).

Positively looking at issues and concerns related to human rights not only in a local but also in a broader global context was always important for Rawls. It certainly paved the way for a better understanding of the need for the promotion and protection of human rights in much wider perspectives. *A Theory of Justice* by John Rawls was published on the heels of a period of intense political questioning and serious challenges to liberalism. In the United States, the Civil Rights and Black Liberation movements, followed by the Anti-Vietnam War movement, brought millions of people into conflict with existing political institutions and policies. They raised fundamental questions about the justice of the existing social order, the unequal distribution of income and the just use of power. Rawls' substantive doctrine was a pure form of egalitarian democracy (Ibid, p. 357).

6 Neo-Negative Liberalism Theory

Liberal as well as neo-liberal attacks on egalitarian principles wanted the state to play a limited role only. Thus, individualism became an important tool for advancing greater freedom, even at the cost of basic human rights, for the larger mass of people. Why should the state become all pervasive in our life situations and interfere in individuals' search for happiness? The minimum role of the state was advocated by liberal and neo-liberal thinkers who were against extending the scope of the state's intervention to private and public lives. Albert Jay Nock, Michael Oakeshott, Friedrich von Hayek, Milton Friedman and Robert Nozick have supported the negative liberal view of the functions of the state and have opposed social-welfare-oriented planning and intervention of the state in economic affairs. Nozick wrote, 'our main conclusion about the state are that a minimal state, limited to the narrow functions of protection against force, theft, fraud, enforcement of contract and so on, is justified; that any more extensive state will violate a person's right not to be forced to do certain things, and is unjustified; and the minimal state is inspiring as well as right' (Jain, 1993, pp. 260–261).

7 Social Welfare Theory

How could people at large should be accorded human rights which in turn could lead to overall growth with justice as a bench-mark for ensuring no one is discriminated against others when we put human rights in to practice. This is how the concept of social welfare theory was conceived. It was recognised by J.S. Mill, G.D.H. Cole, L.T. Hobhouse, Ernest Barker, Harold Joseph Laski, Richard Henry Tawney, Roscoe Pound and Zechariah Chafee Jr. The main contention of this theory is that individuals' rights are limited by social welfare. Individuals are given rights so that they may contribute to the common good. This theory emphasises the social character of rights. It is based on the demands of social justice and on the values of social welfare (Ibid, pp. 322–323).

8 Theory of Dignity

In the absence of dignity, is it even possible to conceptualise and put human rights into operation? The worth of human beings becomes essential to understand the need to grant all human rights to all. This is also to state the fact that human rights cannot become functional in a mechanical way. The state apparatus, society, the economy and polity at large must take into account the need to examine issues and concerns wherein dignity would play an important role. Myres S. McDougal, Harold D. Lasswell and Lung-chu Chen advocate a value-policy-oriented approach based on the protection of human dignity. They argue that demands for the satisfaction of human rights derive from a broad-based international sharing of values. These values are manifested by demands relating to such social goods, such as respect, power, enlightenment, well-being, health, skill, affection and rectitude. All of these values contribute to, and are validated by, the super value of human dignity (Davidson, 1990, p. 37).

9 Marxian Theory

A state-driven initiative that could ultimately lead to a classless society wherein everyone would become equal would result in the granting of equal status and rights for everyone. In Marxist theory, the essence of an individual is that of a social being who uses his ability to satisfy his needs. The fulfilment of these needs in a capitalist society, where the means of production are controlled by the ruling class, is impossible since it results in the alienation of the working class. The true potential of human beings under the Marxist doctrine can only be realised when they are enabled to return to their true nature as social beings. This, however, can only be achieved in a truly communist society where all means of production are held in common and there is an absence of class conflict. Within the Marxian theory, rights are simply instruments or tools to achieve a particular end, i.e. communism. Once that end has been achieved, the tools are no longer needed and may be conveniently disposed of. That is why legal and socio-economic rights are only transformative and provisional in nature. Furthermore, rights have no transcendental or eternal value; they are positive in the sense that rights that are deemed to exist are fixed solely by the state (Ibid, pp. 37–38).

10 New Generation of Rights

In a world situation where the promotion and protection of human rights became an important part of the discourse because of the massive violations reported from different countries, world bodies like the United Nations took this vital step to formulate a declaration on human rights to preserve and protect humanity/human rights and prevent them from declining any further. It was rightly stressed that every violation of human rights, wherever it occurs, is a threat to the welfare and dignity of the entire human family. The protection of human rights, therefore, is a world-wide responsibility that transcends all racial, ideological and geographical boundaries. This is the fundamental belief that gave birth to the international struggle for human rights. The most widely recognised statement of human rights is the United Nations Universal Declaration of Human Rights. This was adopted by the United Nations General Assembly on December 10, 1948, 'as a common standard of achievement for all people and nations'. The declaration has had an immense impact throughout the world. Many nations have included various articles of the Declaration in their constitutions and laws.

The Universal Declaration of Human Rights (UDHR), adopted by the UN General Assembly in 1948, was the first international legal document to set out the fundamental human rights to be universally protected. The UDHR continues to be the foundation of all international human rights law. Its 30 articles provide the principles and building blocks of current and future human rights conventions, treaties and other legal instruments. The UDHR, together with two covenants—the International Covenant for Civil and Political Rights and the International Covenant for Economic, Social and Cultural Rights—make up the International Bill of Rights (UN Office of the High Commissioner for Human Rights, n.d.).

The principle of universality of human rights is the cornerstone of international human rights law. This means that we are all equally entitled to our human rights. This principle, as first emphasised in the UDHR, is repeated in many international human rights conventions, declarations and resolutions. Human rights are inalienable. They should not be taken away, except in specific situations and according to due process. Non-discrimination cuts across all international human rights law. This principle is present in all major human rights treaties. It also serves as the central theme of two core instruments: the International Convention on the Elimination of All Forms of Racial Discrimination and the Convention on the Elimination of All Forms of Discrimination Against Women (Ibid).

Civil and political rights, on the one hand, and economic, social and cultural rights, on the other, have been respectively called the first and second generations of rights. The UN General Assembly has stated on a number of occasions that 'all human rights and fundamental freedoms are indivisible and interdependent and that equal attention and urgent consideration should be given to the implementation, promotion and protection of both Civil and Political and Economic, Social and Cultural rights'. Thus, everyone is entitled to enjoy human rights without discrimination of any kind. The non-discrimination principle is a fundamental rule of international law. This means that human rights are for all human beings, regardless of 'race, colour, sex, language, religion, political or other opinion, national or social origin, property, birth or other status'. Non-discrimination protects individuals and groups against the denial and violation of their human rights. To deny human rights on grounds of cultural distinction is discriminatory. Human rights are intended for everyone across all cultures (Chandra, 1990, pp. XXVI–XXXI).

11 Third Generation or Solidarity Rights

The erstwhile Third World countries have been struggling on several fronts, and because they have remained victims of several strategic as well as geo-political designs of their colonial masters, it was but natural for them to push for a global order that is free from exploitation and accords equal status to different nationalities, along with an equal bargaining power in the global political scenario through the solidarity of all affected countries and people. Thus, the emergence of third-generation or solidarity rights is closely associated with the rise of Third World nationalism and the perception of developing states that the existing international order is weighted against them. It may also be seen as a claim by developing states for fairer treatment and for the construction of a world system that facilitates distributive justice in the broadest Rawlsian sense. Six categories of solidarity rights have been identified (Davidson, 1990, pp. 42–45):

1. The right to economic, political, social and cultural self-determination
2. The right to economic and social development
3. The right to participate in and benefit from the common heritage of mankind and other information and progress
4. The right to peace
5. The right to a healthy environment
6. The right to humanitarian relief

12 The World Conference on Human Rights, June 14–25, 1993

The World Conference on Human Rights took place in Vienna, Austria, on June 14–25, 1993. A pivotal moment in the history of international human rights, the Conference's main outcome was the Vienna Declaration and Programme of Action, a common plan for the strengthening of human rights work around the world. The Conference also made concrete recommendations for strengthening and harmonising the monitoring capacity of the United Nations system. It called for the establishment of the post of High Commissioner for Human Rights by the General Assembly, which subsequently created it on December 20, 1993.

Additionally, the Conference took new steps to promote and protect the rights of women, children and Indigenous peoples by, respectively, supporting the creation of a new mechanism, a Special Rapporteur on Violence Against Women, who was subsequently appointed in 1994; recommending the proclamation by the General Assembly of an International Decade of the World's Indigenous People (1995–2004), which led to the proclamation of another Decade (2005–2014); and calling for the universal ratification of the Convention on the Rights of the Child by 1995.

The Vienna Declaration and Programme of Action marked the culmination of a long process of review and debate over the status of the human rights machinery in the world. This process began in 1961 with a General Assembly resolution designating 1968 as the International Year for Human Rights. The International Conference on Human Rights was held in Tehran, Iran, that same year. Vienna also marked the beginning of a renewed effort to strengthen and further implement the body of human rights instruments that had been painstakingly constructed on the foundation of the Universal Declaration of Human Rights since 1948 (UN Office of the High Commissioner for Human Rights, n.d., 2023).

13 United Nations and Caste Discrimination

Caste-based discrimination, exclusion and violence leading to massive Dalit human rights violations have remained outside the ambit of the human rights mechanisms developed by the UN. This is why caste as a basis for discrimination is not mentioned in the Universal Declaration of Human Rights (UDHR) or in any other international human rights treaties. But it is also a fact that several treaty- and charter-based bodies of the UN have maintained, over the years, that caste-based discrimination falls within the purview of international human rights instruments. An examination of the *travaux preparatoires* of the UDHR shows that caste was explicitly contemplated by the drafters as being encompassed within the more general terminology of the UDHR's foundational non-discrimination provision (Prove, 2003).

It was in 1996 that the UN Committee on Elimination of Racial Discrimination (CERD) made specific reference, for the first time, to caste discrimination, untouchability and Scheduled Castes and Scheduled Tribes under the rubric of 'descent':

> The Committee states that the term 'descent' mentioned in Article 1 of the Convention does not solely refers to race. The Committee affirms that the situation of the Scheduled Castes and Scheduled Tribes falls within the scope of the Convention (UN Committee for Elimination of Racial Discrimination, 1996).

The CERD further observed:

> It is noted that although constitutional provisions and legal texts exist to abolish untouchability and to protect the members of the scheduled castes and tribes, and although social and educational policies have been adopted to improve the situation of members of scheduled castes and tribes and to protect them from abuses, widespread discrimination against them and the relative impunity of those who abuse them point to the limited effect of these measures. The Committee is particularly concerned at reports that people belonging to the scheduled castes and tribes are often prevented from using public wells or from entering cafés or restaurants and that their children are sometimes separated from other children in schools, in violation of article 5 (f) of the Convention (UN Committee for Elimination of Racial Discrimination, 1996: ibid).

The Committee on Human Rights considered the fourth periodic report of India at its 4134th and 4135th meetings, held on July 15 and 16, 2024. At its 4144th meeting held on July 22, 2024, it adopted the Concluding Observations for India. While the Committee appreciated the constitutional and legal measures adopted to prevent, protect and address discrimination and violence against 'Scheduled Castes' and 'Scheduled Tribes', such as the Scheduled Castes and Scheduled Tribes (Prevention of Atrocities) Act, 1989, it expressed concern over reports indicting systemic challenges to the implementation of these measures, such as delayed registration of 'first information reports' (FIRs), inadequate police investigations, lengthy trials and non-compliance with the 60-day case disposal requirement. The Committee remains concerned about multiple reports on widespread discrimination and violence against these groups, including lynching, mob violence, displacement, as well as attacks on Adivasis for practising Christianity and vigilante lynching of Muslims. The Committee is further concerned with the non-extension of Scheduled Caste status and reservation benefits to Dalits who have converted to Islam or Christianity. The Committee acknowledges the State Party's efforts to prevent manual scavenging, including through the Prohibition of Employment as Manual Scavengers and Their Rehabilitation Act, 2013. However, the Committee received information that this is not effectively enforced, and the practice continues in several regions of India, including instances involving local governments (UN Committee on Human Rights, 2024).

Though the Indian government ratified the International Covenant on Civil and Political Rights (ICCPR) in 1979, it was almost 20 years later, in 1997, that the Committee on Human Rights first noted serious shortcomings in the government's performance in guaranteeing basic human rights to Dalits:

> 'The Committee notes with concern that, despite measures taken by the Government, members of scheduled castes and scheduled tribes, as well as the so-called backward classes and ethnic and national minorities continue to endure severe social discrimination and to suffer disproportionately from many violations of their rights under the Covenant, inter alia inter-caste violence, bonded labour and discrimination of all kinds. It regrets that the de facto perpetuation of the caste system entrenches social differences and contributes to these violations. While the Committee notes the efforts made by the State party to eradicate discrimination: it recommends that further measures be adopted, including education programmes at national and state levels, to combat all forms of discrimination against these vulnerable groups, in accordance with articles 2, paragraph 1, and 26 of the Covenant' (UN Committee on Human Rights, 1997).

When the Indian government submitted its first report to the Committee for Elimination of Discrimination Against Women (CEDAW) in 2000, the Committee raised many questions regarding the plight of Dalit women, noting that Dalit women seem to remain an untouched sector. The Committee called for various measures to address the particular issue. It observed:

> The Committee is concerned with the continuing discrimination, including violence, suffered by women of the Dalit community, despite the passage of the Scheduled Castes and Scheduled Tribes (prevention of atrocities) Act of 1989. The Committee urges the Government to enforce laws preventing discrimination against Dalit women and prohibiting the Devadasi system. It urges the Government to introduce affirmative action programmes in such areas as education, employment and health so as to provide life chances to Dalit women and girls and create an environment conducive to their progress. The

> Committee calls upon the Government to set a time-frame for those interventions and provide information on the progress made in the next report (UN CEDAW, 2000).

As a matter of fact, the Child Rights Committee (CRC), in 2000 and again in 2004, and, over the years, other treaty-monitoring committees like CERD, CEDAW and the Committee on Economic, Social and Cultural Rights (CESCR) and other UN bodies like Human Rights Council through the Universal Periodic Review, special procedures and several thematic special rapporteurs have consistently made observations and recommendations emphasising the need to tackle caste-based discrimination, not just in India but also in other countries where caste, work and descent-based discrimination continue. On several other occasions, UN treaty-monitoring bodies have examined India's periodic reports, and after a rigorous review of such reports and after subsequent dialogue with the government delegation, they gave several important observations and a set of recommendations to the State Party India. The details are attached as part of the appendix to this book.

14 Discrimination Based on Work and Descent

During the 52nd session of the UN Sub-Commission on the Promotion and Protection of Human Rights in Geneva in August 2000, Dalit organisations and others, like the Buraku Liberation League from Japan, made several submissions. In response to these efforts, on August 11, 2000, the Sub-Commission, through Resolution 2000/4, declared that discrimination based on work and descent is a form of discrimination prohibited by international human rights law and decided to entrust Mr. Rajendra Kalidas Wimala Goonesekere with the task of preparing, without financial implications, a working paper on the topic of discrimination based on work and descent in order to (a) identify communities in which discrimination based on occupation and descent continues to be experienced in practice; (b) examine existing constitutional, legislative and administrative measures for the abolition of such discrimination; and (c) make any further concrete recommendations and proposals for the effective elimination of such discrimination as may be appropriate in the light of such examination (Thorat & Umakant, 2004, pp. XIX–XX).

Subsequently, at its 53rd session in 2001, the UN Sub-Commission on Promotion and Protection of Human Rights presented Goonesekere's working paper, in which it clearly stated that discrimination based on work and descent has been a long-standing practice in many societies throughout the world and affects a large portion of the world's population. Discrimination based on descent manifests itself most notably in caste-based (or tribe-based) distinctions. These distinctions, determined by birth, result in serious violations across the full spectrum of civil, cultural, economic, political and social rights. Victims of discrimination based on descent are singled out not because of a difference in physical appearance or race but rather due to their membership in an endogamous social group that has been isolated socially and occupationally from other groups in society (Goonesekere, 2001, p. 4). The focus of this paper was primarily on countries in Asia. At the time the resolution was discussed in the Sub-Commission, it was noted that the problem was not limited to Asia alone but also existed in some parts of Africa and perhaps in South America. Notably, there is a serious problem of human rights violations arising from work and descent (Ibid, p. 14).

Following the World Conference Against Racism, Racial Discrimination, Xenophobia and Related Intolerance (WCAR) held at Durban, South Africa, the UN Committee on Elimination of All Forms of Racial Discrimination (UN CERD), at its 61st session held from August 5 to 23, 2002, took a fairly bold position and referred to caste as a form of work and descent-based discrimination. One of the striking features of this session was the representation from a number of African countries, which highlighted discrimination based on caste and caste-like social institutions existing in their countries. CERD's General Recommendation No. XXIX refers to caste in several contexts as follows:

> Confirming the consistent view of the Committee that the term 'descent' in article 1, paragraph 1, the Convention does not solely refer to 'race' and has a meaning and application which complement the other prohibited grounds of discrimination,
>
> Strongly reaffirming that discrimination based on 'descent' includes discrimination against members of communities based on forms of social stratification such as caste and analogous systems of inherited status which nullify or impair their equal enjoyment of human rights,
>
> Noting that the existence of such discrimination has become evident from the Committee's examination of reports of a number of States parties to the Convention,
>
> Having organized a thematic discussion on descent-based discrimination and after having received the contributions of members of the Committee, as well as contributions from some Governments and members of other United Nations bodies, notably experts of the Sub-Commission for the Promotion and Protection of Human Rights,
>
> Conduct periodic surveys on the reality of descent-based discrimination and provide disaggregated information in their reports to the Committee on the geographical distribution and economic and social conditions of descent-based communities, including a gender perspective.

The recommendations of the CERD are fairly comprehensive in nature. Some of these, as mentioned above, are meant to highlight how and in what manner the committee has brought caste-based discrimination and exclusion within its ambit and included caste-like institutions and practices in other Asian, apart from South Asian, and African countries. This, in short, reflects the stated position of UN bodies on human rights, which has evolved over a period of time (CERD General Recommendation XXIX 2002, pp. 1–5).

At the 53rd session of the UN Sub-Commission of Promotion and Protection of Human Rights, wherein the working paper by R.K.W. Goonesekere was discussed, it was also decided to entrust Goonesekere with the preparation of an expanded working paper on the topic of discrimination based on work and descent existing in other regions of the world. But as his term at the Sub-Commission ended, it was decided by the Sub-Commission at its 54th session to assign the preparation of the expanded working paper to Asbjorn Eide and Yozo Yokota (Thorat & Umakant, 2004, p. XXXIII).

The first expanded working paper on 'Discrimination Based on Work and Descent' by Asbjorn Eide and Yozo Yokota noted that discrimination based on work and descent is prevalent in many African countries. Sources show that endogamous groups of musicians and artisans (blacksmith, potters, musicians/bards or 'griots', leather workers, weavers, hairdressers/barbers and other similar groups) are found in over 15 ethnic groups and at least 14 modern states in West Africa—Mali, Mauritania, Senegal, Gambia, Guinea, Guinea-Bissau, northern Cote d'Ivoire, Burkina Faso, Niger, eastern Ghana, parts of Algerian Sahara, some places in northern Cameroon, Liberia and Sierra Leone. As a consequence of the endogamous and social isolation of these caste-like ethnic groups, various kinds of human rights violations take place. As a matter of fact, they face segregation in housing/residence, bans on intermarriages and commensality, restrictions on access to public places and services, poverty, wretchedness and large-scale violence whenever they tried to alter social norms. The literature also revealed that a number of populations in North-East Africa, particularly in southern Ethiopia, exhibit similar patterns of social organisation and discrimination based on work and descent (Eide & Yokota, 2003, pp. 4–6). Further in the same working paper, the experts also discussed Somalia, Yemen and how social outcaste groups like Midgan/Madhiban, Tumal and Yibir in Somalia, Al-Akhdam in Yemen and the Osu/Ozu community in Igbo land in Nigeria face similar kinds of discrimination, exclusion and even violence in society, the economy and polity (Ibid, pp. 6–8).

The Sub-Commission adopted Resolution 2003/22 on August 13, 2003, calling for a further working paper on the topic. The main purposes of this working paper were (a) to examine the legal, judicial, administrative and educational measures taken by the governments concerned; (b) to identify additional communities affected by discrimination based on work and descent; and (c) to prepare a draft set of principles and guidelines for all relevant actors, not only national or federal governments but also local governments, as well as private sector entities such as corporations, schools, religious institutions and other public places where discrimination based on work and descent often occurs, in cooperation and collaboration with relevant international human rights treaty bodies and United Nations organs and agencies, such as the Committee on the Elimination of Racial Discrimination, the International Labour Organization and the United Nations Educational, Scientific and Cultural Organization, taking full account of the contents of CERD's General Recommendation XXIX (Eide & Yokota, 2004, p. 5).

The second expanded working paper by Eide and Yokota thus focused on the legal, judicial, administrative and educational measures taken by governments in Bangladesh, Burkina Faso, India, Japan, Kenya, Mali, Micronesia, Nepal, Pakistan, Senegal, Sri Lanka and Yemen. Additionally, the expanded working paper looked into discrimination based on work and descent within the South Asian and Somali diasporas, caste practices in the state of Yap in the Federated States of Micronesia and the Fuga community of Ethiopia and the set of problems faced by the Roma/Sinti groups in Europe. In the third part of their expanded working paper, Eide and

Yokota focused on a proposed framework of principles and guidelines to help countries affected by work- and decent-based discrimination incorporate them into their national and local administrative structures and assist other relevant bodies in addressing such kinds of discriminatory practices in their societies. It also proposed measures to be taken by international bodies to address problems arising out of traditional norms and practices prevalent in many countries around the world (Ibid, pp. 5–21).

The Commission on Human Rights, taking note of Resolution 2004/17 of August 12, 2004, of the SubCommission on the Promotion and Protection of Human Rights, decided, without a vote, to approve the decision of the SubCommission to appoint Mr. Yozo Yokota and Ms. Chin-Sung Chung as Special Rapporteurs, with the task of preparing a comprehensive study on discrimination arising from work and descent on the basis of the three working papers on this topic (E/CN.4/Sub.2/2001/16, E/CN.4/Sub.2/2003/24 and E/CN.4/Sub.2/2004/31) submitted to the Sub-Commission, the comments made during the sessions of the SubCommission at which those working papers were submitted and the provisions of the above-mentioned Resolution, as well as the responses of governments, national human rights institutions, relevant organs and agencies of the United Nations and non-governmental organisations to a questionnaire to be elaborated and circulated by the Special Rapporteurs. The Commission also approved the request for the Special Rapporteurs to submit a preliminary report to the SubCommission at its 57th session, a progress report at its 58th session and a final report at its 59th session, as well as the request for the Secretary-General and the United Nations High Commissioner for Human Rights to provide the Special Rapporteurs with all the assistance necessary to enable them to accomplish this task (UN Commission on Human Rights, 2005/109).

The first preliminary report was about the elaboration of a questionnaire to Governments, national human rights institutions, relevant organs and agencies of the United Nations system and non-governmental organisations for the purpose of identifying best practices and to obtain more comprehensive information on constitutional, legislative, judicial, administrative and educational measures taken to address discrimination based on work and descent. In order to eradicate this type of discrimination, it is essential that the governments concerned (a) acknowledge the existence of such discrimination; (b) conduct a survey to determine the extent and nature of such discrimination; (c) prohibit any act of discrimination based on work and descent; (d) punish offenders; (e) educate and train government officials, including law enforcement officers; (f) raise public awareness of the issue; (g) provide effective protection and remedies to the victims of this type of discrimination; and (h) take other measures, including affirmative action and special budgetary allocations, to eliminate such discrimination (Yokota & Chung, 2005: E/CN.4/Sub.2/2005/30).

The second preliminary/progress report not only tried to identify the meaning and scope of the term discrimination based on work and descent but at the same time made an attempt to find multidimensional features of sociocultural, religious, economic and political aspects that affect the lives of discriminated communities across the globe, though these issues are much more pronounced in South Asia. In order to find ways and means through which redressal of age old problems could be possibly relied upon, the Rappoteurs looked in to the international human rights mechanism, regional human rights standards and norms as applicable in different parts of the world (Yokota & Chung, 2006: A/HRC/Sub.1/58/CRP.2).

The final report contained in its main part the revised draft Principles and Guidelines for the effective elimination of discrimination based on work and descent. While finalising the draft set of principles, the Special Rapporteurs adopted a broad-based approach to dealing with issues arising from work- and descent-related discrimination. Some of the suggested principles were as follows: discrimination based on work and descent is a form of discrimination prohibited by international human rights law, and discrimination based on work and descent and other forms of discrimination are not only human rights violations but also major obstacles to achieving development. The proposed guidelines advocates for guiding the initiatives by the national and local governments for all necessary constitutional, legislative, administrative, budgetary and judicial measures, including appropriate forms of affirmative action and public education programmes, to prevent, prohibit and provide redress for discrimination based on work and descent in both public and private spheres; and ensure that such measures are respected and implemented by all state authorities at all levels (Yokota & Chung, 2009: A/HRC/11/CRP.3).

15 Human Rights, Democratic Governance and the Right to Development

Democratic governance and the right to development, along with human rights, provide the justification for building an egalitarian system based on the notions of liberty, equality and fraternity in their true sense of the term. To help make human rights possible, democratic governance and the right to development play much more important roles than we could even imagine. The promotion and protection of human rights are largely dependent on a democratic form of governance, along with the right to development. In another sense, this is also to suggest that the incorporation of human rights principles and guidelines is an essential element for ensuring democratic governance and the right to development. It goes without saying that this trinity—human rights, democratic governance and the right to development—complement and supplement each other in a sense that one cannot function without the other. In another sense, it is also important to highlight the fact that human rights are inextricably linked to democratic governance. They both require that people be aware of their rights and duties, that appropriate institutional arrangements facilitate their realisation and that a democratic civic culture has a role in both issues of national importance and those of everyday life (Sagasti, 2013, p. 126).

The period after World War II and the emergence of free and independent states in several parts of the world intensified the struggle to bring changes as far as the question of the right to development is concerned. The adoption of the International Covenant on Economic, Social and Cultural Rights (ICESCR) in 1966 by the UN facilitated future discourse on development cooperation between developed and developing worlds. The adoption of 1986 UN Declaration on the Right to Development succeeded as one key milestone in a decade and a half of struggles by radical Third World states within the UN to pass a package of reforms that would result in a New International Economic Order (NIEO) that was fair to poor countries. The Declaration is non-binding, and some view it as a watered-down version of the radical redistributive measures sought by the NIEO movement. Nonetheless, it does reflect some of the radical politics of that era (Musembi & Cornwall, 2004, p. 8).

It has also been observed that social, economic and political exclusion, which is faced by a large section of society in different countries across the world, is certainly due to the prevalence of conservative sociocultural practices from the past that are still continuing in many ways. Thus, in order to initiate the process of human rights framework to address the social, economic and political exclusion, it is necessary that the state operationalizes the process of social democratisation, productive transformation in the economic sector and a process of legitimisation of State Institutions and citizen participation. Sagasti emphasises that reducing social exclusion through democratisation requires a vigorous and efficient economy that is able to grow and generate wealth as well as a legitimate state capable of creating an environment favourable for economic progress and of redistributing the benefits of growth in an equitable manner, consistent with the right to development (Sagasti, 2013, pp. 128–130).

16 Due Diligence and Accountability as Standards for Ensuring Human Rights

Yakin Erturk, former UN Special Rapporteur on Violence Against Women, presented her third report to the erstwhile UN Commission on Human Rights at its 62nd session on January 20, 2006, focusing on the due diligence standard as a tool for eliminating violence against women. Erturk mentioned how the due diligence standard derived its legitimacy from the Declaration on the Elimination of Violence Against Women, adopted by the General Assembly in 1993, which urged states, in its Article 4(c), to 'exercise due diligence to prevent, investigate and, in accordance with national legislation, punish acts of violence against women, whether those acts are perpetrated by the State or by private persons'. As a matter of fact, the due diligence standard has a long history in international law, and references to the standard can be found in the works of Grotius and other seventeenth-century writers (Erturk, 2006, pp. 6–7).

Over the years, human rights bodies, such as the Committee on the Elimination of Discrimination Against Women (CEDAW), and other treaty bodies, along with different special procedures and regional human rights institutions, have also elaborated on the requirements of the due diligence standard in relation to specific country situations as well as on a more general level (Ibid, p. 8).

The concept of due diligence, as developed within the UN human rights system, would mean, in layman's language, implementing the constitutional provisions and subsequent legislation in their true letter and spirit. In UN terminology, due diligence refers to the responsibility of the state to prevent human rights violations and to protect and promote human rights in their true letter and spirit. Holding the state and non-state perpetrators that indulge in human rights violations accountable for their acts of commission and omission is actually part of the due diligence process. There is general apathy and one could even say very low awareness in India about fixing the accountability and cracking the institutionalised impunity which the state (duty bearers) and non-state perpetrators enjoy.

17 Human Rights from the Dalit Perspective

The practice of untouchability, atrocities, discrimination, exclusion and violence on a regular basis has to be acknowledged whenever we discuss the concept of human rights. It could very well be described as a perspective 'from below'. Human rights are, literally, the rights one possesses simply by virtue of being human. All human beings thus have the same human rights. Since these rights rest on nothing other than one's nature as a human being, there are not only 'natural' and equal rights but also inalienable rights, for one's nature as a human being cannot be alienated. However, the idea that one is entitled to equal concern and respect and a wide range of inalienable personal rights simply because one is a human being is utterly foreign to traditional societies. In fact, in traditional societies, in India as elsewhere, social structures, and the underlying social visions of human dignity, rest not on human rights but rather on social duties and status hierarchies (Donnelly, 1990, pp. 57–58).

Religion has been playing an important role in deciding the fate of people in every society all over the globe. In the case of India too, any attempt to analyse human rights situations need to take the role of religion in to consideration for ascertaining its contribution in deciding every day affair in society, economy and polity. Ambedkar was of the view that religion, as a social force cannot be ignored. Religion has been aptly described by Herbert Spencer as 'the weft which everywhere crosses the warp of history'. This is true of every society. But religion has not only crossed everywhere the warp of Indian history, it forms the warp and woof of the Hindu mind. The life of the Hindu is regulated by religion at every moment of his life. There is no act of the Hindu right from birth to death which is not covered or ordained by religion (Ambedkar, 1987, p. 27).

What is equity, and what does it signify? This is important to understand, or else we may not be able to explain the several root causes of human rights violations. Equity signifies equality. Rules and regulations, rights and righteousness are concerned with equality in value. If all men are equal, all men are of the same essence, and the common essence entitles them to the same fundamental rights and to equal liberty. In short, justice is simply another name for liberty, equality and fraternity. Which of these tenets does Hinduism recognise? It was Ambedkar who made an attempt to examine the concept of human rights in theory and in practice by looking through this perspective.

18 Does Hindu Social System Recognise Equality, Liberty and Fraternity?

Is equality an intrinsic part of Indian society? Could we say that everyone is treated at par with others without any discrimination or exclusion? According to Ambedkar, the question instantaneously brings to one's mind the caste system. One striking feature of the caste system is that different castes do not stand as a horizontal series all on the same plane (Ibid, pp. 25–31). It has been observed for millennia that Hinduism is opposed to conditions in which liberty can thrive. It is therefore a denial of liberty (Ibid, pp. 38–44). With a complete refusal to share the joys and sorrows of life, how can the sentiment of fraternity take root? Hinduism teaches not to inter-dine, not to intermarry and not to associate. These do not constitute the essence of its teaching. The philosophy of Hinduism is a direct denial of fraternity. Thus, from the point of view of justice, the Hindu social system is inimical to equality, antagonistic to liberty and opposed to fraternity (Ibid, pp. 44–66).

It has rightly been observed that it is the state and the Brahmanical social order that are responsible for violating the human rights of Dalits by unleashing violence against them. As a matter of fact, the violation of human rights by the Brahmanical social order is far more subtle and hence can sustain hegemonic and subordinate relations in stronger forms. The ordinary non-violent Hindu does not hesitate to use the utmost violence against Dalits. What could explain why an archaic religio-social doctrine of a caste system continues its stranglehold for generations after generations throughout history? Ambedkar did provide answers to these questions by explaining the essential nature of caste norms and practices: 'If the Hindu observes untouchability, it is because his religion enjoins him to do so. If he is ruthless and lawless in putting down the Dalits rising the established order, it is because his religion not only tells him that the established order is divine and therefore sacrosanct but also imposes upon him a duty to see that this established order is maintained by all possible means. If he does not listen to the call of humanity it is because his religion does not enjoin him to regard the Dalits as human beings. If he does not feel any qualms of the conscience in assaulting, looting, burning and other acts of atrocities against the Dalits, it is because his religion tells him that nothing is sin, which is done in defence of the social order' (Ambedkar, 1989, p. 90). Ambedkar further went on to affirm that 'Psychologically, caste and untouchability are one integral system based on one and the same principle. If the caste Hindus observe untouchability it is because they believe in caste. Untouchability is only an extension of the caste system. There can be no severance between the two. The two stand together and will fall together…' (Ibid, p. 101).

The concept of 'human rights' under the Hindu social order is very unique. In this order of hierarchy and graded inequality, the Brahmins are not only placed at the top but are also considered to be 'superior social beings' worthy of all special rights and privileges, and at the bottom, the untouchables are treated as 'Sub-human' or lesser human beings considered unworthy of any rights.

The Dalit perspective thus seeks the entitlement of societal resources as a means for concretising the right to be human, and therefore, mere legal entitlement is not enough, for the right to be human is to enable a person to satisfy his most basic requirements of 'humanhood'. The Dalit perspective on the right to be human does not take a voluntaristic view, which believes that human rights are given and can be enjoyed by all people. On the contrary, the Dalit perspective makes it clear that the right to be human, unlike the human right, is neither state-constituted nor it is a historical, but is historically constituted through the constant struggle for human treatment led by Phule, Ambedkar and many others. The Dalit perspective thus has to be organised around the honourable conditions of human existence. The Dalit perspective on human rights, in a wider sense, does not ignore specificity; on the contrary, it has the potential to move towards universality (Guru, 1997, pp. 115–116).

References

Ambedkar, B. R. (1987). *Babasaheb Ambedkar: Writing and speeches* (Vol. 3, pp. 27, 25–31, 39, 38–44 & 44–66). Education Department, Bombay, Government of Maharashtra.

Ambedkar, B. R. (1989). *Writings and speeches* (Vol. 5, pp. 90, 92–99 & 101). Education Department, Bombay, Government of Maharashtra.

Asirvatham, E., & Mishra, K. K. (1997). *Political theory* (pp. 353–354 & 357). S. Chand & Company

Chandra, S. (1990). *International documents on human rights* (pp. XXV & XXVI–XXXI). Mittal Publications.

Davidson, S. (1990). *Human rights* (pp. 26, 27, 28, 37, 38 & 42–45). Open University Press.

Donnelly, J. (1990). Traditional values and universal human rights: Caste in India. In C. E. Welch Jr. & V. A. Leary (Eds.), *Asian perspective on human rights* (pp. 57–58). West View Press.

Eide, A., & Yokota, Y. (2003, June 26). First expanded working paper on discrimination based on work and descent. UN Sub-Commission on Promotion and Protection of Human Rights, E/CN.4.Sub.2/2003/24, pp. 4–8. https://digitallibrary.un.org/record/499780?ln=en&v=pdf#files

Eide, A., & Yokota, Y. (2004, July 05). *Second expanded working on discrimination based on work and descent.* UN Sub-Commission on Promotion and Protection of Human Rights, E/CN.4/Sub.2/2004/31, pp. 5-21. https://digitallibrary.un.org/record/526185?ln=en&v=pdf

Erturk, Y. (2006). *The due diligence standard as a tool for the elimination of violence against women.* Sixty-second Session, UN Commission on Human Rights, January 20, E/CN.4/2006/61. https://documents-dds-ny.un.org/doc/UNDOC/GEN/G06/103/50/PDF/G0610350.pdf?OpenElement

Gauba, O. P. (1985). *An introduction to political theory* (pp. 285 & 176). Macmillan India Limited.

Goonesekere, R. K. W. (2001, June 14). *Working paper on discrimination based on work and descent.* UN-Sub Commission on Promotion and Protection of Human Rights, E/CN.4/

Sub.2/2001. https://documents.un.org/doc/undoc/gen/g01/142/20/pdf/g0114220.pdf?token=rjJV7FEnqf7L7MWWCw&fe=true
Guru, G. (1997). Human rights and the Dalits - An enquiry into the human rights discourse in India. *Indian Journal of Human Rights, 1*(1), 115–116.
Jain, M. P. (1993). Political theory (pp. 260–261 & 322–323). Authors Guild Publications.
Madsen, S. T. (1996). *State, society and human rights in South Asia* (p. 3). Manohar.
Musembi, C. N., & Cornwall, A. (2004), *What is the rights based approach all about* (IDS Working Paper 234, p. 8). https://www.ids.ac.uk/download.php?file=files/dmfile/Wp234.pdf
Prove, P. N. (2003). Caste and Universal Declaration of Human Rights. *International Dalit Solidarity Network*. https://idsn.org/un-2/compilation-of-un-references-to-caste-discrimination/
Reiss, H. (Ed.). (1991). *Kant: Political writings* (p. 125). Cambridge University Press.
Sagasti, F. (2013). A human rights approach to democratic governance and development. In *Realizing the right to development* (pp. 126 & 128–130). UN Office of the High Commissioner for Human Rights.
Thorat, S., & Umakant (Eds.). (2004). *Caste, race and discrimination: Discourses in international context* (pp. XIX–XX and XXXIII). Rawat Publications.
UN CEDAW. (2000). *Concluding observation - India*. A/55/38. https://idsn.org/un-2/compilation-of-un-references-to-caste-discrimination/
UN Commission on Human Rights. (2005). *Adoption of Sub-Commission on Promotion and Protection of Human Rights Resolution on Appointment of Two Special Rapporteur on discrimination based on work and descent*. https://ap.ohchr.org/documents/E/CHR/decisions/E--CN_4-DEC-2005-109.doc
UN Committee for Elimination of Racial Discrimination. (1996). *Concluding observations - India*. https://documents-dds-ny.un.org/doc/UNDOC/GEN/G96/183/45/PDF/G9618345.pdf?OpenElement
UN Committee on Elimination of Racial Discrimination (CERD). (2002). UN CERD, General Recommendation XXIX, *https://tbinternet.ohchr.org/_layouts/15/treatybodyexternal/Download.aspx?symbolno=INT%2FCERD%2FGEC%2F7501&Lang=en*, https://tbinternet.ohchr.org/_layouts/15/treatybodyexternal/TBSearch.aspx?Lang=en&TreatyID=6&DocTypeID=11
UN Committee on Human Rights. (1997). *Concluding observation - India*. https://documents-dds-ny.un.org/doc/UNDOC/GEN/G97/177/39/PDF/G9717739.pdf?OpenElement
UN Committee on Human Rights. (2024). *Concluding observation - India*. https://tbinternet.ohchr.org/_layouts/15/treatybodyexternal/Download.aspx?symbolno=CCPR%2FC%2FIND%2FCO%2F4&Lang=en
UN Office of the High Commissioner for Human Rights. (2023). https://www.ohchr.org/en/what-are-human-rights
UN Office of the High Commissioner for Human Rights. (n.d.). *History of Vienna Declaration*. https://www.ohchr.org/en/about-us/history/vienna-declaration
Yokota, Y., & Chung, C.-S. (2005, June 21). *Preliminary report on discrimination based on work and descent, E/CN.4/Sub.2/2005/30*. https://digitallibrary.un.org/record/552131?ln=en&v=pdf
Yokota, Y., & Chung, C.-S. (2006, July 28). *Progress report on discrimination based on work and descent, A/HRC/Sub.1/58/CRP.2*. https://digitallibrary.un.org/record/580654?ln=en
Yokota, Y., & Chung, C.-S. (2009, May 18). *Final report on discrimination based on work and descent, A/HRC/11/CRP.3*. https://www.ohchr.org/sites/default/files/Documents/HRBodies/HRCouncil/RegularSession/Session11/A-HRC-11-CRP3.pdf

Dalit Human Rights in Bihar

Abstract The state of Bihar has been in the news for a long time now for serious violations of Dalit human rights. The chapter explains how and why the situation turned so hostile, leading to Dalit human rights violations on a large scale. Along with this, an attempt has also been made to highlight specific cases, from the Belchi massacre of 1977 to the Laxmanpur Bathe massacre in 1997. The chapter also details the miserable life conditions of Dalits in the erstwhile central Bihar.

Keywords Dalit human rights in Bihar · Caste carnage at Belchi · Killing fields in Bihar · From Belchi to Laxmanpur Bathe and beyond · Operation Black Rain

Like other states in India, Bihar also has a long history of caste animosities and conflicts. These have permeated almost every aspect of socio-religious-cultural-economic-political life, to the extent that caste hatred and caste rivalry seem to have become quite naturalised within its society. The caste exclusivity seen in other parts of India can also be seen in Bihar in its full glory. Any attempt to alter traditional norms and practices has every chance of being crushed quite ruthlessly. The Scheduled Castes (SCs) in Bihar, as elsewhere, have been in the grip of commutative inequality. They suffer not only from social disabilities but also from the impact of economic, educational and political inequality. Untouchability, in both overt and covert forms, remains in practice in many areas of Bihar. A survey carried out in 1980 identified ten districts as relatively more prone to untouchability practices. Broadly speaking, untouchability has been found to be more evident in rural areas of both north and south Bihar. In rural areas where people have been more tradition oriented and where the practice of untouchability has also been a facet of the exercise of power, social disabilities were found in more overt forms. Taking water from a well or tea at roadside tea shops or entry into a temple have been the usual disability to which the Scheduled Castes were subjected in rural areas. In the Rohtas

UMAKANT, *Dalit Human Rights in India*, People, Cultures and Societies: Exploring and Documenting Diversities,
https://doi.org/10.1007/978-981-95-5751-6_3

district, Scheduled Castes were, in several cases, even prevented from taking marriage processions through village streets (Sachidananda, 1997, pp. 166–167).

Do Dalits have a freedom of choice? The freedom of choice to live a life in their own terms and conditions has never been allowed to the wretched of the earth—the Dalits—in Bihar and elsewhere in India. Dalits' position in the caste hierarchy makes them vulnerable to all kinds of human rights violations and indignities, which they are forced to face as fait accompli. They are there to serve those above them in hierarchy and not to demand equal treatment, rights and status. With no recourse to escape from such dehumanising situations, socio-religious dictates forced Dalits to accept their status as slaves, in both physical and mental sense, and this easily became a vicious circle, wherein generations of Dalits were made victims in this kind of oppressive system.

The ramifications of caste-based discrimination and exclusion can be found in several forms, be it socio-economic or political. In another survey on the social disabilities of Dalits conducted in the districts of Nawada, Rohtas and Madhubani, different areas recorded different forms of social disabilities faced by Dalits, depending on the attitude and behaviour of caste Hindus towards them and the dominance of upper caste people. In the Nawada district, the social disabilities faced by Dalits were found to be limited in public places, but at the same time, caste Hindus of the area—particularly Rajputs and Bhumihars—still maintained a casteist attitude towards them. In the Rohtas district, social disability and untouchability existed to a much greater extent. Dalit children were not allowed to attend schools, and if admitted, they were not allowed to sit together with the children of caste Hindus. In Madhubani, Dalits were not allowed to utilise bathing ghats, tea stalls and public temples used by caste Hindus. The social disabilities faced by Dalits were regarded as customary by caste Hindus, particularly Brahmins, forcing Dalits to lead a sub-human life. In a nutshell, social disability and untouchability, by and large, existed in both overt and covert forms in various parts of Bihar (Prasad et al., 1987, pp. 42–44).

It is quite an abusive life that Dalits have been forced to accept as a fait accompli. The magnitude of the abusive relationship between the touchables and untouchables was and remains deeply embedded in society. The manifestation of the deep hatred towards the lowest of the low has always been used as an instrument to control and brow-beat them in to an exploitative structure in society. The manner in which this abusive behaviour continues reflects the graded inequalities embedded in society. All those above the Dalits in the social hierarchy vociferously stick to the code of conduct as practised in a caste-based societal universe. Not only the upper strata people but even those belonging to the Shudra category, when part of a dominant caste group, treat Dalits, without any hesitation, in the most dehumanising way (Table 1).

The pattern of ownership of land according to caste cannot be seen as surprising, especially at the top and bottom ends of the social hierarchy. Most big landowners have been members of twice-born castes, and most of the Scheduled Castes have been poor landless labourers. Poverty and unemployment have been quite alarming in Bihar. Most seriously affected by these were SCs, as more than 86% were

Table 1 Land Ownership by caste in Bihar

	Big landowners	Midsize landowners	Small landowners	Landless labourers
	(Over 10 acres)	(2.5–10 acres	(0–2.5 acres)	
Twice-born castes	80	231	217	32
Backward castes	18	89	457	392
Scheduled castes	0	7	203	477

Source: Prasad and Rodgers (1983), Class, Caste and Land Holding in the Analysis of the Rural Economy, Population and Labour Policies Programme, Working Paper No. 140, Geneva, World Employment Programme Research, ILO

dependent on the agriculture sector for their livelihood. However, the preponderant majorities did not own any land. They were either completely landless or worked on leased lands as a sharecropper or as an attached or bonded labourer to a landlord. The bulk of Scheduled Caste families were found to be in debt. The absence of stable assets, the uncertainty of obtaining work as agricultural labourers, the dwindling prospects of caste occupation and the inability to receive the prescribed minimum wages have all led to families being in debt. Their habitation areas lacked drinking water, sanitation, electrification, roads, etc., and they were constantly exposed to harassment and heinous atrocities (NCSCST, 1998–1999 Vol. II: 20).

1 Dalits and Education

Education has been and remains one of the key strategies for acquiring liberty, equality and fraternity for any society that aims to build an egalitarian order/system. Education is a means for better living conditions not only to an individual but to every sections of society, if provided an opportunity, for advancing on the path to liberation from slavery and bondage of a traditional society.

Table 2 presents the literacy rate of social groups—Scheduled Castes (SCs), Scheduled Tribes (STs) and Non-SC/ST—in Bihar, as recorded in the decennial Censuses of 1961, 1971, 1981 and 1991.

The general condition of education among Scheduled Castes has been quite pathetic. The educational empowerment of Scheduled Caste peoples has remained an unfulfilled dream not only in Bihar but also all over the country. In 1961, the literacy rate among the Scheduled Castes in Bihar was only 5.96%. It increased to 6.53% in 1971 and 10.40% in 1981, whereas in 1991, the literacy rate among the Scheduled Castes in Bihar was only 19.49%, which happened to be the lowest in India. The female literacy rate among the Scheduled Castes has been extremely low in Bihar and stood at 7.07% in 1991.

Even by the 2001 Census, literacy rates among Scheduled Castes and Scheduled Tribes had not improved much. The overall literacy rates of SCs and STs were 28.5% and 28.2%, respectively, as per the Census of 2001. While the literacy rate of SC/ST males was about 20% lower than the overall male literacy rate of Bihar, SC/

Table 2 Literacy rate of social groups in Bihar

Literacy rate					Male				Female			
	1961	1971	1981	1991	1961	1971	1981	1991	1961	1971	1981	1991
SC	5.96	6.53	10.4	19.49	11.2	11.9	18.0	30.64	0.92	1.0	2.51	7.07
ST	9.16	11.64	16.99	26.78	15.2	18.5	26.2	38.4	3.18	4.85	7.75	14.75
Non- SC/ST	18.4	9.9	26.2	38.48	29.8	30.6	38.1	52.49	6.9	8.7	13.6	22.89

Source: Report, NCSCST 1996b–97 & 1997–98 and 1999–2000 & 2000–2001, New Delhi, Government of India

ST female literacy rate was all the more unfavourable—it was less than half for both SC (15.6%) and ST (15.5%) females as compared to the 33.1% overall female literacy rate in the state. Male literacy among SCs and STs constituted 40.2% and 39.8%, respectively, as compared to the overall male literacy rate of 59.7%. The overall literacy rate of the state was 47%, with male literacy and female literacy standing at 59.7% and 33.1%, respectively (Government of Bihar, 2012a, pp. 21–22).

Within Scheduled Castes, some groups accounted for extremely low literacy rates. For instance, Musahars had an overall literacy rate of only 9%, while females among Musahars accounted for a literacy level of only 3.9%. About half a dozen castes included in the Mahadalit had a female literacy rate of less than 5% (Ibid: 21).

Among the literates, 39.7% of SCs in Bihar were either without any educational level or had attained education below the primary level. The proportion of literates who had attained education up to primary and middle levels constituted 28.4% and 13.1%, respectively. Only 15.1% SC literates had studied up to matriculation, secondary or higher secondary level etc. The Table 3 below reflects that only 3.6% of SCs were able to attain graduate and above levels, while only 0.1% were able to achieve non-technical and technical diplomas (Ibid: 21–22).

2 Precarious Economic Situation of Dalits in Bihar

In 1993–1994, Bihar had the highest percentage of Scheduled Castes (70.66%) in rural areas living below the poverty line. During the same time period, 55.16% of Scheduled Castes in urban areas were also below the poverty line (NCSCST, 1999–2000 & 2000–2001, p. 41).

As a matter of fact, even a decade ago (1983–1984), about 71.10% of the Scheduled Castes in rural areas and 52.20% in urban areas in Bihar lived below the poverty line (NCSCST, 1994–1995 & 1995–1996, p. 128).

According to Agriculture Census 1985–86, 91.2% of the Scheduled Caste landholders in Bihar belonged to the marginal category, 5.30% in the small category, 2.58% in the semi-medium category, 0.81% in the medium category and 0.07% in the large category (NCSCST, 1996c–1997 & 1997–1998, p. 148).

The minimum wages for Scheduled Caste agricultural labourers and for other labourers have been quite low. It was Rs. 4.50 (with one meal/breakfast) for

Table 3 Levels of education among Scheduled Castes (SCs) and Scheduled Tribes (STs) in Bihar

Caste and Tribe	Literates without educational level (%)	Below primary (%)	Primary (%)	Middle (%)	Matric, higher secondary (%)	Tech–non-tech diploma (%)	Graduate (%)
SC	6.6	31.1	28.4	13.1	15.1	0.1	3.6
ST	5.8	31.3	28.2	14.4	16.3	0.2	3.8

Source: Census of India 2001

un-irrigated areas and Rs. 5.00 (with one meal/breakfast) for irrigated areas from July 1975 onwards (Commissioner for Scheduled Castes and Scheduled Tribes, 1980–1981, p. 38).

The distribution of rural labour households by size class of land cultivated is helpful to know the size-specific incidence of rural labour households among the Scheduled Castes and other groups.

Table 4 shows that in 1993–1994, there was a major concentration of rural labour households in the landholding size category of less than 1 acre. In the case of Scheduled Castes, 87% of landowning labour households fell within the less-than-1-acre-size category. The proportion declined to 9.10% in the 1-to-2.5-acre category and 3.90% in the 2.50-above-acre-size category for Scheduled Castes.

3 Access to Agricultural Land

The implementation of land reform measures remained far from adequate in Jehanabad and other districts in the erstwhile central Bihar, which were rife with tension over disputes concerning the distribution and control of ceiling-surplus lands as well as of gairmazarua (government) lands. Notwithstanding the tall claims of the state government, the fact remained that the poor and impoverished Dalits did not benefit much from these measures. In Jehanabad district, a total of 581 acres of land had been declared surplus—i.e. in excess of the landowning limits imposed by ceiling laws—by the end of 1986–1987. Out of this, 428 acres had been acquired and distributed among 516 landless persons. But a breakdown of this distribution revealed that the pattern of distribution was not uniform, and it appeared that people belonging to the Scheduled Castes were blatantly discriminated against. Equally bleak was the implementation of another land reform programme, i.e. the settlement of gairmazarua (government) lands in favour of the landless. Around 40,870 acres of land were declared gairmazarua, of which 19,515 acres were classified as 'gairmazarua aam' and 21,355 acres as 'gairmazarua malik' lands. However, only 14,932 acres of gairmazarua malik land, or 70% of the total land of this type, had been settled in favour of the landless till 1987. On the other hand, only 657 acres of gairmazarua land, or only a little more than 3.1% of the total land of this type, were settled till 1987. Taking together the two types, the settled gairmazarua land came to be around 38% of the total gairmazarua land (Bharti, 1988, p. 2519).

Table 4 Percentage distribution of the estimated number of labour households with cultivated land by (hectors): 1993–1994, Bihar

Social groups	(<1 acre) (<0.4)	(1–2.5 acre) (0.4–1)	(>2.5 acre) (>1)
General	76.40	17.30	6.30
SCs	87.00	9.10	3.90

Source: Rural Labour Enquiry (1993–1994)

However, the major part of such distribution and settlement existed only on paper. The physical reality was quite different and spoke of another tale. Surplus and gairmazarua lands had been acquired and distributed, and settled holdings continued to be occupied by landlords. There were about 70 villages that continued to be illegally captured by landlords in Jehanabad district. The landless labourers, on the other hand, have been demanding the implementation of laws enacted by the state government to dilute the iniquitous pattern of landholdings. However, powerful rural elements have suppressed every such demand through violent methods. This has led to the numerous killings of innocent Dalits in the recent past (Ibid: 2519–2520).

Feudal structures from the past have not been dismantled at large in rural areas. The socio-religious structure played a much larger role in the agrarian sector of rural areas and has continued to influence the dominant caste hegemony, wherein the lowest of the low have always found to be at the receiving end in every possible sense of the term. The semi-feudal relations of production that existed in states like Bihar have been found to be the main reason for the underutilisation of vast irrigation potentials, the low level of inputs and the lack of enterprise and initiative on the part of farmers. Endemic sharecropping, exploitation by moneylenders and the tilting of the balance of political power against weaker sections resulted in unspeakable atrocities, including arson, rape, mayhem and mass murder against whole groups of families of sharecroppers, who tried to establish their rights to the land they we were cultivating (Subramanian, 1987, p. 22).

Lack of sincerity in implementation of land reforms thus added to the tension-three decades after zamindari (Landlordism) was abolished, as only 1.26% of surplus cultivable lands were acquired in Bihar and less than half of that distributed. But the situation in the central districts was even worse. In Patna district itself, for example, a mere 0.3% of cultivable land had been acquired and distributed by 1984. The then Home Commissioner B.K. Singh admitted quite frankly: 'Extremism in this pocket was deeply rooted in the poor implementation of land reform laws.' Minimum wages were another fractious issue. The minimum wage for unskilled agricultural labour was Rs 8.50, but landlords rarely paid more than Rs 3. In areas where wages were paid in kind, landlords paid merely about 1.25 kg of food grains instead of the mandated minimum of 3 kg (India Today Magazine, 1986a, b).

The pitiable conditions of the landless Scheduled Castes in Bihar reflects a situation in which a very low rate of land reforms/distribution of government lands was initiated and much more than that the landowning castes' blatant and violent activities resulting in to even killing of innocent Scheduled Castes has been a pointer to the fact that the wretched of the earth have not been provided with any means to live a life of dignity. According to B.B. Mohanty, 'It appeared, as pointed out by a number of studies [Appu 1996, Mearns 1998, Patel 1974, Deshpande 1998, Murdia 1975], that the inherent loopholes and ambiguities in the legislative measures, slow proceedings at all levels of bureaucracy, lack of updated land records, the ignorance and illiteracy of the scheduled population and the escaping attitude of the large landowners were the major reasons that hindered fair distribution of land by allowing the bulk of landowners to avoid expropriation. Even a slow process of passing of the land to the Scheduled Castes and Tribes and its resultant upliftment became intolerable and non-acceptable to the dominant groups. They resisted the allotment of land by committing atrocities on members of Scheduled Castes and Tribes through well organised groups, like the Ranveer Sena, Brahmarsi Sena, Bhumi Sena and Lorik Sena. In Bihar, a number of Dalits have been killed by the Ranveer Sena alone in recent years owing to issues relating to land allotment [Diwakar 1999:75]. Evidence of this type of inclement resistance abounds across the states. Because of this problem the poor Scheduled Caste and Tribe person found it difficult to occupy the land after allotment' (Mohanty, 2001, pp. 3862–3863) (Table 5).

The above table highlights the allocation of funds and their non-utilisation/partial utilisation. This reflects gross negligence on the part of the government in failing to spend the allocated budgetary funds for the socio-economic and educational welfare of the Dalit community. The NCSCST also highlighted in this report that Bihar was among the states (along with Assam, Gujarat, Haryana, Kerala, Maharashtra, Rajasthan, Tamil Nadu, West Bengal, Delhi, Punjab and Andhra Pradesh) that lagged in proper allocations under the Special Component Plan (SCP) and performed very poorly due to underutilisation of allocated funds.

How should we look at the overall socio-economic status of Dalits in India, in general, and in Bihar, in particular? Dalits, the lowest of the low in social hierarchy, have been found to be at the receiving end in every sense of the term as far as the question of land or any indicator of development is concerned. In a similar vein, Anand Chakravarti said: 'Caste continues to be the fundamental basis of social inequality in contemporary Bihar. Due to a range of factors, both the traditional and new dominant castes have privileged access to material and political resources, and constitute the dominant class. As a consequence those who belong to the depressed social groups are denied access to such resources. The circumstances of birth into a low-ranking caste, therefore, tend to determine their social and material conditions. They thus constituted a vast rural underclass, subject to caste and class exploitation, as well as state repression. In the ultimate analysis the continuing oppression of the underclass in Bihar has been a consequence of the organic linkage between dominant castes in the society at large—who constituted the dominant class- and the structures of the state' (Chakravarti, 2001, p. 1459).

Some of the core issues from the socio-economic sector are being highlighted here to emphasise the need for an all-inclusive approach to issues related to

Table 5 Special component plan (SCP) outlay and actual expenditures by Bihar (1992–2002)

		(Rs in crores)
Year	Outlay	Expenditure
1992–1993	180.09	95.05
1993–1994	104.00	94.74
1994–1995	166.69	152.23
1995–1996	470.91	110.34
1996–1997	260.30	144.17
1997–1998	354.79	0.00
1998–1999	627.97	0.00
1999–2000	549.36	389.00
2000–2001	386.13	Not available
2001–2002	384.36	Not available

Source: Report, National Commission for Scheduled Castes and Scheduled Tribes (NCSCST), 1999–2000 & 2000–2001, New Delhi, Government of India, 29

economic growth and prosperity across different social groups (Institute for Human Development, 2012b, pp. 14–16):

- The incidence of poverty, based on estimates using the Expert Group Methodology, declined from 62.2% in 1983 to 55.0% in 1993–1994 and further to 41.4% in 2004–2005. Tentative estimates from the recent National Sample Survey Office (NSSO) 66th Round Survey of 2009–2010 showed that in spite of the high growth achieved during the recent years or so, the level of poverty (measured using the Tendulkar methodology) continued to be about 54% as against 32% for India as a whole.
- About 80% of the surveyed households did not have electricity connections, and even in the most advanced districts, only one-third of the total households had electricity connections.
- Open defecation was found to be the norm, and only a small minority of households had toilets.
- There was widespread social exclusion, which was most evident in the denial of land to lower-caste groups. On average, 81% of Scheduled Caste households were landless, while Other Backward Classes (OBC-I), 65%.
- In general, the rural areas of Bihar suffered from relatively high mortality and malnutrition, particularly among women and children, and there was a wide prevalence of several kinds of diseases.

4 Rising Numbers of Caste Atrocities in Bihar

An examination of atrocity-related information and subsequent analysis can help us understand the grim realities of caste-based hostilities and human rights abuses that Dalits have been facing in Bihar. How the situation turned so badly needs to be understood so as to make an overall assessment of the worsening Dalit human rights situation in the state and in the erstwhile central Bihar. The incidents of atrocities against Dalits were not happening on a large scale as reported during pre 1970s decade and that may have been because the total number of atrocity related cases were not filed up in proper way. Overall, the situation in Bihar did not reach alarming proportions. But it did not mean that caste-based discrimination, exclusion and violence were not happening. The reported official figures were not high, and that was the only saving grace. It would be instructive to quote the Commissioner for Scheduled Castes and Scheduled Tribes annual report during this time period to understand this new trend in Bihar. According to 1979–1981 reports by the Commissioner for Scheduled Castes and Scheduled Tribes, Bihar did not figure among the 12 states with the highest number of atrocities against Dalits between 1967 and 1974. And quite surprisingly, in that period, Bihar made its first appearance as the sixth worst state; in 1974, it was ranked fourth and then third for four consecutive years, from 1976 to 1979. As a matter of fact, from the middle of the 1970s onwards, sharp clashes were reported between landowners, on the one hand, and Dalit and other low-caste agricultural labourers, on the other. The landed gentry set up their own caste militia to demonstrate their superiority and did not hesitate to unleash a reign of terror and killings so as to teach rebellious low-caste labourers a hard lesson by finishing them off in the most brutal manner. This resulted in a spike in crimes against the Dalits in Bihar from 1977 onwards: 681 cases were reported in 1977; 1911 in 1978; 2152 in 1979; 1890 in 1980; and 10,873 from 1981 to 1986 (Table 6).

From 1977 to 1986, a total of 17,437 cases of crimes against Dalits were reported. Atrocity reports appeared to be unavailable from 1987 to 1988. The state of Bihar reported 997 atrocity cases in 1989, 744 cases in 1990 and 511 cases in 1991 (NCSCST, 1992b–193, p. 98) (Table 7).

From 1992 to 1997, a total of 8885 cases of crimes against Dalits were reported in Bihar. Thus, the total number of reported crimes committed against Dalits from

Table 6 Number of cases of crimes against the Scheduled Castes committed by members of non-Scheduled Castes in Bihar from 1977 to 1986

Year	No. of cases registered
1977	681
1978	1911
1979	2152
1980	1890
1981	2033
1982	2073
1983	1809
1984	1845
1985	1452
1986	1661
Total	17,437

Source: Report of the Commissioner for Scheduled Caste and Scheduled Tribes from 1977 to 1986, New Delhi, Government of India

Table 7 Number of cases of crimes against the Scheduled Castes committed by members of non-Scheduled Castes in Bihar from 1992 to 1997

Year	No. of cases registered
1992	1295
1993	1016
1994	1724
1995	1867
1996	1865
1997	1118
Total	8885

Source: Annual Report (1992–97), Scheduled Castes, Scheduled Tribes and Minority Cell, Crime Investigation Department, Patna, Government of Bihar

1977 to 1997 (except 1987 and 1988) in Bihar was 28,574 (17,437 + 2252 + 8885). These figures are based on reports from government agencies only, and it is a fact that many cases do not get registered at police stations due to several factors. Thus, there is a possibility of more cases happening during this time period. These figures represent all cases of untouchability and atrocities and not only killings.

On the other hand, for the same time period (1992–1997), the National Crime Record Bureau (NCRB), in its annual report 'Crime in India', documented 4394 cases of crimes against the Dalits in Bihar. This is almost half of what was reported by the Scheduled Caste Cell of the Bihar Police for the same time period. The discrepancy in number of cases registered for crimes against Dalits in two different reports by the government agencies revealed the fact the atrocity related data compilation work was not being carried out in a proper way. But what is more important to note here is the fact that even with the lesser number of crimes reported and published in government reports, these figures still present a broader picture of the crimes committed against the Dalits (Table 8).

The rise of backward caste politics in many ways also led to atrocities against Dalits being committed even by backward caste people. One of the main reasons for retaliation by agricultural landholders could be the redistribution of land among the Dalits in Bihar, which was not favoured by them to a large extent. As there is an ascending order of reverence and a descending order of abhorrence, which is the hallmark of the hierarchical system of caste, it is not a surprise that they would not hesitate to follow the socio-religious and cultural dictates prevalent and practised in society at large. This is how the system of graded inequality works in Indian society, and the behaviour of backward caste people towards Dalits is certainly not an exception. Graded inequality also gets reflected in the officials/duty bearers who discriminate against Dalits whenever they have an opportunity to do so. For example, wastelands were distributed to Dalit landless labourers, but these lands turned out to be of no use to the beneficiaries. It has also been found that the better off sections of society have never favoured any welfare measures intended for people belonging to untouchable castes. The non-implementation of several welfare programmes and policies bears testimony to this gross violation of Dalit human rights.

Table 8 Number of cases of crimes against the Scheduled Castes committed by the non-Scheduled Castes in Bihar from 1992 to 1997

Year	No. of cases registered
1992	617
1993	721
1994	789
1995	747
1996	810
1997	710
Total	4394

Source: 'Crime in India' (1994–97), National Crime Record Bureau, Ministry of Home Affairs, New Delhi, Government of India

In most villages and districts in the erstwhile central Bihar, the government initiative for land redistribution and other anti-poverty programmes led to several incidents of direct clashes between the old established caste order and the new and bolder initiatives that had become a ray of hope for the betterment of Dalits' lives. In a situation where most Dalits were forced to work as landless labourers, any chance of improving their socio-economic lot was further blocked by several cases of caste-based atrocities and violent killings by dominant landowning communities. The hegemonic control exercised by these landowning communities/castes afforded them several privileges. In Bihar, with different districts and regions often with dominant landowners belonging to one or another particular caste, the identity of caste provided to the dominant sections the means through which it could exert its power of monopoly control over land and thus over employment. It also enabled the consolidation of this power in numerical terms by uniting large and small landowners of the same caste together. This benefited all these landowners by permitting a pittance to be paid as agricultural wages, extraction of a large share of the produce in tenancy (*bataidari*) contracts, binding down the rural poor with debt bondage and subjecting them, especially the womenfolk, to barbaric oppression (PUDR, 2016, p. 6) (Table 9).

Landlords in particular organised many armed outfits, called *senas*, to enforce their writ. These *sena*s were usually organised on caste lines, with some having the support of more than one caste. The Bhumi Sena functioned as an army of Kurmis, the Lorik Sena of Yadavs, the Sawarna Liberation Front (SLF) and the Ranveer Sena of Bhumihars, the Sunlight Sena of Rajputs and so on. In each case, the role of the police and the administration ranged from complicity to callous disregard in connection with the criminal activities of these senas (Ibid: 6–7).

5 Caste Carnage Writ Large: Selected Cases from the Killing Fields of Bihar

Some of the major incidents of caste carnage, starting from Belchi in 1977 to Laxmanpur Bathe in 1997, are cited here as examples of the killing fields prevalent in Bihar, which have put a question mark not only on the state of civil society but

Table 9 The landlord armies

Name	Year of establishment	Caste affiliation	Region of operation
Kisan Suraksha Samiti	1979	Kurmi	Patna, Jehanabad and Gaya
Kuer Sena	1979	Rajput	Bhojpur
Bhumi Sena	1983	Kurmi	Patna, Jehanabad, Nawada and Nalanda
Lorik Sena	1983	Yadav	Patna, Jehanabad, Nalanda
Kisan Sangh	1984	Rajput, Brahmin	Palamu, Aurangabad, Patna
Sunlight Sena	1989	Rajput, Pathan	Gaya, Palamu and Garhwa
Swarna liberation front	1990	Bhumihar	Gaya, Jehanabad
Kisan Morcha	1990	Rajput	Bhojpur
Ganga Sena	1990	Rajput	Bhojpur
Ranveer Sena	1994	Bhumihar	Bhojpur, Rohtas, Patna, Jehanabad, Gaya, Aurangabad

Source: Report (2016), p. 6

also on the governability of the state. The cases mentioned below are meant to highlight violations of Dalit human rights, though they are not a comprehensive list. It is also a fact that caste killings that happened in Bihar in three decades or so became an example of caste war for which parallels may be difficult to find in other states. The other sad truth was that it has not been possible to compile all the cases as massacres had become a recurring feature. During this period, Bihar witnessed scores—and perhaps thousands—of caste killings, and sadly enough, the governments in the state and also at the centre do not have the exact number of Dalits killed in caste-based massacres during the three decades of caste wars.

6 Patna District

Patna district, despite being the capital of the state, witnessed incidents of caste-based killings over a period of three decades, serving as a testament to how lawlessness became normalised and how state intervention to curb the growing caste-based killings turned out to be most ineffective. Belchi represented a classic example of caste tyranny in the most brutal manner on May 27, 1977, in which eight Dalits and three members of the backward castes were shot down and thrown into a funeral pyre. The alleged culprits were part of a gang comprising Kurmi and Dhanuk landlords. On this fateful day, Mahabir Mahto collected his entire gang with the intention of wiping out Singheshwar Paswan, alias Singhwa, and others who posed a threat to their caste hegemony. Two other gangs, one led by Inderdeo Choudhary and the other by Parsuram Dhanuk, were also involved in this carnage. Ultimately, they caught Singhwa and ten others, allegedly shot them and subsequently burned them (Bhushan, 1977, p. 974).

On August 1, 1977, the absconding accused Parsuram Dhanuk, accompanied by about 40 others, tried to attack Belchi at 10 o'clock in the morning. The Bihar Military Police stationed in the village managed to chase them away after crossfiring. Singhwa Paswan was the leader of the agricultural labourers and was actively involved in opposing the tyranny of figures like Mahabir Mahto. Mahto had managed to file two criminal cases against Singhwa by falsely implicating so as to get rid of him (Sinha, 1977, p. 1244). The situation in the village turned quite bad. Most of the Kurmi caste families were hostile to the SCs in the village. Because of the reign of terror following the gruesome killings, several SC families started to leave for safer places in other areas (Narayan, 1979, p. 188).

The response from the central government, on the basis of a report sent by the state government, was a knee-jerk reaction that described the incident as an example of gang warfare. The Union Home Ministry said in a press note that gang warfare between two rival groups of criminals was responsible for the May 27 incident in Belchi village near Patna in which 11 persons were killed. It completely denied the fact that the incident was a caste-based killing perpetrated by the landed gentry of the village (Indian Express, 1977a). Charan Singh, the Union Home Minister, said: 'It was a clash between two groups of hardened criminals having long standing rivalry... It had no caste, communal, agrarian or political overtones. No atrocities on weaker section were committed' (Bhardwaj, 1977, p. 18). This kind of response from the government was also critically reported in other media outlets. The May 27, 1977, massacre of the landless in Belchi village in Bihar demonstrated once again the orgy of violence that the caste-ridden landed class could still perpetrate in free India against the village poor, particularly in areas where an outdated socio-economic order still prevails. Eleven of the poorest of the poor were murdered in that tiny hamlet in broad daylight in cold blood. The Bihar government took belated notice of the crime and, having recognised its brutal nature, tried to explain it away as a case of mere retaliation by one of the criminal gangs against another and not an atrocity committed by the landed caste against the weaker sections of society (Sharma, 1977, p. 4).

However, there were others who were not ready to accept the government's response to this ghastly killing of the poor and helpless Scheduled Caste people at Belchi in Bihar. It was certainly far from the truth and was rightfully disputed by many. The Parliamentary committee headed by Mr. Ramdhan, which conducted an enquiry at Belchi, thus observed: 'The committee is of the opinion that nowhere in the world persons were characterized as hardened criminals on mere suspicion. The government version that these gruesome murders were not based on caste hatred and social inhibitions was also totally incorrect' (Bhardwaj, 1977: op. cit). The committee came to the conclusion that the Bihar government's report stating 'that there was a clash between two groups of hard-core criminals having long standing rivalry was totally false'. According to the committee, it was rather a case of pre-meditated, well-planned mass murder of landless Scheduled Castes by a large gang of Kurmis, prosperous farmers of the area who had secured firearms through the influence of a local political leader. There was no encounter. The murderers caught hold of their 11 victims, tied them up with ropes, poured kerosene on them and threw them into a mass pyre (Indian Express, 1977b). The committee, during it fact-finding mission, also found that five days before the killings, the Mahabir Mahto gang had attacked SC people and shot Sakal Paswan, who later succumbed to his bullet injuries and died. Even though a police case was lodged, there was no action from the local police, which emboldened the perpetrators, Mahabir Mahto and his gang members, to carry out even more gruesome crimes against the SCs in Belchi on that fateful day (Mitta, 2023, p. 487).

This incident of brutal killings of Dalits and other lower-caste people, which happened in more ways than one, actually lit the fire that remained un-extinguished for more than three decades in Bihar. The collusion of the local police and support from politicians emboldened the landed gentry to commit atrocities on Dalits and other rebellious lower-caste people with impunity. This had become a regular feature in the area for quite some time. The massacre was perhaps waiting to happen, and the manner in which it was carried out had only one objective: to eliminate any threat to their hegemony.

The Commissioner for Scheduled Castes and Scheduled Tribes, along with a team of officers, visited Belchi on August 29, 1977, and met with officials, non-officials and the dependents and relatives of the victims. Some sort of conflict had been going on between the leader of the deceased Singheshwar Paswan and the landlords about cultivation of lands as well as regarding protecting the interests of the agricultural labourers. Minimum wage requirements were being violated by landlords, yet no case was filed against them. It did not appear tenable to characterise any of the victims as hardened criminals. The committee thus observed: 'There were reasons to believe that it was a case of atrocities committed on Scheduled Castes. Though no apparent political motives could be ascribed to this incident, there were definite economic and social motives. Well-to-do sections among the Kurmis wanted to maintain their unchallenged economic and social supremacy and tried to be ruthless in dealing with persons of Scheduled Castes community who posed any threat to their over lordship. Killing of 11 persons in broad-day light could be accomplished only by hardened criminals and just because some of them were involved in criminal activities against their own caste men should not be taken as indication that they did not carry out atrocities on Scheduled Castes and indulged in criminal warfare only' (Commissioner for Scheduled Castes and Scheduled Tribes, 1975–1976 and 1976–1977, pp. 110–11).

On May 19, 1980, a Patna trial court delivered its verdict in the Belchi massacre case. The Additional Sessions Judge sentenced 17 of the accused to life imprisonment and imposed the death penalty to two of them, Mahabir Mahto and Parsuram Dhanuk (The Times of India, 1980). The verdict was challenged in the Patna High Court, which confirmed the death sentences of the two accused and upheld the life imprisonment of the others convicted in the mass murder (The Times of India, 1982). The High Court's verdict was challenged in the Supreme Court, where the case lingered for 3 more years. Finally, on November 9, 1983, the duo, Mahabir Mahto and Parsuram Dhanuk, were executed by hanging (The Times of India, 1983).

Another day brought yet another case of caste conflict reported from Patna district. On January 1, 1979, about two dozen people were reported to have attacked the Scheduled Castes in Mahuli village under the Barh police station, and their houses were set on fire due to a dispute over fishing rights on a public pond (National Commission for Scheduled Castes and Scheduled Tribes, 1978–1979, p. 154). In the same month, on January 26, Scheduled Caste girls were burnt by landlords at Bahor village under Naubatpur police station 10 as a result of a land dispute (Ibid: 155). On the other hand, at Bahuara village under the Naubatpur police station, ten houses of the Scheduled Castes were burnt by the musclemen of landlords on February 26, 1979. This incident arose from a resentment over the allotment of land to Scheduled Caste persons (Ibid: 154).

Pipra became a target of caste-based killings on the night of February 25, 1980. The invaders, numbering about 500, were armed to the teeth, mostly with firearms. They set on fire 27 houses of the untouchables—which were made mostly of mud and straw—shot them indiscriminately, looted their belongings and burnt their cattle alive. The Kurmis were avenging the murder of one Bhola Singh, a large landowner from Kalyanchak. It was alleged that Bhola Singh was slain by Naxals, who were supposed to be organising the untouchables of the area against the tyrannies of the landowners. The Kurmis suspected that the untouchables of Pipra were in complicity with the Naxals (Prasad, 1985, p. 37).

Bhutali Ramdas, the 65-year-old leader of the community, was dragged out of his house. His head was chopped off, and his body was thrown into the fire. Altogether, 14 people were killed in this attack, including seven women and five children (PUDR, 1983, p. 6). The raiders surrounded the houses in the hamlet and set them on fire, and when the men, women and children fled outside, they were tossed right back into the inferno (India Today Magazine, 1986a).

Patna Additional Sessions Judge S.C. Mukherjee sentenced 50 people on August 5, 1981—the largest collective conviction ever—to life imprisonment for the Pipra carnage that took place in February last year. Apart from the unusually high number of convictions, what was remarkable was the fact that several powerful people in the village hierarchy were booked. Among them were mukhiyas, sarpanchs, landlords and student leaders, who, normally, as modern-day rural czars, think nothing of using money and political links to buy freedom. If the verdict was out of the ordinary, so too was the crime that invited it. Fourteen people, including women and children, were gunned down or burnt alive in what was described as a premeditated attack by about 500 well-armed men with the intention of wiping out the entire village of Pipra (India Today Magazine, 1981).

On April 13, 1986, Ramanand Yadav and his Lorik Sena gang member attacked Jeenpura at midnight and shot dead six Dalits. This gruesome killing was a reaction to Mazdoor Kisan Shakti Sangathan (MKSS) helping the poor and Dalit landless agricultural labourers in the village (PURD, 1986, pp. 31–32).

Fourteen Dalits were killed at Tiskhora on January 19, 1991, because of a brutal attack orchestrated by the Kisan Sangh. More than 100 armed men, accompanied by police personnel from Tulsi Chak Camp and Charma Camp, launched a violent assault on the village and killed Dalits and OBCs who were attending a marriage ceremony (Outlook Magazine, 2023). In another incident, on September 23, 1991, seven poor Dalits were gunned down by members of the Kisan Sangh at Karkatbigha in Paliganj (PUDR, 1992a, p. 1).

On March 23, 1997, about ten or 11 landless Mushahar caste members were killed in Haibaspur village, apparently for aligning themselves with the CPI (ML) Party Unity. Before leaving the village, the Ranveer Sena inscribed its organisation's name in blood on the rim of a dry well (Outlook Magazine, 1997). It is alleged that alcohol and the rape of Dalit women by Bhumihars played a key role in provoking the attack on the village. Although the police were informed immediately of the Haibaspur killings, they did not arrive on the scene until the following morning, after hearing that the Chief Minister was due to visit the site (The Hindu, 1997).

Describing this gruesome killing, a former bureaucrat thus explained: 'A batch of five-to-six Ranveer Sena men dropped in at that nondescript Musahar toli on the eve of Holi (the festival of colours). Posing as guests, the Ranveer Sena cadres had demanded drinks to mark the hospitality and revelries of Holi. The Musahars, too overwhelmed with the unexpected visit of their respectable high caste guests at night, did everything possible within their modest means to entertain them in their huts. At the end of the fun and frolics following bouts of home-brewed drinks, the visitors requested the unsuspected Musahars to accompany them for some distance and guide them out of their village. A dozen or so Musahars walked alongside their visitors in compliance, as desired. Half-a-kilometre away from their hamlet, the wolves in sheep's clothing threw off their pretension, whipped off their sophisticated weapons and emptied them on the poor hospitable Musahars leading the unprovoked killers as their guides. The field with standing ripe golden wheat crop saw massacres of innocent men in the pre-dawn of the Holi in 1997. The full moon above flooded the entire landscape in glorious ecstasy that night of the bloodbath' (Biswas, 2009).

In an on-the-spot enquiry conducted by the National Commission for Scheduled Castes and Scheduled Tribes (NCSST), it was found that the incident was well planned but still could have been averted if the district administration had been vigilant and quick to respond. Though the case was filed under the Indian Penal Code (IPC), Arms Act and SC and ST PoA Act, the victims were not provided relief in cash, kind or both, as per the provisions of the SC and ST (Prevention of Atrocities) Rules, 1995. It was also found that the case was investigated by a police inspector and not by a deputy superintendent of police (DSP), as required under the provisions of the PoA Rules (NCSCST, 1998–1999, p. 27).

7 Nalanda District

On November 22, 1978, an SC member was alleged to have been murdered by a landlord at Srurgaon village due to a dispute over irrigation of land (Commissioner for Scheduled Castes and Scheduled Tribes, 1978–1979, p. 155). On the same day, another incident was reported in which an SC person was killed at Dhargaon village under Ekangarsarai police station on account of a dispute over a piece of land. In the same Dhargaon village, another SC was killed on November 27, 1978, due to a dispute over the harvesting of crops (Ibid: 154).

Three SC individuals were alleged to have been shot dead by an armed gang of dominant OBC caste farmers at Kaila village under Chandi police station on December 9, 1978. The incident stemmed from a long-standing dispute over 14 acres of land between the deceased SC person and members of the Kurmi caste. It was discovered through a field study that individuals hired by the Mahto community had mercilessly killed the victim by chopping off his head with sharp weapons (Ibid: 154). The Kurmis gathered a mob and mounted a surprise attack on the Harijans. Some of those killed had nothing to do with the quarrels between the Harijans and the Kurmis. The attack took place despite the fact that there was a police camp in the village. After killing the Harijans with sharp weapons, the Kurmis fired on the walls of several huts to terrorise them. The Kurmis greatly resented equal rights given to the Harijans lest they may become less amenable to exploitation (Sachidananda, 1979, pp. 32–33). In the Kaila killings, a charge sheet was submitted in February 1979, but prosecution commenced only 20 months later. Ultimately, three accused received a life sentence, while eight were sentenced to various jail terms (India Today Magazine, 1981).

On April 16, 2000, two SC members were killed and four were injured by Bhumihar landlords at Panki village under Silaw police station. A month and a half later, on June 1, 2000, two other SC members were killed by a gang hired by landlords at Palni village (Current Agrarian Situation in Bihar, 2008, p. 124).

8 Nawada District

Mauji Paswan was speared to death by a gang of big Bhumihar farmers of Bikku village under Hisua police station. His death occurred after he protested against the destruction of his improvised hut on the outskirts of his village. The gang wanted his hut to be burnt during the *Agja* fire ceremony on the eve of the Holi festival. The gang was drunk and armed with lethal weapons. The protest by the poor Harijans was too much of an affront to the landlords. How does a Harijan talk back to Bhumihars? Mauji was attacked twice with a spear. As a result of this, he died on the spot. Four others who spoke in favour of Mauji were also injured. All the suspects were still at large and very much present in the village but not arrested by the police (Narayan, 1978, p. 10).

On May 3, 1978, about 50 houses belonging to Scheduled Caste families were reported to have been burnt down by landlords at Tirwan village under Pakribarawan police station following a dispute over the cutting of trees (Commissioner for Scheduled Castes and Scheduled Tribes, 1978–1979 op. cit: 154).

An SC individual was allegedly killed at Thalpos village on November 12, 1978, as a result of a dispute arising from encroachment on fallow land (Ibid: 155).

9 Rohtas District

On March 25, 1978, three lower-caste persons were killed by an armed group of landlords in Bishrampur. In connection with this case, the Commissioner for Scheduled Castes and Scheduled Tribes deputed a team in April 1978 to enquire into the incident. The team report submitted to the Commissioner highlighted the most condemnable role of the police in handling the situation in Bishrampur. They took an inordinately long time to reach the village, and even after reaching there, they were reported to be hiding in agricultural fields to protect their own skin. The district police sent a reinforcement team, but they also failed to control the ground situation and managed to apprehend only two persons from the site of the crime. The enquiry committee also observed that it was wrong on the part of the Bihar government to classify the Bishrampur incident as gang warfare between two groups. It emphasised, instead, that this incident was an act of atrocity committed against the Scheduled Castes in Bishrampur village, and the government of Bihar should compensate the survivors' families without further loss of time. Also, the government should consider allotting land to the SC families who have lost their kith and kin on account of this unfortunate event (Commissioner for Scheduled Caste and Scheduled Tribes, 1977a–1978, p. 112).

In relation to the case, a charge sheet was submitted in April 1978, but the trial began only in July 1980, and the verdict was delivered in April 1981. A total of 27 persons were sentenced to life imprisonment (India Today Magazine, 1981).

On August 28, 1978, two Scheduled Caste individuals were alleged to have lost their lives at Pipri village in Rohtas district on account of a long-standing land dispute (Commissioner for Scheduled Castes and Scheduled Tribes, 1978–1979, p. 154). A simmering enmity over the allotment of government land culminated in the killing of two Harijans at Pipri village in Rohtas district on August 28, 1978, according to official sources. The Communist Party of India and Congress Party leaders described the Pipri killings as an extension of the Belchi incident. Two Harijan families headed by Mr. Sukhvilas and Jamuna Ram were each allotted 0.7 hectares of government land in 1976. Rich farmers objected, and the Harijans filed a case against them. All this led to several clashes and a boycott of Harijan labourers by the farmers. Mr. Sukhvilas told a visiting *United News of India* (UNI) correspondent at the backward caste dominated village, some 30 kilometres away from Sasaram, that ever since the allotment of land, farmers in the village have been troubling us. A police official said that trouble had been brewing since the Harijans closed a channel dug by farmers a year ago. Mr. Sukhvilas further explained that they had to close the channel as it passed by the side of their huts, threatening the foundation of the colony. Wage dispute was another problem in this village. The farmers decided not to give work to Harijan labourers in the village and instead started borrowing workers from neighbouring villages. Matters came to a head when Ramprit Ram and Saryu Ram, brother and nephew of Sukhvilas, were going to another village in search of work. On the way, they were attacked and shot dead. Sukhvilas managed to escape from the village and filed a First Information Report

(FIR) with the Karahghar police station, some 6 kilometres away from the village (National Herald, 1978).

Samhauta (1979), Gaganbigha (1984) and Panchkhori in Baghela (2000) all witnessed the killings of Dalit agricultural labourers. Four SC individuals—Suresh Pasi, Tulsi Pasi, Sawarath Pasi and Kalika Ram—were shot dead by Rajput landlords in Samhauta village on June 22 and 23, 1979 (New Age, 1979, p. 7). Five Dalits were killed in Gaganbigha and four in Panchkhori by Rajput landlords and Ranveer Sena, respectively (Current Agrarian Situation in Bihar, 2008, p. 126).

On June 29, 1980, a large army of landlords, their musclemen and police personnel, numbering around 500 in total, surrounded the Kerserwa village in Rohtas district. This operation, conducted in search of an alleged dacoit Mohan Bind, continued for about 18 hours. Unable to find him, they picked up four young Dalits, tied them up and rode horses over their chest before finally killing them (PUDR, 1983, pp. 6–7).

10 Jehanabad District

On the night of February 6, 1980, armed landlords raided the village of Parasbigha in Jehanabad, which was still part of the Gaya district. The attackers set fire to almost all lower-caste houses in the village. They first bolted the doors from outside and then poured kerosene over the reed and thatch huts and set fire to them. People who were fleeing the houses were shot dead. Altogether, 12 people were killed in the attack, including four women and five boys (PUDR, 1983 op. cit: 6). They were roasted alive after being held up inside (India Today, op. cit, 1986). On February 10, 1981, Bhumihar landlords again attacked this village and killed 11 Dalits (Current Agrarian Situation in Bihar, op. cit: 127).

The Arwal massacre on April 19, 1986 should remain as an atrocious example of mishandling of the situation by the state and its police in one of the most brutal manner. It led to the killing of 21 persons, and this figure reached 23 by the end of the month. The brutal incident arose out of a dispute between nine families (eight Scheduled Castes and one Backward Caste) and an executive engineer (belonging to one of the Scheduled Castes) over a tiny marshy and uncultivable piece of land. The land was in dispute for over 9 years, and in spite of the court verdict against the engineer, he managed to take possession of the land due to his excellent rapport with the police and state administration. In January 1986, he demolished the huts of nine families and erected a concrete wall around the plot with the help of the police. In protest against this, a strong mob of MKSS demolished the wall. The place where the participants of the protest movement were holding an entirely peaceful meeting was combed by the police in such a manner as to prevent the peaceful dispersal of the gathering. This incident culminated in what can be called the 'Jallianwala Bagh massacre' (Pathak, 1993, pp. 90–94).

At the protest site, the police started firing from the western exit leading to the main road. The southern and eastern sides of the ground were also blocked by the police. As the firing began, there was total chaos as people tried desperately to escape the deadly crossfire of bullets. When firing was over, the police started a brutal lathi charge. And even the injured were not spared, but somehow, many of them managed to escape. Once the firing was over, a few people were called to identify the dead bodies. At least four bodies could be identified immediately. The police took the dead and injured to Patna in police vans. When they arrived in Patna, eight more had succumbed to their injuries and died. The police did not hand over the dead bodies to their family members but rather disposed of them by cremating them so as to prevent further protest. By the end of April, the official toll had increased to 23 as more injured persons succumbed to their injuries (PUDR, 1986a, pp. 38–41).

In the aftermath of this ghastly killing of lower-caste people, massive protests took place in several places. The Association for Protection of Democratic Rights (APDR) conducted a fact-finding mission after its team visited and interacted with several people in Arwal. It found that the police-firing incident that occurred on April 19 and resulted in the death of a large number of people was the outcome of a high-level conspiracy hatched at the ministerial and secretariat levels of the Bihar government. Its purpose was only to terrorise and suppress the legal and democratic movement of poor peasants and agricultural labourers, and this massacre was staged without any provocation. The state government's allegation that the police fired in self-defence when an armed mob attacked the police station was utterly baseless (APDR, 1986c, p. 1).

The Bihar police and its chief, Director General of Police S.B. Sahay, said in an interview to the press that 'the force (police) was fully determined to go to any length to disperse the meeting of the extremists and clearly affirmed the resoluteness of the police to liquidate the extremists' (Indian Nation, 1986). Chief Minister Bindeshwari Dubey continued to publicly defend and justify the police action. Civil rights activists described the firing as part of a concerted plan to systematically eliminate those mobilising the poor by branding them as 'Naxalites' and killing them in stage-managed 'encounters'. When the state government submitted its preliminary report on the carnage incident to the central government, Minister of State for Internal Security Arun Nehru rejected it, according to informed sources in the state secretariat, and Prime Minister Rajiv Gandhi deputed a trusted aide, Scheduled Castes and Scheduled Tribes Commissioner B.D. Sharma, to tour the area and present to the government his own report. Sharma spent 3 days in the area, refusing state government facilities and assistance and reportedly returning convinced that landless peasants were being eliminated under the pretext of crushing Naxalites (India Today Magazine, 1986b).

B.D. Sharma mentioned in his report that there was a wide gulf between state policies and their implementation in general and minimum wages and the distribution of government lands in particular. And that is how a long history of extremist movement existed in this part of Bihar, which has been sustained by the gruelling poverty, ruthless exploitation and untold atrocities experienced by the weaker sections. The state government needed to streamline the administrative set-up, and police support should be assured to the weaker sections of the community. Numerous senas that have sprung up should be declared illegal. Issues related to minimum wages and land distribution should be taken up on a priority basis by the state government (Commissioner for Scheduled Castes and Scheduled Tribes, 1986b-1987, pp. 250–252).

Another massacre took place at Nonhi on June 16, 1988, in which 16 Dalits, including children, were gunned down by local landowners following an agricultural wage dispute prior to the paddy cultivation season. About 50 armed attackers sneaked into Nonhigarh-Bhagalpur Tola village, marked out seven houses and cold-bloodedly gunned down people sleeping in their houses. Ten minutes later, the murderers moved to Nagwan. They shot dead two Dalit youth—Ravindra Mochi, 17, and Karu Mochi, 25—and injured four others (India Today Magazine, 1988).

Nawal Sharma, the main accused of the massacre, continued to dodge the police and was declared an absconder. Those found guilty of committing mass butchery against the Dalits were Jodha Singh, Mohan Yadav, Bipin Sharma, Rajendra Yadav, Sidheshwar Yadav, Ramprit Yadav, Prabhu Yadav, Jang Bahadur Yadav, Jadu Yadav, Deenanath Yadav, Ram Bahadur Mahto, Kirit Yadav and Ramashis Yadav. All these were convicted by the Additional District and Session Judge of Gaya (The Times of India, 2003).

On September 21, 1991, seven landless labourers were taken to the village of Sawanbigha and killed by members of the Sawarna Liberation Front (PUDR, 1992a, p. 1). The Sawarna Liberation Front also killed two other Dalits on December 22, 1991, at Rampur Chai (Current Agrarian Situation in Bihar, 2008, p. 127).

In the worst-ever carnage in Bihar, at least 61 people, including 33 women and 13 children, were gunned down by banned Ranveer Sena activists at Laxmanpur Bathe village, situated on the bank of the Sone River, on the night of December 1, 1977 (The Times of India, 1997b). According to one account of the events of that evening, a group of more than 100 members of the Ranveer Sena, a 'private army' of upper-caste Bhumihar landlords, alighted from two boats coming from the Bhojpur side. They took by surprise three mallahs who were fishing. The next morning, these three were found with their throats slit. Two other mallahs, one of whom had been sleeping on the sand, were found a little further up, also with their throats slit. Another mallah who witnessed the scene from a distance was able to save his life and fled. It was only in the case of these five that the assailants did not use their guns; clearly, they did not want to alert the unsuspecting members of the tola they were about to attack. Without electricity, the tola was pitch dark. Any outsider unfamiliar with the layout would find it impossible to find his way. But not only did the assailants find their way, but they were also successful in breaking into 14 specific houses and shooting the occupants from close range. Among the 61 massacred were members of four families who were completely wiped out. Nineteen men, 27 women and 15 children less than 10 years old were killed; the youngest victim was 1 year old. Among the women, eight were pregnant. Five women were found in positions suggesting rape; three had their breasts cut (Bhatia, 1997, p. 3242).

The National Commission for Scheduled Castes and Scheduled Tribes (NCSCST) immediately took up the matter with the state government, and a member of the Commission visited the site of the ghastly killings. The incident revealed the pathetic condition of the weaker sections of society and their exploited position. They urged the state government to take prompt action to prosecute the accused and provide all relief and security to the victims and their dependents. The underlying causes of conflicts, such as land disputes, non-payment of minimum wages, lack of education, poor infrastructure, etc., also need to be taken care of so as to strengthen the hands of the weaker sections (NCSCST, 1996c–1997 & 1997–1998, p. 244).

Another version of this ghastly killing reported that 'On the night of 1 December 1997, a mob of Ranveer Sena men attacked the dalit tola in the village Laxmanpur-Bathe in Arwal block of Jehanabad district. The men barged into houses, firing and shooting indiscriminately. At the end of the carnage, 58 men, women and children were dead. The majority of the victims were dalits and backward castes. The youngest was a one year-old infant. After the mayhem, the killers left the village shouting slogans in the name of Ranveer Baba, killing five poor fishermen who lived near the river Sone on the way' (PUDR, 2016, p. 23).

There was much confusion about the total number of people killed in the Laxmanpur Bathe massacre. The Counsel for the Bihar State informed the Patna High Court that 58 persons were selectively killed in the village of Laxmanpur Bathe on December 1, 1997, at about 10:30 p.m. while asleep, and seven others were injured in 13 different houses situated in a row. Out of the 58 killed, 53 belonged to the Dalit section of society, and five were fishermen (Judgment, 2013, p. 79).

The National Commission for Scheduled Castes and Scheduled Tribes (NCSCST) conducted an on-the-spot enquiry into the atrocities committed against the Dalits in Laxmanpur Bathe village. The victims were innocent and poor. The incident was pre-planned and organised. There was no immediate cause for the incident. The crime was reported to be committed by the supporters of the so-called Ranveer Sena. The case was registered under the IPC, Arms Act and PoA Act and was investigated by a deputy SP rank officer. Financial assistance and other relief measures were provided by the state government. However, it was observed that the next of kin of the SC victims were not rehabilitated in accordance with the provisions of the SC and ST (PoA) Rules, 1995 (NCSCST, 1998–1999, pp. 27–28).

11 Gaya District

Two Scheduled Caste individuals were killed, and six, including a woman, were injured when a landlord opened fire following a dispute over land on December 11, 1978, at Chainpur village in Gaya district (Commissioner for Scheduled Castes and Scheduled Tribes, 1978–1979, p. 155).

On April 25, 1981, armed landlords attacked Bira village, under Ghosi block, in Gaya district (now part of Jehanabad district). The attackers entered the village at night and began setting fire to the houses in Musahar locality. As villagers woke up and started running helter-skelter in panic, the landlords fired at them. Three old women—Bhatani Devi (80 years), Mahagi Devi (80 Years) and Bhagiya Devi

(60 years)—a young boy aged 15 years and a young girl aged 12 years were killed. A week later, on May 1, 1981, three alleged Naxalites, including a woman, were killed in an encounter with the police at Deoramath village under Ghosi block (PUDR, 1983, p. 9).

In Jamuk in Jehanabad (then under Gaya District), a procession of landless labourers organised by MKSS was attacked by armed landlords in the presence of the police on July 2, 1981. Two agricultural labourers—Siddheshwar Manjhi and Pujan Paswan—were killed on the spot. In another incident at Kadirchak village on July 3, 1981, MKSS activist Gyanchand Bhagat was killed by landlords (Ibid: 9–10). A gang of landlords armed with rifles and guns attacked Bhagwanpur village in Jehanabad on August 10, 1981. They kidnapped three MKSS activists—Lakhan Manjhi (20 years), Sandesh Manjhi (19 years) and Kishor Manjhi (15 years)—who were tortured to death (Ibid: 10).

At Neelampur village in 1986, five Dalit agricultural labourers were killed by Lorik Sena (Current Agrarian Situation in Bihar: 130). Seven members of a family of sharecroppers in Tindiha, a settlement of Ramdohar Panchayat in Gaya, were dragged out of their houses in the middle of the night on October 1, 1991, and their throats were slit. The Sunlight Sena is believed to have perpetrated this attack. The Dalit tolas of Men and Barsiwan in Gaya were attacked by members of the Sawarna Liberation Front on the night of December 23, 1991, in which ten persons were killed (PUDR, 1992a: 1, 24 & 28).

12 Aurangabad District

In the year 1984, three Dalit agricultural labourers at Ambari and six Dalit agricultural labourers at Kharakpura were killed by Rajput landlords (Current Agrarian Situation in Bihar 2008: 129). In Kachpa, four Dalits were killed by Rajputs on October 6, 1985 (Ibid). And on December 31 1984, ten people described as extremists were killed in Kaithi Bigha in an alleged encounter involving the Central Reserve Police (CRP), Bihar Military Police and the district police from Aurangabad and Gaya. In this encounter, a policeman was also allegedly killed (India Today Magazine, 1985). A fact-finding team of PUDR revealed in its report that on the evening of December 31, 1984, a few CPI (ML) members were holding a meeting at the house of a Dalit (Nanku Ram). Local police from Obera police station arrived and demanded their surrender. The alleged extremists inside Nanku Ram's house told them to go away as they were political workers, but the local police started moving towards the house, and in an ensuing gunfire from both sides, a police constable died. After a while, with the reinforcement of CRP and BMP, the district police chief started a so-called encounter. According to local residents, the police team was also joined by landlords from Kaithi Bigha and nearby villages. The police firing and crossfiring from the ML activists continued till the evening of January 1, 1985. The police and the local landlords also set the mud houses on fire. People who were trying to flee from there were beaten up mercilessly, resulting in the death of a woman and her young girl. Several people were arrested, of whom at least five were alleged to have died in police custody. In all, ten Dalits were killed in this operation (PUDR, 1985, p. 5). According to the villagers, Lakhan Paswan (50 years) and Prahlad (30 years) were shot and thrown into the fire. Three brothers—Suresh Mistry (13 years old), Umesh Mistry (15 years old) and Satyendra Mistry (9 years old)—were also thrown into the fire. Later, the police caught Faguni Paswan, Lalchand and Narsingh Paswan, a known peasant leader of the area, and two others and took them to the police station. The villagers feared that they were shot either on the way or in the police station (Sinha, 1985, p. 343).

A militant movement of landless labourers resulted in intense conflict between the landlords and the landless labourers in parts of Aurangabad district in early 1982. On June 27 of that year, a mob led by landlords attacked the Dalit basti in Gaini village, in which seven people were killed (PUDR, 1983, p. 9). On August 18, 1982, five activists were killed by landlords at Tarari village. Then there was the infamous Pananiya killings, in which five innocent villagers were shot dead and seven others injured by the police. In November 1982, six more Harijans were killed by landlords at Goh (Sinha, 1985 op. cit, p. 344). Four years later, 12 Dalit agricultural labourers were killed at Gaini in 1986, whereas in Parasdih, five Dalit agricultural labourers were killed in the same year (Current Agrarian Situation in Bihar op. cit: 129).

13 Bhojpur District

In the month of October in 1977, four Dalits were killed by Rajputs in Dharampura village. Rajput landlords also killed four Dalits at Brahmpur in the same year (Ibid: 132). These were clearly due to a long-standing dispute over the non-payment of minimum wages and sharecropping.

Three Dalit agricultural labourers were killed by upper-caste landlords in 1979 at Bajitpur village (Ibid: 132). Three landless labourers belonging to the SC community were shot dead by landlords in Katharaini village on October 5, 1978, while they were engaged in earth work under a Food-for-Work programme (Commissioner for Scheduled Castes and Scheduled Tribes, 1978–1979 op. cit: 154).

At Birampur village, a conflict started when SC labourers took possession of government land that was allegedly held by landlords. This act was perceived as a challenge to landlord hegemony. On June 26, 1981, an armed party led by the Zamindar and his men attacked the Harijan locality and set fire to four huts. They were joined by the police as well. One person, Shyam Dayal, was killed in the incident (PUDR, 1983, pp. 7–8).

In 1984, 22 Dalit agricultural labourers were killed at Danwar-Bihta by upper-caste landlords (Current Agrarian Situation in Bihar op. cit: 132). Again, in 1989, the Jwala Singh gang killed 22 Dalits in Danwar-Bihta. Fourteen Dalit villagers in Deochand and Sahiara in Bhojpur district were slaughtered in their sleep in 1991 because the local landlords belonging to Jwala Singh gang suspected them of being behind the murder of three of their henchmen; the principal accused in the 1989 murder by Rajput landlords of 22 Dalits in Bhojpur's Danwar-Bihta area. What was the Dalits' crime? They dared to vote in the 1989 election. The Kisan Sangh, another upper-caste militia, struck in the same village and killed another 14 Dalit agricultural labourers in 1991 (Ibid). Following these massacres, Chief Minister Laloo Prasad Yadav handed out ex gratia payments and jobs, while Union Welfare Minister Sitaram Kesari offered yet more money and announced a welfare programme. But what Yadav failed to do was act against Jwala Singh, a 70-year-old Rajput landlord responsible for unleashing a reign of terror in Danwar-Bihta and who was the main suspect in the 1989 massacre. When Jwala Singh, better known as *adamkhor* (man-eater), was given anticipatory bail, security forces were sent to protect not the Dalits but Jwala Singh (India Today Magazine, 1991). It is also a known fact that the dreaded Jwala Singh was given protection by the state's chief minister when the Danwar-Bihta massacre took place in 1989. 'The magistrates and police officers (deputed in the village in the wake of five killings) were treated to a feast at night by Jwala Singh (Tarari block pramukh) and his caste men. Then they organised a systematic massacre, as claimed by M.A. Ibrahimi in "My Experience in Governance". The exact number of victims could never be known as the hacked bodies were alleged to have been thrown into the Sone River, and the police did not make any attempt to fish them out'. Ibrahimi, a 1978-batch Indian Administrative Service (IAS) officer who retired in 2012, rues that the massacre took place despite the presence of forces, including the Border Security Force (BSF), which did not fire a single round. 'The BSF officer told me when he heard noise and cries (of people) in the night, he contacted the SDPO, only to be told to relax as everything was normal', the writer said. He added that the Sub-Divisional Police Officer (SDPO) was of the same upper caste to which the massacre accused belonged (The Times of India, 2014).

Four Dalit agricultural workers were killed by Bhumihar landlords in Ekwari in 1993 (Current Agrarian Situation in Bihar op. cit). This area had been a witness to several conflicts between the Naxalites and the landed upper-caste gentry. On April 1, 1997, the Ranveer Sena killed four Dalit women (Ibid). On the morning of April 10, 1997, members of the Ranveer Sena gunned down ten Dalits of Ekwari village in Bhojpur district in an operation that lasted for 2 hours. Police officers stationed nearby forced open the villagers' houses and then stood by and watched as the massacre took place (The Times of India, 1997a, b).

On April 4, 1995, three Dalit agricultural labourers were killed by Bhumihar landlords at Khopira village. And in Sarathua, on July 25, 1995, six Dalits were killed by Ranveer Sena, whereas in Chandi on February 7, 1996, the Ranveer Sena killed another four Dalit agricultural workers (Current Agrarian Situation in Bihar op. cit: 132).

Nanaur is situated close to the river Sone in the old Sone Canal area, to the east of the Ara-Sahar road. Five people, all children and teenagers, were killed by the Ranveer Sena on April 22, 1996. Nanaur falls under Nadhi panchayat and comprises six tolas, with roughly 400 households in all—60 Bhumihars, 30 Rajputs, 65 Muslims, 63 Paswan and 20 Musahars households, besides some Yadav and other

OBCs. There was no specific tension in Nanaur prior to this incident. On the night of April 22–23, 1996, a crowd of about 500 villagers was watching a video film show under a shamiana. At about 12.45 a.m. on April 23, firing began from the canal side. About 15 of those watching the film got injured. Five people were killed: Haisamuddin (15 years old), Khurshid Alam (11 years old), Naseem (8 years old), Kallu (19–12 years old) and Manoj Kumar (12–13 years old). The attackers, numbering about 50–60, were of the Bhumihar caste from neighbouring villages. A police case was filed, and subsequently, some of the Bhumihars were arrested but were released later on bail. Ten thousand rupees were given to each victim's family as compensation. Houses were also built under the Indira Awas Yojana. Of the injured, only those who had lost limbs received 5000 rupees as compensation (PUDR, 1997, p. 2).

Nadhi is located very close to Nanaur. The village was the site of two clashes between lower castes, led by the CPI (ML) Liberation, and Bhumihar landlords, on May 5 and May 19, 1996, which killed at least 11 people and left several people injured. The village comprises several upper-caste people, Muslims, OBCs and Dalit households. Eight Bhumihar landowners were killed on May 5, 1996. As retaliation to this killing on May 19, 1996, the Ranveer Sena killed three Dalits through firings in the Dalit hamlets. All of them were shot point blank. Crossfiring occurred between the police and Ranveer Sena as well. The police arrested 15–20 Ranveer Sena members and beat them up. No compensation was given to any of the victims' families. The tension continued in the village as CPI (ML) Liberation imposed a blockade on Bhumihar landowners (Ibid: 3–5).

Even for Bihar's Bhojpur district, wrecked periodically by caste clashes, the now infamous July 11 massacre of 19 Dalits in Bathani Tola came as a numbing surprise. The killings were a part of the periodic bloodletting between the notorious Ranveer Sena of the upper castes and the so-called Red Army of the CPI-ML (Liberation), comprising Dalits and landless locals. Matters were not exactly helped by Union Home Minister Indrajit Gupta, who initially sought to play down the incident and, after a visit to the village, observed that 'such incidents are commonplace in rural Bihar'. He later went on to blame the 'system', the failure of land reforms and the 'ill-trained' state police for the carnage. Gupta's remarks angered Chief Minister Laloo Prasad Yadav, who, while announcing Rs. 1 lakh in compensation, asserted that 40 persons had already been arrested (India Today Magazine, 1996).

According to another version, in the afternoon of July 11, 1996, 19 poor Dalit and Muslim women and children were killed, while five sustained bullet injuries and deep cuts from swords and other sharp implements. Two of the injured succumbed to their injuries the following month, bringing the toll of the massacre to 21 (out of the eight children who were killed, two were less than a year old). The assailants attacked from three sides, and from the sound of their shots, it was clear that they were moving closer every second. Soon, the rising flames from the northern and western ends of the tola signalled that two houses on that side had been torched. In the next half an hour, six more houses were burnt. The houses had been on fire for around half an hour when it started pouring. And in the rain, the rampage of killings began. The assailants were armed with not only guns and rifles but also swords and other traditional weapons (Bhatia, 2013, p. 42).

Even though the police and other high officials reached the village not long after, the fard-bayan was recorded only at 4:30 a.m. the next day. The time at which the FIR was registered is not known, but it was finally placed before Chief Judicial Magistrate (CJM) Bhojpur 3 days later, on July 14, 1996. After almost 2 years, in January 1998, charges were framed against 62 persons under various sections of the IPC, Arms Act and SC & ST (Prevention of Atrocities) Act. But when the trial commenced in November 2000, the proceedings were launched against 53 accused only as some had died, some had absconded and some proceedings had been quashed and/or dropped (PUDR, 2016, p. 20).

Barki Kharao is one of the few villages in Bhojpur and Central Bihar, with both Bhumihar and Rajput presence (60 houses each) as well as in terms of land ownership. Besides these two dominant castes, other numerically strong castes included Muslims (35 houses), who lived next to the Rajputs before shifting; Yadavs (25); Koeri (20); Sav (25); Paswan (40); Chamar (20); and Dhobi (20). A combination of issues over a period of time culminated in the massacre. To begin with, it was the political assertion of the Dalits, which manifested itself in the election of a Muslim as a mukhiya in the panchayat election of 1978. Later, struggles over wages started, culminating in the wage strike of 1988, which lasted for about 4 months. They demanded a daily wage of Rs 21, along with traditional breakfast and lunch, instead of approximately half *paseri* (1 kg and 750 gm of coarse cereals). Finally, a settlement was reached at Rs 20. Prior to the strike, the harvesters received 1 *bojha* (head load) for every 21 *bojhas* of harvested crop. After the strike, this changed to 1 *bojha* for every 10 *bojhas* (Current Agrarian Situation in Bihar, 2008, pp. 96–97).

The immediate cause was the Karbala land under the control of some upper-caste landlords. To contest this possession, CPI (ML) organised Karbala Mukti March in February 1996, in which two upper-caste men from Barki Kharao were killed. From then on, the situation got really tense. On April 24, 1996, Gyanchand Bhagat (Ganeri Caste) of the nearby Dhanchua village was found murdered in the fields at 2 o'clock in the afternoon. On the same night, a meeting of the Ranveer Sena was held in Barki Kharao village. Early next morning, Sultan Miya, a youth in his early 20 s who was on his way to a local shop, was killed by five Rajputs from the same village. After this murder, the 35 Muslim households located next to the Rajput houses, fearing for their lives, decided to seek refuge in the neighbouring Bathani Tola, a CPI (ML) stronghold. It was followed by several incidents of violence and murder over the next 2 months. One thing led to another, culminating in the Bathani Tola massacre on July 11 (Ibid).

On December 12, 1996, five people were shot dead in the Musahar tola of Khanet by a group of about 40 Bhumihar men organised by the Ranveer Sena. The Khanet village comprises about 300 households, which include 100 Bhumihar households, about 80 Yadav households, 70 Chamar households, 25 Musahar households and ten Teli households. The Musahars do not own any land and were engaged as landless labourers only. On the night of December 12, 1996, close to midnight, a large group of fully armed Bhumihar men, numbering about 40, headed towards the

Musahar tola. One group of about 20 entered the tola, whereas the other group remained outside to provide security cover. They shot dead Rajandhari Ram; his brother; his wife, Bhola; and his infant daughter, Kanapi. The police case that was filed included 12 names as accused. The main accused absconded, while some of the co-accused were arrested (PUDR, 1997, pp. 6–7).

The above-mentioned selected cases of caste-based killings bears testimony to the fact that despite the country having a modern constitution and sets of legislation outlawing caste-based discrimination, exclusion and violence, the upper echelons of the Hindu society and a section of dominant OBCs had a free hand in dealing a death blow to the wretched of the earth, the lowest of the low—the Dalits—in the most unimaginable ways, not only on a few occasions but also on countless number of days/nights, year after year, for almost more than three decades in the erstwhile central Bihar. How could the state and society at large permit such mayhem to continue for such a long time? Though this question may have remained unanswered as neither the state nor society at large seems bothered much about the reasons behind the gruesome killings of Dalits, the answer clearly remains in the deep-rooted casteist mindset of the people who have been at the helm of affairs, whether in governing the state or in playing dominant roles in societal affairs.

These cases also highlight the complicity of the state, its different agencies and society at large in allowing ghastly crimes to take place again and again. When and how such kinds of barbarism would come to an end may be difficult to answer, but what is for sure is the fact that as long as the caste system remains the guiding force, fully backed and sanctioned by religious and cultural norms and tradition, its pernicious influence would remain alive and ticking in several forms even under changed circumstances. What also remains certain is the fact that an iniquitous socio-economic and political system would keep at least a quarter of its people, the Dalits and other low-caste individuals at the receiving end in every possible sense of the term.

14 Operation Black Rain: Cobrapost Exposé on the Ranveer Sena

Cobrapost, a web news portal, captured on camera the confessions of perpetrators of six major massacres of poor, unarmed Dalits in the erstwhile Central Bihar, revealing how the Ranveer Sena militia planned and conducted these indiscriminate killings with impunity and how they twisted the long arm of the law, who trained them, armed them, financed them and lent them political support. In a year-long investigative undercover operation, Cobrapost captured on camera six commanders of the dreaded outfit Ranveer Sena confessing to their involvement in six major massacres of Dalits in Central Bihar, namely Sarathua (1995), Bathani Tola (1996), Laxmanpur Bathe (1997), Shankar Bigha (1999), Miyapur (2000) and Ekwari (1997). In all, 144 were killed in these six massacres, including several women and children. The six Ranveer Sena men were Chandkeshwar, Ravindra Chaudhary, Pramod Singh, Bhola Singh, Arvind Kumar Singh and Siddhnath Singh (Cobrapost, 2015).

Though an exposé like this may lack credibility as it was purely based on a sting operation conducted by a web news portal that claims itself to be engaged in investigative journalism, looking at an overall assessment of the situation under which the mass killings of Dalits by Ranveer Sena militias occurred in the erstwhile Central Bihar from 1994 onwards, this report, in the form of investigative journalism, points fingers not only at private militia like Ranveer Sena and the brazenness that became its hallmark, but at the same time, the role of the state, the police and the judiciary, as well as the political support for these kinds of non-state actors/ organisations, has come under cloud.

This report was released at a press conference held in New Delhi, wherein several journalists and social activists were present. Some of the journalists were quite agitated, arguing that the killings in Bihar should not be unnecessarily projected as examples of caste-based killings; rather, they should be projected as normal killings that happen anyway. It is also a fact that not many media outlets, whether print or visual, gave enough coverage to the Cobrapost exposé. This press meet was followed by a panel discussion. Moderated by Anirudh Bahal, the editor of Cobrapost, the panel comprised journalists Siddharth Varadarajan, Manoj Mitta, Urmilesh, lawyer Prashant Bhushan and activists V Ramesh Nathan, Asha Kowtal and Kavita Krishnan. Quoting statistics, both Nathan and Kowtal contended that justice paralysis, when it came to Dalits and lower castes, was an institutionalised feature. Bhushan was even more scathing in his critique of the Indian justice system. 'It is an illusion that the country works under a system of law—there is a deeply entrenched caste/class bias,' he said. Bhushan further lamented that no one spoke about judicial reforms or questioned the selection process of judges (Saikia, 2015).

The Cobrapost exposé failed to elicit much response from the media, the government, the police and even the judiciary. Is this a sign of hopelessness that has set in across society at large? How shocking and traumatic it is to be told publicly that India's Prime Minister empowered an anti-Dalit private mafia like Ranveer Sena with supplies of sophisticated arms and ammunition from Indian Army depots? There were Union Ministers, Members of Parliament, and Ministers of Bihar, too, in league with the same conspirators! The conscience of the nation is either dead or in a comatose state. In any other country that does not have a caste system, people would have perhaps risen in tumultuous rebellion against the treachery and violation of the oath of office and secrecy committed by these men (Biswas, 2016).

References

Bhardwaj, N. (1977). The Harijans: Victims of Socio- Economic Oppression and Political Hypocrisy, *Secular Democracy*, *X*(XVI), August (II), 18.

Bharti, I. (1988, November 26). Farce of Land Reforms in Jehanabad, *Economic and Political Weekly*, 2519.
Bhatia, B. (1997, December 20). Massacre on the Banks of the Sone, *Economic and Political Weekly*, 3242.
Bhatia, B. (2013). Justice not vengeance: The Bathani Tola massacre and Ranveer Sena in Bihar. *Economic and Political Weekly, XLVIII*(38), 42.
Bhushan, S. (1977). The Belchi Killings. *Economic and Political Weekly, 12*(25), 974.
Biswas, A. K. (2009, October 31). Musahar-Maoist Combination: Are the Poorest Asserting themselves in Bihar? *Mainstream, XLVII*(46). Retrieved from https://www.mainstreamweekly.net/article1730.html
Biswas, A. K. (2016, July 02). A Tale of Elusive Justice, *Mainstream Weekly, LIV*(28). Retrieved from https://www.mainstreamweekly.net/article6517.html
Chakravarti, A. (2001, April 28–May 04). Caste and Agrarian Class: A View from Bihar, *Economic and Political Weekly, 36*(17), 1459.
India Today Magazine. (1981, September 15). *Jagannath Mishra administration lauded for speedy disposal of cases concerning atrocities on Harijans*. Retrieved from https://www.indiatoday.in/magazine/indiascope/story/19810915-jagannath-mishra-administration-lauded-for-speedy-disposal-of-cases-concerning-atrocities-on-harijans-773242-2013-11-11
India Today Magazine. (1985, January 31). *Kaithi-Bigha incident raises issue of caste and social tensions, rural poverty in Bihar*. Retrieved from https://www.indiatoday.in/magazine/crime-stories/story/19850131-kaitha-bigha-incident-raises-issue-of-caste-and-social-tensions-rural-poverty-in-bihar-769750-2013-11-22
India Today Magazine. (1986a, December 31). *Root cause of almost all rural conflicts in Bihar attributed to land*. Retrieved from https://www.indiatoday.in/magazine/special-report/story/19861231-root-cause-of-almost-all-rural-conflicts-in-bihar-attributed-to-land-801564-1986-12-30
India Today Magazine. (1986b, May 31). *Arwal massacre: Bihar CM Bindeshwari Dubey justify police action*. Retrieved from https://www.indiatoday.in/magazine/indiascope/story/19860531-arwal-massacre-bihar-cm-bindeshwari-dubey-justify-police-action-800894-1986-05-30
India Today Magazine. (1988, July 15). *Bihar: Nonhigarh-Nagwan massacre of Dalits foxes officials*. Retrieved from https://web.archive.org/web/20230513214923/https://www.indiatoday.in/magazine/indiascope/story/19880715-bihar-nonhigarh-nagwan-massacre-of-dalits-foxes-officials-797451-1988-07-14
India Today Magazine. (1991, July 31). *Bhojpur carnage exposes victimization of Harijans in Bihar*. Retrieved from https://www.indiatoday.in/magazine/special-report/story/19910731-bhojpur-carnage-exposes-victimisation-of-harijans-in-bihar-814593-1991-07-30
India Today Magazine. (1996, August 15). Killings by Ranbir Sena brings into renewed focus conflicts over land and power in Bihar. Retrieved from https://www.indiatoday.in/magazine/indiascope/story/19960815-killings-by-ranbir-sena-brings-into-renewed-focus-conflicts-over-land-and-power-in-bihar-833679-1996-08-14
Indian Express. (1977a, July 16). *The Belchi Massacre*.
Indian Express. (1977b, June 09). *Belchi Killings Result of Gang Warfare*.
Indian Nation. (1986, April 26). *cited in APDR's Report on Arwal Massacres*, 12–13.
Judgment. (2013). *Patna High Court, Death Reference No. 5 of 2010*. https://patnahighcourt.gov.in/viewjudgment/MjgjNSMyMDEwIzEjTw==-Snu8Zq8w8S8=
Mitta, M. (2023). *Caste pride: Battles for equality in modern India* (p. 487). Westland Books.
Mohanty, B. B. (2001, October 6–12). Land Distribution among Scheduled Castes and Tribes. *Economic and Political Weekly, 36*(41), 3862–63.
Narayan, H. (1978, April 28). *Killing of a Harijan, Mainstream*, 10.
Narayan, H. (1979), Belchi Now, *Economic and Political Weekly, 14*(5–6), 188.
National Herald. (1978, September 02). *Pipri Killings: Extension of Belchi*.
New Age. (1979, July 01). Four Harijans Shot Dead by Landlords, *XXVII*(26), 7.

Outlook Magazine. (1997, April 09). *Caste Bullets Ricochet*. Retrieved from https://www.outlookindia.com/national/caste-bullets-ricochet-news-203326

Outlook Magazine. (2023, September 03). *From Bathani Tola to Lakhawar: Revisiting Unbridled Massacres of Bihar*. Retrieved from https://www.outlookindia.com/national/from-bathani-tola-to-lakhawar-rivisiting-unbridled-massacres-of-bihar-weekender_story-315492

Pathak, B. (1993). *Rural violence in Bihar* (pp. 90–94). Concept Publishing Company.

Prasad, N. (1985). *Rural violence in India* (p. 13). Vohra Publishers.

Prasad, P. H., & Rodgers, G. B. (1983). *Class, Caste and Land Holding in the Analysis of the Rural Economy, Population and Labour Policies Programme, Working Paper No. 140, Geneva, World Employment Programme Research*. ILO.

Prasad, A., Varma, R., & Thakur, A. K. (1987). *Social disabilities of the Harijans in Bihar* (pp. 42–44). A.N. Sinha Institute of Social Studies.

Report. (1975–76 and 1976–77). *Commissioner for Scheduled Castes and Scheduled Tribes*, New Delhi, Government of India, 110–11.

Report. (1977a–78). *Part- II, Appendices, Commissioner for Scheduled Castes and Scheduled Tribes*, New Delhi, Government of India, 112.

Report. (1977b–86). *Commissioner for Scheduled Castes and Scheduled Tribes*, New Delhi, Government of India.

Report. (1978–79). *Commissioner for Scheduled Castes and Scheduled Tribes*, New Delhi, Government of India, 154–55.

Report. (1980–81). *Commissioner for Scheduled Castes and Scheduled Tribes*, New Delhi, Government of India.

Report. (1983). *And Quite Flows the Ganga: A Documentary Report on the Political Killings in Rural Bihar* (p. 6, 7, 8, 9 & 10). People's Union for Democratic Rights (PUDR).

Report. (1985). *Massacre in Bihar: An Inquiry into the Killing of 10 People in a Harijan Village-Kaithi Bigha* (p. 5). People's Union for Democratic Rights (PUDR).

Report. (1986a). *Behind The Killings in Bihar* (p. 31–32, 38–41 & 43). People's Union For Democratic Rights (PUDR).

Report. (1986b–87). *Commissioner for Scheduled Castes and Scheduled Tribes*, New Delhi, Government of India, 250–52.

Report. (1986c, May 11). On Arwal Massacre, Calcutta, Association for Protection of Democratic Rights (APDR), 1.

Report. (1992a). *Bitter Harvest: The Roots of Massacres in Central Bihar* (pp. 21–29). People's Union for Democratic Rights (PUDR).

Report. (1992b–93). *National Commission for Scheduled Castes and Scheduled Tribes (NCSCST)*, New Delhi, Government of India, 98.

Report. (1992c–1997). *Crime in India, National Crime Record Bureau*, New Delhi, Government of India.

Report. (1993–94). *Rural Labour Enquiry*, New Delhi, Government of India.

Report. (1994–1995 & 1995–1996). *National Commission for Scheduled Castes and Scheduled Tribes*, New Delhi, Government of India.

Report. (1996a–1997). *National Commission for Scheduled Castes and Scheduled Tribes*, New Delhi, Government of India.

Report. (1996b–97 & 1997–98 and 1999–2000 & 2000–2001). *National Commission for Scheduled Castes and Scheduled Tribes*, New Delhi, Government of India.

Report. (1996c-97 & 1997–98). *National Commission for Scheduled Castes and Scheduled Tribes (NCSCSST)*, New Delhi, Government of India, 244.

Report. (1997). *Agrarian conflicts in Bihar and the Ranveer Sena* (p. 2, 3–5, 6–7). People's Union for Democratic Rights (PUDR).

Report. (1998–99). *National Commission for Scheduled Castes and Scheduled Tribes (NCSCST)*, New Delhi, Government of India, 27–28.

Report. (1999–2000 & 2000–2001). *National Commission for Scheduled Castes and Scheduled Tribes*, New Delhi, Government of India.

Report. (2008). *Current agrarian situation in Bihar*. Patna.
Report. (2012a). *Status of Backwardness of Scheduled Castes and Scheduled Tribes in Bihar', SC & ST Welfare Department* (pp. 21–22). Government of Bihar.
Report. (2012b). *Social and economic change in rural Bihar and the emerging policy framework* (pp. 14–16). New Delhi.
Report. (2015, August 16). Operation Black Rain: Revisiting the Killings of Dalits of Bihar and Confessions of Their Killers, *Cobrapost*. Retrieved from https://www.cobrapost.com/blog/operation-black-rain-revisiting-the-killings-of-dalits-of-bihar-and-confessions-of-their-killers/895
Report. (2016). *Harvesting death: Massacres in Bihar and the question of justice* (pp. 6–7 & 23). Peoples Union for Democratic Rights (PUDR).
Sachidananda. (1979). *Bihar's Experience, Seminar, No. 243*, 32–33.
Sachidananda. (1997). The Harijans in Bihar. In Sachidananda, K. K. Verma, & M. Lal (Eds.), *Social realities in Bihar* (pp. 166–167). Novelty & Co..
Saikia, A. (2015, August 18). Why do we refuse to accept that caste is still a reality and an ugly one at that? *News Laundry*. Retrieved from https://www.newslaundry.com/2015/08/18/how-ranvir-sena-killed-dalits-an-expose-by-cobrapost-and-some-more-delusionary-denial-of-the-existence-of-caste
Scheduled Caste Cell. (1997). *Crime investigation department*. Patna.
Sharma, N. (1977, July 02). *Harijans are for burning, Mainstream*, 04.
Sinha, A. (1977). Belchi Revisited. *Economic and Political Weekly, 12*(32), 1244.
Sinha, U. (1985). Teaching the landless a lesson. *Economic and Political Weekly, 20*(9), 343 & 344.
Subramanian, K. S. (1987, July 25). *Behind Rural Violence, Mainstream*, 22.
The Hindu. (1997, March 26). *Police Arrived Late at Carnage Scene*.
The Times of India. (1980, May 20). *Death Sentence for Two Accused in Belchi Case*.
The Times of India. (1982, January 13). *Sentences in Belchi Carnage Case Upheld*.
The Times of India. (1983, November 12), Convicts Hanged.
The Times of India. (1997a, April 13). *Ekwari Carnage was Backed by Police*.
The Times of India. (1997b, December 03). *Ranveer Sena Activists Mow Down 61 in Bihar*.
The Times of India. (2003, June 06). *13 Convicted for Nonhi-Nagwan Massacre*.
The Times of India. (2014, October 26). *Ex- DM Puts 1989 Ara Blood Spill in Black and White*.

Radical Groups and Voluntary Organisations: An Assessment of Their Role in Creating Awareness About Dalit Human Rights

Abstract From 1977 up to 1997 and even after this time period, several radical and democratic groups emerged in Bihar that were struggling to secure a safe life and demand justice in a society where an iniquitous social structure has been playing havoc with Dalits. What the gains were and what their fallouts have been have also been explained in this chapter.

Keywords Maoist Naxalit groups in Bihar · CPI (ML) · Indian People's Front (IPF) · Bihar Pradesh Kisan Sabha (BPKS) · Mazdoor Kisan Sangharsh Samiti (MKSS) · Chhatra Yuva Sangharsh Vahini (CYSV) · Bodh Gaya Land Movement · Bihar Dalit Vikas Samiti · Nari Gunjan

A society based on an unequal relationship among its different sections is bound to be lawless in its dealings in many ways. The characterising feature of Bihar's society is violence that feeds on itself and reaches depths of brutality and barbarism, which makes a cruel mockery of the concept of a civilised society. Arson, rape, loot, pillage, massacre and mayhem—these are the themes of reports emerging from Bihar with revolting regularity. Terror stalks the land; in a state where more than 2000 years ago blood sport was put to an end, Dalit hunting has become its popular pastime. These are classic examples of insensitivity embedded in society, the economy and polity towards the lowest of the low in the caste hierarchy. Nothing else could perhaps explain why such barbaric actions are allowed to happen in a civilised world.

The ramifications of caste-based discrimination, exclusion and violence could also permeate the economic field. The basic idea is to keep not only the hegemony of the upper strata of society that is in control of economic resources but also its stranglehold on the people belonging to low-caste groups and exploit them for cheap labour and other purposes, which may include exploitation of various kinds. In Bihar, caste, along with poverty, has created its own culture of dehumanisation.

UMAKANT, *Dalit Human Rights in India*, People, Cultures and Societies: Exploring and Documenting Diversities,
https://doi.org/10.1007/978-981-95-5751-6_4

The state with its rigid caste structure and its obnoxious practices and also with one of the lowest per capita income, the largest percentage of people below the poverty line and with millions of people eking out existence at the margins of subsistence is bound to have a situation where human beings are reduced to animals existence (Das, 1987, pp. 8–9).

Dalits are placed unfavourably in terms of ownership of productive assets as well as distribution of income. Inequalities tend to be cumulative in their case. The idioms in which landlords address the untouchables are those of ridicule, abuse and contempt. The situation has been so unfavourable for Dalits that in the absence of an effective mechanism for redress, they found themselves inclined to organise under the leadership of left extremists. The situation that led to the rise of violent uprising is evident from the following portrayal of Dalits' predicament in Ekwari, Bhojpur: 'Put yourself in the position of a slave in Ekwari and you will understand the urge to reach out for a gun. You are not considered a man at all. Born a slave, your life is strictly tied to spade, sickle and the lord's feet, you produce everything that the lord boasts of. Yet your children are drumming the aluminium plates. Every day one landlord or other takes away your wife and your daughter. If your working daughter is not spoiled in the fields in the day, the son of the landlord will break into your single room mud hovel in the night, and humiliate her right there. For you the best course is to pretend deep slumber. How long, you will ask yourself, I will take this? Is this my fate?' (Sinha, 1978, p. 73).

The growth of modern civilisation seemed to have stopped somehow in this part of the world. The antiquity and continuity of the casteist and feudal social structure have maintained its stranglehold, and there is no sign of modernity and civilised behaviour taking root in any meaningful sense. In stark contrast to its glorious past, Bihar today finds itself in the throes of economic chaos and unprecedented social tension. It has the dubious distinction of being one of India's most crime-ridden states, with 14 murders a day and one kidnapping every 4 h. As in other Indian states, people in Bihar are divided by the age-old caste system, wherein the Dalits or untouchables are at the bottom of the ladder. Dalits constitute around 15% of the state's population, but they hold less than 2% of the cultivated land. Social tensions are largely due to agrarian inequality and often result in clashes between the landed gentry and landless Dalit labourers. Active Dalit resistance in Bihar started in the 1960s, when landless labourers aligned themselves with Maoist Naxalite groups. Landlords and other upper-caste people formed their own private armies to assert their supremacy. Women, children and old people were often the victims of these caste-based massacres. The state administration, irrespective of which party is in power, is powerless to control these clashes, which have been going on for the last three decades (Das, 1999, p. 8).

Though legally free, Dalits continue to be socially and economically dependent on landowners for their subsistence, and given their caste hierarchy, they are also victims of social oppression. The absence of industrialization, of even agro-based industries which could provide alternate employment and better bargaining power to the Dalit labourers have been the major contributing factor in this relation of dependency. This kind of unsavoury life conditions pushes Dalits to the brink, and that is why an urge to get out of an exploitative and dehumanising social order/ system keeps creeping into their mindset.

The region has known many peasant movements originating from the inequalities of the agrarian structure. But these have mainly been led by and benefited the upper and backward castes. During the decades of the 1970s, 1980s, 1990s or so, a significant movement of the agrarian poor emerged on the scene, mainly because of inequitable distribution of land and oppression based on caste and gender. Organisations that were/are presently active in the region belong to a wide political spectrum, ranging from socialists to Naxalites.

Researchers and analysts write regularly about these happenings. Bela Bhatia's comments reflects this kinds of developments in the erstwhile central Bihar. The Liberation group functioned in approximately 30 districts of undivided Bihar and Jharkhand, including 11 districts of central Bihar. Even though the Liberation group considered itself the true inheritor of the CPI (ML) legacy, its political line has changed dramatically from that of the original CPI (ML). The Indian People's Front (IPF) and the Bihar Pradesh Kisan Sabha (BPKS) were formed in the early 1980s. The aim of BPKS was to lead the peasant movement in Bihar, while the goal of the IPF was to intervene in the national political scene. Both organisations flourished (Bhatia, 2005, pp. 1536–1537).

1 Peasant Struggle in Central Bihar

Peasants in Bihar over a period of time became more aware of their need for a better deal as far as their working conditions were concerned. An awareness of this kind also led to the formation of peasant associations at local levels in districts where left-oriented peasant groups were already active. According to a CPI (ML) document, the movement in the erstwhile central Bihar spread across seven districts: Bhojpur, Rohtas, Patna, Gaya, Jehanabad, Aurangabd and Nalanda. The struggle started for an increase in the wage of agrarian labourers who account for 30–40% of rural population in these areas. The forum of struggle usually resorted to was strike for better wages and better treatment by the landowners and which often developed into armed confrontations. In this struggle the target range was narrowed down to the possible minimum. Generally, the middle sections possessing vested lands were spared and the course of persuasion and exerting pressure was adopted in the case of rich peasants. The seisure of lands, crops and ponds and assertion over fishing rights in canals, rivers, etc. often led to armed confrontations (Report, CPI (ML), 1987, pp. 60–63).

The Naxalite groups justified the use of counter-violence to seek justice. But counter-violence could prove to be counterproductive and a very costly affair as far as fighting on behalf of resourceless people is concerned. However, did they have any other option? Again, this is a question that has remained unanswered. It is true that social strife became a regular feature in the rural areas of Bihar, especially in the erstwhile central Bihar, but at the same time, in this struggle for supremacy between two sets of social elites—the feudal casteist people on the one hand and the upper-caste-led Naxalite/peasant movement on the other—Dalits and other lower-caste people had been made targets of attacks by casteist-feudal militias for more than three decades. Violence always begets violence.

The Bihar Pradesh Kisan Sabha (BPKS) came into existence on February 23, 1981. Its formation was declared in Patna during a mammoth rally attended by 15,000 peasants from different districts of Bihar. By now, the influence of the Kisan Sabha and its sister peasant organisations had spread over 26 districts, covering nearly 25 lakhs of rural population, the majority being agrarian labourers and poor and middle-class peasants. The mass economic struggle of peasants has mainly centred on issues like seisure of crops and lands, control over fishing and irrigation and demands for fair wages. There were also occasional movements for sharecropping rights and against usury and mortgage (Ibid: 85–87).

The strategy to organise the peasantry was done through local people's participation in consultations on issues affecting their living conditions as peasants in the erstwhile central Bihar. What was also important to note is that these strategic manoeuvres were being carried out in quite a democratic manner, and decisions were arrived at only after discussing all the pros and cons of the issues/problems. Other sources relating to their style of functioning revealed that the most important form of mobilisation by the Bihar Pradesh Kisan Sabha (BPKS) was through chaupal meetings. A chaupal meeting was a gathering of the village's poor to address various problems, which range from minor thefts to long-standing land disputes. Problems with landlords, such as the payment of wages, and problems with corrupt and inefficient public officials were all taken up in these meetings. The chaupals also dealt with social evils affecting the poor, such as alcoholism, gambling, eve teasing, sexual exploitation of women and quarrels (Singh, 1995, p. 152).

During a fact-finding visit, the People's Union for Democratic Rights (PUDR) team found that BPKS had become active in a number of villages in at least seven blocks of Patna district: Punpun, Bikram, Masaurhi, Dhanarua, Fatua, Pali and Naubatpur. In these villages, BPKS organised village chaupals to solve cases related to crimes committed in the area, which also covered social and other problems. It was, in many ways, not only able to control local criminal activities but also helped poor people get instant justice. On September 24, 1981, a Patna-based newspaper, Indian Nation, carried a headline saying that Naxalites had formed a 'parallel government' in nine blocks of Patna district and were moving around with sophisticated weapons and collecting taxes from landlords. On October 31, 1981, another newspaper, Pradeep—a Patna-based Hindi daily—published Photostat copies of letters purported to be BPKS letters asking its branches to collect taxes from landlords. However, BPKS maintained that these news items were propaganda against the growing popularity of their organisation and that their organisation functioned through subscription and donations (PUDR, 1981, pp. 13–14).

The above-mentioned account of different activities undertaken by the BPKS, from their standpoint, looks very impressive on face value. Their definition of 'peasant' men and women must be questioned to begin with. It is pertinent to ask: since when did landless labourers become 'peasants'? This definition needs to be explained so as to clarify that their understanding on this issue was quite confusing. It is not proper to Club together a section of middle caste agriculturist along with landless labourers and claim unification of peasants.

The main economic thrust of BPKS struggle were rightly centred on question of land, wages, irrigation and corruption, which were intimately connected with the basic interests of the broad peasant masses. To achieve this, a policy change at the level of state administration through an effective mass pressure did not take place. Adequate emphasis should have been given for a consistent mass struggle through a broad network for mounting pressure on the government for implementing land reforms and minimum wages legislations. Various human rights violation of Dalits except landlessness and the consequent exploitation were thoroughly neglected by BPKS.

2 Mazdoor Kisan Sangram Samiti

The internal rivalry among state leadership within peasant organisations like BPKS and CPI (ML) led to the formation of splinter organisations in the erstwhile central Bihar. Thus, we see that in addition to the BPKS, another organisation that was prominent in mobilising the rural poor in erstwhile central Bihar was Mazdoor Kisan Sangram Samiti (MKSS), which was established in early 1981. The activities of the MKSS were largely confined to three broad areas: resisting the illegal occupation of government land by landlords; forming mass resistance committees against organised crimes; and organising agitations, including total strikes, by agricultural labourers to demand better wages. The MKSS also effectively raised issues like resistance against dacoities and the protection of women's honour, which made them very popular with the masses, especially in many villages of Jehanabad (Singh op. cit: 153–154).

During this period of agricultural upheaval, several news reports highlighted the ongoing struggles of MKSS, as reported from different areas in the erstwhile central Bihar. MKSS was outlawed following the Arwal incident, in which 23 landless labourers were killed in police firing. In an interview with United News of India (UNI), head of MKSS Dr. Vinayan said that they have no armed gang and that 90% of their workers had participated in the JP movement in Bihar. He further stated that his organisation did not subscribe to the Naxalite theory of liberating villages from state control. According to him, their movement, which has spread to a number of villages despite the ban, is aimed at arousing poor peasants and making them aware of their rights under the law of the land. The idea was to build public pressure on a corrupt administration and police force to stop shielding landlords who were exploiting the landless poor. The gap between the landed class and the poor in Bihar has widened, and there is agrarian unrest everywhere in the state. Dr. Vinayan also stressed that they do not claim to be non-violent. When landlords are armed and use all forces at their command against the poor, they have to defend the poor, he argued. To talk of non-violence when the class enemy is out to crush you is hypocrisy, he claimed (Times of India, 1988).

Whereas on the other hand, the Bihar police maintained that ultra-leftist MKSS was banned as it went about liberating villages to set up its own council to administer them and also started collecting levies. There was a reign of terror in many villages, with MKSS workers unleashing violence against those refusing to pay and cooperate. The police–MKSS encounter took place at Kaithi village in Aurangabad district in 1978. Between 1984 and 1986, the MKSS snatched 300 firearms from the police after attacking their outposts. In March 1986, the MKSS attacked the Hassanbazar police outpost and killed two policemen. At the height of its movement, the MKSS had its 'Lal Sena' moving from village to village, grabbing land held by landlords and distributing it among the landless peasants. The police also maintained that the MKSS operated from its underground headquarters in Jehanabad and Dehri-on-Sone (Ibid).

For a brief period of time, there was unity among some ultra-left organisations, like CPI (ML)—Liberation, CPI (ML)—Party Unity, IPF, MKSS, etc. But soon they broke away and started indulging in violence among themselves. On December 25, 1993, at least eight people were killed and 30 injured in different incidents of firing between activists of the Indian People's Front (IPF) and the Mazdoor Kisan Sangram Samiti (MKSS) in Dhamani village in Haspura police station in Aurangabad district. The police fired 50 rounds to disperse the warring groups. Trouble began when IPF activists objected to MKSS activists holding a meeting at the nearby Panchmukhi bazar fired indiscriminately at them. Two MKSS activists, Lalan Ram and Ahilya Devi, died in this violence. In retaliation, MKSS men raided the Dhamani village and opened fire, killing Malti Devi, Chirmania Devi, Khan Bahadur, Lilawati Devi and Parsuram Paswan. Meanwhile, the police firing, which resulted in the killing of at least two people, prevented 25 houses from being burnt by the MKSS men (Times of India, 1993).

In many areas of Gaya and Jehanabad, the Party-Unity-controlled MKSS and the IPF-controlled BPKS came to blows because of serious differences over many issues. To cite one example, in April–May 1988, the Party-Unity-controlled MKSS compiled a list of 18 people from Bhawanichak village in Jehanabad district whom they alleged to be members of the Bhoomi Sena, warning that if they did not surrender by May 22, 1988, strong action would be taken against them. The IPF-controlled BPKS opposed this move by the MKSS and contended that all those people belonged to the Kurmi caste but were not members of the Bhumi Sena. Because of this episode, a cold war began, which continued for a long time, between these two radical groups. On various other occasions, BPKS, IPF and CPI (ML) Liberation have accused MKSS and Party Unity for giving protection to noted criminals and landlords in the Jehanabad district (Urmilesh, 1991, pp. 137–39).

The CPI (ML) faction led by Vinod Mishra claimed to be active in 60 blocks. The MCC has been mainly active in Aurangabad district—where, ironically, it was led by a Rajput ex-teacher, Ramadhar Singh, and a Brahmin ex-quack, Pramod Mishra. The third—and mainly underground—organisation was the Party Unity Group, which worked through the MKSS. Another umbrella organisation of 89 ML groups, the Indian People's Front (IPF), was quite active in about 28 districts in Bihar, and its main concentration was the central districts (Ahmed & Kumar, 1986).

The Naxalites' struggle to counter the age-old exploitation and oppression of the poor in Central Bihar, the repression of this movement by caste senas and police and paramilitary forces and the further resistance to that repression led to a spiral of violence. It can be argued that this was an inevitable part of a revolutionary struggle. However, the negative influences of the series of violent activities were found to be manifold. To start with, the revolutionary struggle was reduced to a 'politics of revenge'. Often at the peak of conflict between caste senas and one of the Naxalite factions, the revolutionary activity was reduced to a mere tit-for-tat strategy. In the process, other activities were neglected because most of the energy and time were focused on defence and retaliation. Also, the price for this retaliatory and counter-retaliatory violence was paid, first and foremost, by Dalits and other downtrodden sections of society. Many parts of the erstwhile central Bihar fell into a war-like situation, where people lived in constant terror and suspicion and were regularly exposed to the worst forms of violence.

While reflecting on the successes and failures of radical organisations, Bela Bhatia observed: 'Like everyone else, landless agricultural labourers also longed for an improvement in their everyday existence: better food and housing, education for their children, adequate employment, freedom from fear and violence, leisure and laughter. In that respect the outcome of the Naxalite movement has been mixed. Empowerment has been achieved only at the cost of considerable suffering. Naxalite leaders have taken little interest in enhancing the quality of life in the villages, arguing that all reform would have to follow revolution. In fact, development efforts like building roads have often been hindered, e g, by extracting taxes from the contractors. Some even considered that the more underdeveloped the region, the better were the prospects of revolution. They regarded development as antagonistic to revolutionary consciousness. Also, darkness and inaccessibility (in the absence of roads and electricity) meant physical safety and some protection from state repression' (Bhatia op. cit: 1547).

There did not seem to be any emphasis on the educational development of Dalits and other marginalised caste groups by these Naxalite organisations that were active in the region. In another study, Bhatia found that in 33 villages in two districts—Bhojpur and Jehanabad—in 1995–1996, most school buildings and classrooms were unfit for human use: filthy premises, dilapidated furniture, assorted clutter, broken windows, leaking roofs, uneven floors and inadequate lighting were common. Classes were held in only a few schools. Due to caste–/class-based conflict, which had existed for almost three decades in the erstwhile central Bihar, the condition of schools had become pathetic due to several factors. On many occasions, school buildings were occupied by the police to set up camps in villages as part of their efforts to counter Naxalite–landlord violence. Due to the several carnages that had taken place during this period, schools became a safe refuge for villagers seeking shelter. Neglect of education by several Naxalite organisations operating in the erstwhile central Bihar was pointer to the fact that it was not part of their strategy to empower people for whom they were engaged in a class struggle against the oppressive landlords (Bhatia, 1998, pp. 27–31).

Could these radical left organizations- BPKS, CPI (ML) Liberation or MKSS, CPI (ML)-Party Unity and even Maoist Coordination Committee (MCC) explain that poor people belonging to different castes in the social-religious hierarchy face same/similar kinds of problems in society, economy and polity? Does caste play any role in differentiating poor people belonging to different castes and sub-castes? Could a poor upper-caste/middle-caste person do the job of any Dalit-caste person, like a cobbler, manual scavenger, and several other degrading works as prescribed/ascribed under the Brahmanical order/system? There could be several other questions addressed to these left-oriented groups/associations which were faulted with putting the lives of helpless Dalits in danger as they became soft target of attack on their life and dignity by the casteist-feudal forces for more than three decades or so in several areas of the erstwhile central Bihar.

3 Chhatra Yuva Sangharsh Vahini

The Bodh Gaya Land Struggle, led by the Chhatra Yuva Sangharsh Vahini, was inspired by the ideas of Ram Manohar Lohia and Jay Prakash Narayan. The Vahini was established in January 1975 and was proclaimed by Jay Prakash Narayan (popularly known as JP) as a national organisation on September 30, 1978 (The Telegraph, 1978).

The struggle was launched by the Vahini on April 8, 1978, against the illegal control of land by the Bodh Gaya Math. Driven by the ideas and inspiration of JP, Vahini activists resolved to liberate the Math land through a sustained peaceful movement (Singh, 1995, p. 159). The control of powerful religious-feudal establishment of Bodh Gaya Math had not only perpetuated an iniquitous pattern of land control but also maintained chains of servitude and bondage (The Times of India, 1986).

The struggle launched by the Vahini activists challenged the traditional socio-religious authority of the Math and demanded immediate distribution of its land among the rightful tillers. The Vahini led the Musahar and other lower caste people to sustain their agitation against the Bodh Gaya Math for almost a decade. The Chhatra Yuva Sangharsh Vahini (CYSV) members, along with local landless lower-caste labourers, carried out a survey and found out that the Math had 6000 acres of uncultivated surplus land in four blocks of Gaya district. During the sowing seasons, the labourers, under the guidance of the Vahini, together cultivated about 2000 acres of land (India Today Magazine, 1980).

In the year 1980, CYSV and Mazdoor Kisan Samiti took possession of Math land at Katorwa village in Bodh Gaya and had sown paddy and arhar on about 2000 acres of land. When the crop was ready for harvesting, the Math acquired police assistance to deprive the tillers of the produce. The hired labourers brought from neighbouring villages went straight to the field and started harvesting the crop, which was yet to be ready. At least one-fourth of a 4-acre plot was already harvested (Indian Express, 1980). The land movement, however, continued to secure land rights and also succeeded to an extent, though not wholly, in getting land deeds distributed to the landless labourers in Bodh Gaya and other three blocks in Gaya district.

Though 6000 acres of land were liberated due to the pressure created by the movement, hardly 2000 acres were acquired for distribution among the landless labourers. Of this, only 91 acres were actually distributed among 192 families in Gasainpesra village on October 31, 1980, and another 300 acres were kept under government control. Subsequently, 140 acres were distributed in Kusha-Beeja and Pipparghatti (The Telegraph, 1980).

Women contributed significantly to this struggle. The movement was not only centred on issues of agrarian grievances, but it campaigned against social evils as well. Women beating, child marriage, concubinage and alcoholism—all these issues formed an integral part of the struggle, which provided a stronger foundation for sustaining mobilisation. Throughout the movement against the Math, women constituted 30 to 40% of those actively engaged in the struggle. They were leaders in struggles in the villages of Gasainpesra, Pipparghatti and Shekhwara of Bodh Gaya. Hundreds of women faced the Math's opposition as well as state police bullets. Many of them were injured in the fights against the Mahant, and more than 100 were arrested (Kelkar, 1991, p. 40).

The women activists launched two major campaigns: one against liquor consumption and another against wife beating. They formed women's vigilance committees, with the assigned tasks of keeping watch on wife beaters and liquor dens. Men who beat their wives were to be smashed by women themselves. Even children were drafted. Their job was to expose their fathers and other men who beat up their wives. Suggestions were made in some of the village meetings that wife beaters should not be allowed to join the Vahini or the struggle and that to curb male violence, women of the landless and marginal peasantry must have land in their own names (Ibid: 41).

Land rights can make a notable difference to women's bargaining power within the home and community, enhance their self-confidence and self-worth, enable them to negotiate better deals in the wage labour market, increase the respect they command within the community, facilitate their participation in village decision-making bodies and so on. Empowerment in one or more of these forms has emerged wherever social movements or non-governmental organisations (NGOs) have helped women gain access to land. Now that we have land, we have the strength to speak and walk (Manimala, 1983, pp. 2–16).

It was in 1981 that the government of Bihar identified about 1000 acres of land for redistribution to agitating farmers/landless labourers. The Vahini drew up a list, giving priority to landless labourers, the disabled, widows and small peasants. Women other than widows did not figure in the list, so they protested their exclusion: 'We were in the fore-front of the fight, carrying our children in the womb and in our arms. We went to jails, and faced police lathis (sticks); we also did all house work. But when land was re-distributed, we were pushed back and we did not even come to know by which rules the land was re-distributed' (Ibid).

Almost 3 years passed before women were finally allocated land in their own names. In time, the entire Math's illegal landholding was distributed, and women received land in various ways: through individual titles; by joint titles with husbands; as widows, destitutes and disabled persons; and (without precedent), in some cases, as unmarried adult daughters. Each person received about 1 acre of land. Indeed, the significance of the Bodh Gaya Land Struggle from women's perspectives not just lies in being South Asia's first land struggle, where women's land rights received explicit attention. It also lies in the process by which this was achieved. It is noteworthy that a largely illiterate peasant community discussed at length such as women's independent rights in economic resources, domestic violence, female education and post-marital residence and on several counts resolved them in favour of women. Thus, the question of gender equality began to be seen by many not as divisive but as integral to the movement's success (Agarwal, 2002, pp. 8–9).

However, the movement started by this socialist organisation never challenged the Brahmanical norms, customs and codes that were practised then and are in practice even now in Bihar and elsewhere. How could women and landless men be liberated without annihilating/eliminating the monster called the caste system? An anti-Brahmanical and anti-caste ideology and strategy for liberation and emancipation of the lowest of the low in the social hierarchy has never been part of this socialist organisation, and that is why despite some successes, it could not and shall not claim to be a truly liberating force, as the edifices of the Brahmanical order/system are still playing havoc with Dalits' lives, not only in Bihar but also everywhere else in the country.

It has also been observed that due to the strong influence of centuries-old caste untouchability practices, it is practically difficult for any untouchable community to disengage itself from the oppressive Brahmanical socio-economic and political order in their rural/urban universe. The long-term sustainability of gains made through a successful redistribution of land by virtue of the Bodh Gaya Land Movement has proved to be quite a challenging task for Dalits in the area. Evidence suggests that Dalits' assertions of their legal rights do not translate into an equitable distribution of material resources or a mitigation of social segregation, even when the state attempts to redress their historical socio-economic marginalisation by building facilities that should have given them equal access to water, electricity, housing and schools. Dalits and non-Dalits continue to operate in a caste hierarchy that keeps everyone in their place, physically and socially. Although Dalit villagers have successfully asserted their rights to access basic resources and thereby altered the more blatant enforcements of the untouchability code and blurred the edges of spatial segregation, every gain they make remains precarious, and their autonomy is threatened in rural Bihar (Prasad, 2021, p. 150).

4 Bihar Dalit Vikas Samiti

This is one of the first non-governmental initiatives aimed solely at the development of the most backward community of Dalit caste people in the state of Bihar. The Bihar Dalit Vikas Samiti (BDVS)—an action programme originally initiated by the Indian Social Institute in New Delhi—is a non-political voluntary organisation wedded to the task of uplifting the downtrodden. It is an important organisation engaged in social awareness, economic uplifting and political consciousness among the neglected section of the population (Lal, 1997, p. 13). A fresh strategy for mainstreaming Dalit rights and issues was an initiative that BDVS undertook in a state like Bihar, where caste discrimination and caste violence remain rampant. It was perhaps also realised that state intervention is not enough, and there is a need to work on creating awareness about holding the state as well as society at large accountable for not doing enough to address issues concerning the most neglected and most exploited sections. It is thus a new initiative to chart out newer paths on which Dalits and other disadvantaged sections could walk as equal citizens with equal rights.

Creating consciousness among the deprived sections of society is one of the most essential tasks for uplifting disempowered and deprived people. Thus, the spread of social consciousness and the organisation of the inert, dispersed masses seem to constitute Samiti's primary concern. Its central objective is the collective empowerment of 'Dalits' in order to enable them to struggle for their rights through the aggregation of the limited resources at their disposal. The Samiti is oriented to make people aware of their power through providing them an organisation and education. It intends to raise the consciousness among the inert sections of society to enable them to assert their rightful place in society.

Samiti has a distinctive approach to mobilising the depressed sections of society around issues that are of direct concern to them. It is a participatory organisation of the rural poor, emphasising local initiatives. It seeks transformation in the socio-economic order through people's power. It operates among distant, uncared, politically dispossessed and economically distressed inhabitants in remote rural areas and neglected urban centres. Included within its ambit are issues and areas of human activities that have been accorded scant attention. As an institutional network of support to the disadvantaged, it has often stepped into government shoes to operate as an important supplement to its delivery system. A.K. Lal, in his book about this organisation, identified the detailed objectives of the Samiti, some of which are mentioned below: 'To work for the integrated development of the oppressed all over India. To end untouchability in all its forms. To enable the oppressed to avail of governmental facilities for their social, economic and educational development and to awaken their political consciousness. To mobilise people against injustice and exploitation and to ensure the oppressed—justice and protection. To try to avail governmental facilities for the educated unemployed, to set up cottage and village industries and to conduct training programmes in tailoring, electronics, computer etc.' In sum, the BDVS is engaged in grassroots activities aimed at advancing the downtrodden's progress (Ibid: 14–15).

How Dalits could be made agents of change is the ultimate challenge, and BDVS is engaged in overcoming the barriers that have deprived Dalits and other marginalised sections for centuries. Thus, we see that it represents a people-oriented radical approach to the problems of Dalits. It helps Dalits from a situation of crisis to demanding immediate intervention for redressal of their grievances. Its basic intent is to organise Dalits who are in search of justice and equality, and it functions among the depressed sections in the unorganised sector.

How Dalits and other disadvantaged people could become involved while ensuring support from government agencies is another area in which BDVS has been actively engaged in several areas in Bihar. Its involvement in state-sponsored programmes is certainly strategic. It seeks to foster people's power to enable Dalits to acquire rights guaranteed in the Constitution. It is aimed to usher in a process of empowering the weak to ensure a process to transform the local situation. In a sense, its efforts represent an educative process that prepares the poor to strike at the structural roots of poverty. Socially conscious and organised masses have sharper political articulation. Its ultimate aim seeks to make Dalits self-reliant by acquiring the needed political resources. The Samiti has gone beyond charity orientation characterising the orientation of the voluntary organisations in the past (Roy, 1992, p. 91).

Violent means could never be an instrument to bring change in a society where inequality reigns. Thus, BDVS is found to be non-violent and orderly in its struggle against injustice. While creating a new space for Dalits in society, it is not entrapped in unnecessary and avoidable confrontation with the state or political parties. As part of a practicle strategy to deal with several kinds of situations in their work they do resort to oppose the exploitative power structure at grass root level and occasional conflict with corrupt officials at times lead the Samiti to adopt a confrontational approach too. Following a different strategy in other situation it seeks to extend its activities for nurturing a non-confrontational orientation among its workers. It adopts a conflictive approach in situations of discrimination and exploitation and pursues a reconciliatory approach in supporting the implementation of state-sponsored programmes for Dalits. Its activities seem to be oriented not towards accentuating social contradictions and class conflict but towards fostering class collaboration. In a broad sense, it belongs to the large section of voluntary organisations that have the objective of 'pursuing an independent and local pro-people role co-operating with appropriate and fighting against it when necessary' (Pandey, 1991, p. 232).

There are possibilities for involving Dalit people for their rightful claim to the development process and that is how the BDVS is consciously pursing it as their strategy for empowering people who are the most deprived. The concern for the poor and programmes for Dalits to enable them to meet their priority and needs constitute the important components of the programmes pursued by them. Its ultimate goal is to ensure people's participation fundamental to a genuine process of developments have been quite impressive. It has helped in the collective institutionalisation of Dalit activities. It has helped them to assert for their rights and participatory development approach. Initiated as an outsider's programme, it has adopted strategies to foster leadership qualities among its participants. Its respect for local perspectives has led it to orient its programmes to suit local needs and aspirations. It has helped in preparing people for participation and has encouraged the emergence of decentralised leaderships among Dalits. People's involvement at the decision-making level has been quite marked. By and large, BDVS has made a mark in instilling confidence among the downtrodden to fight for an egalitarian socio-economic and political order.

5 Nari Gunjan

Nari Gunjan is a voluntary/non-governmental organisation working to empower women and girl children from the most disadvantaged Dalit community, especially the Musahar (rat-eating) caste near Patna, the capital city of Bihar. It was started by Sister Sudha Varghese of the Notre Dame Sisters group, who left her teaching job at Notre Dame Academy and relocated to Jamsaut, a village of the Musahar community in Danapur on the outskirts of Patna, in 1987.

While living with the Musahars at Jamsaut, she realised the need for a targeted intervention to bring education to Dalit girls and help Dalit women by creating self-help groups. That is how 'Prerna' (Inspiration), a residential school for Dalit girls started with little support from here and there and subsequently with support from the Government of Bihar and most important of all, the UNICEF, Prerna the residential school has become a Nari Gunjan model of imparting education and other skills to Dalit girl child. At Nari Gunjan, most girls are first-generation learners who have to acquire grade-III-level competence before being sent to regular schools. Centre in-charge Asha Devi says: 'All these girls face tremendous pressure to get married. But now they have found the voice. Now they are role models back in their villages.' Sister Sudha, who has won a Padmashree, states: 'It came in small steps. We fought inch by inch to restore their dignity and create self belief. And it came despite the open discrimination practiced by people all around.' Aged between 6 and 16, the girls come from homes where their education is frowned upon (Hindustan Times, 2008).

Focusing on Dalit girls' education in a society where not many people are even literate was certainly a huge challenge. Today, Sister Sudha's organisation runs 50 educational centres for Musahar girls, where about 1500 students learn academics and vocational skills, such as stitching, embroidery, nursing and preliminary medical assistance. The emphasis is on helping them develop economically valuable skills. 'I have a lot of hope that this group of girls will be agents for changing the community', she said. The winds of change have already started sweeping, with Musahar working girls bringing positive transformations to their society (India Today, 2008). Apart from imparting education and skills to Dalit girls, Nari Gunjan also works on women empowerment for the youths through Mahila Dastak and Yuva Dastak. Sudha Varghese, being a practising lawyer herself, also fights cases of Dalit atrocities reported from surrounding areas. Nari Gunjan has been helping Musahar women in cultivating rice, wheat and vegetables on lands taken on lease. This has brought economic empowerment in the community, with more than 5000 women having their own success stories in this regard (Mathrubhumi, 2023).

References

Agarwal, B. (2002). *Are We Not Peasants Too?: Land Rights and Women's Claim in India, No. 21, Seeds*, 8–9.

Ahmed, F., & Kumar, A. (1986, December 31). Root cause of almost all rural conflicts in Bihar attributed to land, *India Today*. Retrieved from https://www.indiatoday.in/magazine/special-report/story/19861231-root-cause-of-almost-all-rural-conflicts-in-bihar-attributed-to-land-801564-1986-12-30

Bhatia, B. (1998, April). Rethinking Revolution in Bihar, *Seminar 464*, 27–31.

Bhatia, B. (2005, April 09). The Naxalite Movement in Central Bihar, *Economic and Political Weekly*. 1536–37 & 1547.

CPI (ML) Liberation. (1987). Political- Organisational Report, *Fourth Party Congress*. Retrieved from https://www.marxists.org/reference/archive/mishra/1987/x01/x01.htm

Das, A. N. (1987). Caste Killings and Naxalite Alibi, *Mainstream*, June 20, 8–9.

Das, A. N. (1999). Dire Poverty and Oppression Are the Grim Facts of Life for the Dalits (The Untouchables) of India's Most Backward State', *The UNESCO Courier*, February, 8.

Hindustan Times. (2008, January 01). *Sister brings girls to school in Bihar.*

India Today Magazine. (1980, December 15). *Labourers demand share to the crops grown on landed property held by Bodh Gaya Mahant.* Retrieved from https://www.indiatoday.in/magazine/indiascope/story/19801215-labourers-demand-share-to-the-crops-grown-on-landed-property-held-by-bodhgaya-mahant-773639-2013-11-30

India Today Magazine. (2008, November 18). *Marginalized girls find hope in Sudha.* Retrieved from https://www.indiatoday.in/web-exclusive/story/marginalised-girls-find-hope-in-sudha-33586-2008-11-18

Indian Express. (1980, November 16). *Harijan Crops Destroyed: Gaya Math Runs Amok.*

Kelkar, Govind (1991), "Agricultural labour, women and land rights in Bihar", 23, 4, Peace Research, 40–41.

Lal, A. K. (1997). *Dalits in action* (pp. 13–15). Concept Publishing Company.

Manimala. (1983). "Zameen Kenkar? Jote Onkar", Women's Participation in the Bodh Gaya Land Struggle. *Manushi, 14*, 2–16, cited in Agarwal, Bina (2003), "Gender and land Rights Revisited: Exploring the New Prospects via the State, Family and Market, Vol. 3, No. 1 & 2, Journal of Agrarian Change, 197.

Mathrubhumi. (2023, February 03). *Rat Eaters to Farmers: How Sudha Varghese Changed Face of Untouchables in Bihar.* Retrieved from https://english.mathrubhumi.com/special-pages/mbifl-2023/rat-eaters-to-farmers-how-sudha-varghese-changed-face-of-untouchables-in-bihar-1.8277506

Pandey, S. R. (1991). *Community action for social justice* (p. 232). Sage Publications.

Prasad, I. (2021). Caste-ing space: Mapping the dynamics of untouchability in rural Bihar, India. *CASTE: A Global Journal on Social Exclusion, 2*(1), 150.

Report. (1981). *Agrarian unrest in Patna* (pp. 13–14). People's Union for Democratic Rights (PUDR).

Roy, B. (1992). Voluntary agencies and government: The Indian experiences. In A. Bhatia & P. Bumka (Eds.), *Images of rural India* (p. 91). Sterling Publications.
Singh, D. K. (1995). *Agrarian transformation* (p. 152). Rawat Publications, 153-54 & 159.
Sinha, A. (1978). The awakening in Bhojpur. In S. Sen et al. (Eds.), *Naxalbari and after* (p. 73). Kathashilpa.
The Telegraph. (1978, October 05). cited in Singh, D. K., op.cit, 158.
The Telegraph. (1980 November 02; 07; 08). cited in Singh, D. K., op. cit. 166.
The Times of India. (1986, May 15). *Mahant: A Terror in Gaya.*
The Times of India. (1988, February 09). *Guns End Bihar Naxalite Unity.*
The Times of India. (1993, December 27). *Clashes in Bihar Claim Eight.*
Urmilesh. (1991). *Bihar Ka Sach (Hindi)* (pp. 137–139). New Delhi.

Role of the State, Political Parties, Judiciary and Media

Abstract What role did the state play while massive violations of Dalit human rights were being violated? The role played by different political parties which were actively pursuing their political ideology and agenda during this time period has been assessed too. While examining the role of state it has looked in to the role played by local and state level administration and more importantly the police and their ways of handling during this time period. The role played by the judiciary and media is also an important aspect which has been given prominence in this chapter.

Keywords State's failure in protecting Dalit human rights · National Commission for Scheduled Castes and Scheduled Tribes (NCSCST) · Failure of police in protecting Dalit human rights · Role of judiciary and media on issues related to Dalit human rights

1 Role of the State, Its Agencies and Political Parties

The state and its agencies could function effectively only in a situation where religio-cultural and social customs are relegated in the background. The overarching influence of traditional social structure is bound to create obstacles for the state to usher in a new dawn for a new republic. If a modern state keeps falling back to its traditional means and ways for conducting its day-to-day affairs, then it is surely bound to go down the drain. In other words, it is to be noted here that not adhering to constitutionalism could lead to utter chaos wherein the democratic set-up itself would remain endangered. Thus Atul Kohli remarked, "In the process of breakdown of political and social order, the declining effectiveness of the state and the increase in violence in the society at large has played a major role. The undisciplined power struggles among the competing elites, the absence of economic development and the growing de-legitimisation of traditional caste domination due to spread of

UMAKANT, *Dalit Human Rights in India*, People, Cultures and Societies: Exploring and Documenting Diversities,
https://doi.org/10.1007/978-981-95-5751-6_5

democratic politics and the growing agrarian conflicts have altogether been responsible for the crisis and governability in the state of Bihar" (Kohli, 1992, pp. 236–237).

As far as the human rights of Dalits are concerned, the state of Bihar has failed on many counts. Prevalence of untouchability, economic backwardness, non-implementation of land reforms, political ascendancy and lumpenization/criminalization of backward castes has all contributed to the growing violation of the Dalit human rights. The indifferent administration, police, political parties, judiciary and media have also played their part in the worsening of pitiable condition of the Dalits in Bihar. It has been very difficult for the Dalits to have an equitable share in the benefits generated by the development process. As a result their socio-economic condition has remained almost unchanged, if it has not worsened further. As a matter of fact, inequality is a question not merely of unequal distribution of resources but a basic idea and a value. The stigma of pollution is always attached to Dalits. Because of this stigma, their intercourse with caste Hindus is limited, and they are segregated in settlements outside the village. Discrimination and material deprivation are the hallmark of the socio-economic and political order. The extreme poverty and wretchedness of Dalits are related to an economy of scarcity. The extreme poverty has resulted in severe economic exploitation, sometimes leading to bondage and loss of freedom to seek independent work.

Not acknowledging the pernicious impact of caste system in the policymaking exercise leads to perpetuation of the already entrenched barriers which forces Dalits to remain outside the purview of any actual development-related initiatives of the government in power. It is also worth noting in this regard the role played by the casteist mindset of the officials who prepare the policy intervention and who are also entrusted with policy implementation tasks. In the name of development packages, what is provided is nothing sort of charity and that too the casteist manifestation of their arrogance. It is quite instructive to note here the observations made in a report prepared during the post-emergency phase. During the Janata regime in Bihar, the Antyodaya programme was started for the poorest of the poor. In a study conducted by the A.N. Sinha Institute of Social Studies of Patna, "it was found that no proper procedure was followed to identify the prospective beneficiaries. More than half of the beneficiaries were given cows and buffaloes. Some people were given aid to start their own caste occupation. Some people received bullocks and some others received rickshaws and hand drawn carriages. In most cases, the beneficiaries had to undergo unnecessary harassment and delay in the disposal of work. The beneficiaries were not satisfied with the cost and the quality of animals supplied to them. Since marketing for milk or other finished products was not attended the beneficiaries could not reap the desired benefits. Some families which were on the margin of the poverty line did cross it, but the bulk of the beneficiaries did not, as the increase in the income were not enough to meet the minimum requirements" (Sinha, 1987, pp. 173–174).

In the 1980s, the Antyodaya programme was replaced by the Integrated Rural Development Programme (IRDP), which was more or less similar in nature. A survey of the Dalit beneficiaries in the Rajauli Block of the Nawada district revealed that the programme had helped 48% of them to cross the poverty line. The provision of assets to the beneficiaries had not only changed their economic status but had also led to a change in their occupation in the case of 32% of beneficiaries. The bulk of the beneficiaries who were earlier agricultural labourers had changed over to rickshaw pulling, shoemaking, etc. The scheme was not been very successful because no proper assessment was ever made about the ability of the beneficiaries to derive maximum benefits from the assets provided to them. The marketing of finished products was always neglected. It was also discovered that there was lot of leakage in the funds meant for the purchases of assets (Verma, 1987, p. 174).

During the sixth plan period, the Special Component Plan (SCP) was mooted for the benefits of the Scheduled Castes to be supported by the state plans as well as Special Central Assistance received from the government of India. In a survey it was found that the implementation of the Special Component Plan (SCP) had been uneven from the point of view of its allotment, disbursement and coverage. Under the present stage of development of Dalits, SCP did not provide an independent and remunerative occupation and income. A large drawback in the structure of SCP was that the distribution of assets among the beneficiaries was exceedingly uneven and inferior in quality. During the field visit it was also noticed that very few assets given to the beneficiaries under the programme were of durable nature. The subsidies provided to the beneficiaries were subject to leakages at different levels. Some cases of mortgage were also reported during the survey. The problem of implementation of SCP was of improper and untimely utilization and disbursement among the beneficiaries. The survey revealed that 30–50% of the allotted funds for this purpose were not utilized by the block officials mainly due to lack of perspective and sincerity among them from top to the bottom in discharging their duties as the agents of change. The participation of Dalit women also appeared to be negligible in the Special Component Plan (Prasad, 1986, pp. 77 & 87–89).

In Bihar Dalits have benefited least from the development programmes as their share in the development schemes has always been nominal. Poverty alleviation and employment generation tend to be elusive in spite of the operation of programmes wedded to these ends. The relationship between the landowner and the tiller tends to be pre-commercial "having their harshest impact on members of the Scheduled Castes" (Kohli op.cit: 203). The state has failed to ensure minimum wages recommended by it from time to time. The wages have been found to be as low as Rs. 4 a day in many areas of Bihar (Bharti, 1990, p. 1512). This together with the limited days of employment in the villages made it difficult to lift them from the condemned life of bondage.

The Land Reforms Act of 1950 and the subsequent Land-Ceiling Act have proved to be defective in the state of Bihar. Large-scale eviction of tenants occurred during the hiatus between the adoption of Zamindari Abolition and its enforcement as law. Zamindars who had maintained a direct interest in supervising their estates were often able to retain all the land they held prior to abolition except only that land to which an occupancy raiyat had incontrovertible documentary evidence in support of their claim (Jannuzi, 1974, p. 33). Moreover under-tenure holders of absentee zamindars, who had managed the far-flung holdings of the great Raja, were among those in the best position to enter their own names in the land records as occupancy tenants.

The power of the landed gentry to undercut land reforms was further demonstrated in the case with which they delayed passage of a land ceiling bill from 1955 to 1962 and then ensured that the Bihar Land Reforms (Fixation of Ceiling Areas and Acquisition of Surplus Land) Act was studded with every possible loophole to scuttle effective implementation. Beyond this, notices of enforcement of the 1962 Act were issued to the big landholders only in 1965. They had, therefore, some 10 years to arrange partitions among family members, transfer lands to fictitious persons (benami), prepare false documents of sale, instigate relatives to file false court claims against land acquired and otherwise alter the land records in collusion with the local revenue officials to evade the law (Pandey, 1979, pp. 35–43). Approximately 400,000–500,000 acres of surplus lands were hidden through fictitious transfers alone during this period (Ojha, 1977, p. 122). On the other hand, whereas some segments of the backward Shudra castes like Yadavs, Kurmis and Koiris made considerable gains in some region as they became landholders, the other groups like untouchable's claim for land remained unaddressed by the land reform measures.

Landlords flouted the law in dealing with bataidars (sharecroppers) who were of low caste or Scheduled Caste background. According to the Batai Land Reforms Section of the 1961 (Fixation of Ceilings) Act, rental in kind, by division of the produce, was limited to one fourth of the crop; all other cesses (abwabs) were illegal; occupancy rights were to vest in under raiyats holding land continuously for 12 years, and eviction could not be carried out except in execution of a decree. The landlords shifted tenants from one plot to another every 3 or 4 years to prevent a bataidar from claiming occupancy rights. They also demanded division of the crop on their own premises, where they took 50% of the produce, deducted payments for production and consumption loans and, in some cases, also extracted abwabs. Often, the sharecropper was left with a nominal amount of grain or a negative balance. In that case he/she had to render free labour at the house of the landholders (Mohsin, 1984, p. 60). Tenants who objected to these practices were forcefully evicted.

Landlords dealt even more callously with agricultural labourers especially those from among the Scheduled Caste. The 1947 Privileged Persons Homestead Tenancy Act, as amended in 1970, provided that all persons with less than 1 acre of land should receive occupancy rights in developed homestead land of 200 square yards as well as a grant of Rs. 200 towards construction of a hut. Fragmentary data collected in the 1980s suggested that a minority of those eligible actually received a "parcha" (paper) from the block office conferring occupancy under homestead scheme, that few received as much as 200 square yards and that none received the subsidy. Even some labourers who received the "parchas" (paper) were forcibly evicted by the landholders in case they refuse to do begari or did not give votes during election as per their demand (Frankel, 1993, p. 96). The situation was perhaps worse with respect to implementation of the Minimum Wages Act which was operational in the state by 1959 (with upward revision in the rates in 1966, 1975 and

1982). Except at harvest, a time of peak labour demand, landowners did not pay minimum wages per day (Ibid: 97).

Commenting on the overall failure of the state, police and even the judiciary, Anand Chakravarti observed that the nexus between class power and the state compounded the oppression of the underclass in Bihar. There were two principal respects in which the operation of the state reinforced the connection between caste and class: (i) laws, such as land reform laws or those pertaining to the payment of minimum wages, which were designed in principle to benefit the disadvantaged, were subverted because of the sway of vested interests over the state's politics and administration, and (ii) wherever the underclass were politicized and mobilized to demand the implementation of the laws designed for their benefit, they were subjected to brutal repression by dominant caste militias and the police. It was indeed ironical that the very state that was instrumental in the enunciation of the programme was also the chief instrument of its subversion. The subversion applied to all aspects of the programme, including the abolition of intermediary interests, tenancy reform and land ceilings (Chakravarti, 2001, p. 1453).

Dhar made the scathing observation, on the basis of a number of case studies, that through "various unscrupulous methods, such as benamdari (fictitious transfers of land), collusion with revenue officials and politicians, coupled with their social status and power...the ex-zamindars of Bihar succeeded, by and large, in protecting their class interests" (Dhar, 2000, p. 125). The failure of land reform was also attributable to the enabling role of the judiciary in protecting vested interests, though this is not unique to Bihar. One of Dhar's cases showed how a large zamindar used the law courts to try and prevent the government from taking over his estate (Ibid: 128–32). Though he ultimately lost the case, but was compensated monetarily, Dhar pointedly observed that "this was done well after the (zamindar), and through him his class, had exhibited their might to use legal and political institutions to protect their interests" (Ibid: 131). Indeed, the judiciary in the country as a whole has been categorically denounced by another writer for its tendency to maintain the status quo: "India is the only country where the judiciary has played a crucial role in frustrating and stultifying land reform laws" (Appu, 1993, p. 53). A report on incidents of agrarian violence in central Bihar in the early 1990s suggested that the rural elites in contemporary India possessed the capacity to "(appropriate)... the paraphernalia of the state" to further their interests (PUDR, 1992, p. 30).

The questions of caste and land have played havoc on the life of Dalits in the post-independence era and more so from 1977 onwards in Bihar. Not only the upper castes and some section of backward castes that have been playing with the dignity and life of Dalits, but as a matter of fact even successive governments in Bihar have failed on this count. As a result of this, large-scale violations of human rights of Dalits have taken place, which portrays the government of Bihar in a bad light.

How precarious have been the life condition of Dalits in Bihar was highlighted in a much more pronounced manner by the National Commission for Scheduled Castes and Scheduled Tribes (NCSCST) when it made an observation like this: "the level of poverty and unemployment in Bihar is alarming. Most seriously affected by these problems are SCs as more than 86% of the SCs, subsist on agriculture, though the majority of them do not own any land. They are either completely landless or work on leased land as share-croppers. Besides, historically, SCs have been settled on lands where productivity is low and uncertain i.e. flood prone and drought prone areas. SC and ST dominant villages still lacked basic amenities like drinking water, sanitation, electrification, roads, etc. The law and order situation has also been deteriorating day after day due to which the SCs and STs became more vulnerable to heinous atrocities. The Scheduled Castes (SCs) and the Scheduled Tribes (STs) have been largely deprived of benefits intended to accrue to them under the Special Component Plan (SCP) and Tribal Sub Plan (TSP)" (NCSCST, 1998a–99, pp. 20–22). It also highlighted the failure of the state government on several counts (Ibid: 29–30).

2 The Role of Police

Merely enacting laws is of little use unless they are put into action properly. In this crucial task the role of police cannot be over emphasized. Unfortunately the credibility of the police has been at its lowest ebb in contemporary times. Justice P.N. Bhagwati thus wrote: "The poor also suffer innumerable hardships, humiliations and sufferings at the hands of the police and other public officers. Instances are not unknown where complaints by SCs and STs and landless peasants against persons belonging to higher castes and rich powerful landlords or contractors are not registered by the police and poor have to continue to suffer injustice silently and helplessly. Not only are the economically dominant sections of the community provided immunity against the law by wrong and unjust exercise of discretion by police and other public officials, sometimes out of corrupt motives, sometimes on account of political pressure and sometimes on account of social and economic alignments" (Bhagwati, 1984, pp. 20–24).

The third Police Commission had also taken similar views about the police and the weaker sections. It noted that "complaints against the police in their handling of cases arising from atrocities against Scheduled Castes often relate to refusal to register complaints, delayed arrival on the scene, half-hearted action while investigating specific cases, extreme brutality in dealing with accused belonging to weaker sections, soft treatment of accused persons belonging to influential sections, making arrests or failing to make them on malafide considerations, etc." (National Police Commission, Government of India, 1980, p. 4).

Though several changes have been made over the years, the police set up in the country are guided mainly by the Police Act of 1861. The policing and maintenance of public order are to be carried out by the police. The "law and order" is listed under state list, and that is why it is the responsibility of each respective state government to bring reforms keeping under consideration the changing scenario and the need for better policing. However, there have been several attempts by the Central Government through constituting commissions and committees to bring forth the much needed police reforms. The Gore Committee on Police Training

(1971–1973), The National Police Commission set up in 1977, the Ribeiro Committee on Police Reforms (1998), the Padmanabhaiah Committee on Police Reforms (2000), the Group of Ministers on National Security (2000–2001), the Malimath Committee on Reforms of Criminal Justice System (2001–2003), the Soli Sorabjee Police Act Drafting Committee (2005–2006) and even the Administrative Reforms Commission headed by Veerappa Moily (2005–2007) had a report on public order with several recommendations on police reforms (Umakant, 2012).

A writ petition filed in 1996 in the Supreme Court and heard over a period of 10 years resulted in a landmark "Seven Directives" for immediate compliance so as be operative till such time a new model Police Act is prepared by the Central Government and/or the State Governments passed the requisite legislations. The landmark judgement of the Supreme Court delivered on September 22, 2006, still remains not complied with fully by several state governments/union territories. Neither a single state nor the union territories comply fully with the directives in true earnest signaling the Central Government's non-compliance too. The failure to comply with the directives reveals the extent to which elected governments are resisting police reform across the country. The much required checks and balances that the directives seek to instil to make policing more professional and accountable are being stymied in multiple ways (CHRI, 2021, p. 2). Year after year and with the not so satisfactory role of the police set-up in containing communal, caste and other kinds of disturbances along with its normal functioning, there does not seem to be any urgency on part of the Central Government as well as the respective state governments and union territories. What is preventing the Central Government in promulgating a new model Police Act? It is quite baffling (Umakant op.cit)!

All the allegations against police and other public officials in the dealings with the weaker sections of society hold true even now as it was in the past. Specific examples have been cited in this section from 1977 onwards to substantiate the role of police and others in the human rights violations of Dalits in Bihar. The Parliamentary Committee headed by Mr. Ramdhan which probed the Belchi massacre not only castigated the report of Bihar government in which it had termed the massacre as the result of criminal gang warfare as false and baseless but at the same time the committee observed: "We are of the definite opinion that the police were in league with the culprits and deliberately delayed their (own) arrival in the village". The report also spoke of a police officer demanding an inducement of Rs. 500 to go to the spot when some villagers informed him of the impending massacre. The committee felt that had the alleged co-conspirators in uniform taken prompt action, the tragedy would have been averted (Indian Express, 1977).

Eleven Special Police Thanas (Station) were set up by the Bihar government with the main objective of exclusively dealing with cases related to atrocities against Dalits. The special police station at Patna with the whole of Bihar under its jurisdiction was set up on August 25, 1978 (Table 1).

With the establishment of the special police station, it was assumed that unreported crimes on the Dalits would be regularly booked in these police stations. But the facts reveal an altogether different story about these police stations. The cognizable as well as non-cognizable crimes either do not reach these police stations or

Table 1 The headquarter and jurisdiction of ten other special thanas

No	District	Headquarter	Jurisdiction
1	Nalanda	Biharsharif	Nalanda
2	Rohtas	Sasaram	Rohtas
3	Bhojpur	Ara	Bhojpur
4	Gaya	Gaya	Gaya, Aurangabad and Nawada
5	Vaishali	Hajipur	Vaishali, Muzaffarpur, Sitamarhi, Saran, Siwan, Gopalganj, East and West Champaran, Motihari and Bettiah
6	Samastipur	Samastipur	Samastipur, Darbhanga and Madhubani
7	Begusarai	Begusarai	Begusarai, Khagaria, Katihar, Purnea, Madhepura and Saharsa
8	Bhagalpur	Bhagalpur	Bhagalpur, Dumka and Gopalganj
9	Munger	Munger	Munger
10	Ranchi	Ranchi	Whole of Chota Nagpur

get hushed up in the process for one reason or another. Large jurisdiction area of these police stations makes it practically difficult for Dalits to register cases of atrocities after travelling long distances. Moreover the staff posted in these police stations were found to be most inefficient and at times even biased against Dalits. These police stations have neither proper place nor the staff in full strength for an effective functioning. The special police station at Patna is still functioning in a rented house and even without proper facilities. In many cases it was found that these police stations even refused to register cases deliberately. On the other hand most of the cases were still lying for investigation, and only few were charge sheeted in time. These special police stations have utterly failed in discharging their duties (Daftuar, 1986, pp. 9–20).

The rising number of atrocities against Dalits during Janata party regime was thus reported by a national daily: "To say that caste tensions are not unknown to Bihar is an understatement. But the fact remains that the disease has become chronic and has assumed a malignant form since the Janata Party came to power in Bihar last year. The tragedy is that Scheduled Castes and Scheduled Tribes have been at the receiving end. Atrocities at which 20th century should hang its head in shame have been committed on them in the past 19 months. The middle or the peasant castes are up in arms to protect their privileges. Their claim is that they swept the Janata Party into power and that is why the government should pay more attention to them. A considerable part of the ruling party's predicament can be traced to that claim" (National Herald, 1978).

The incident of atrocity at Kaila village of Nalanda district in which three Scheduled Castes were killed, two of them beheaded by the armed musclemen of the affluent rich farmers of the area, was worse than the Bajitpur or Belchi in some respect because here everything happened in the presence of a police party headed by a Magistrate which remained a silent spectator to the ghastly crime on December 9, 1978 (New Age, 1978, p. 3).

In at least seven blocks of Patna district in Bihar, the state government and its police, with the active support of landlords and with the explicit or implicit cooperation of all major political parties, were attempting, systematically, to suppress a mass-based democratic movement of poor peasants and agricultural labourers whose only demands were the guarantee of the rights granted to them by the Constitution and the implementation of various laws promulgated by the government. This was the conclusion of a team of academicians and journalists who were part of a fact-finding team by the People's Union for Democratic Rights (PUDR) in to agrarian unrest in Patna. They made a study tour to seven blocks of Patna district, namely, Masaurhi, Bikram, Pali, Dhanarua, Punpun, Fatuha and Naubatpur. The police were regularly conducting raids in several villages in these blocks and harassing Dalit landless labourer's family. Between October 30, 1981, and November 05, 1981, seven people were killed in police firing at Narihi-Pirihi in Bikram block, Kajra and Bahuara in Naubatpur, Beshwarpur in Masaurhi and Parhbigha in Dhanarua block, and several others were arrested by police (PUDR, 1981, pp. 4, 21 & 28).

Massive police repression on MKSS activists who were trying to organize a conference of peasants and agricultural labourers in Jehanabad area of the erstwhile central Bihar was reported in a cross section of media in and around the third week of May 1983. An important dimension of the intense contradictions of the area was the fact that almost all landless labourers belonged to untouchable Dalit castes. Thus the age-old tradition of social discrimination added up to intense economic exploitation. In the night of May 08, 1983, the local police shot dead Pradeep Bind in Patadia village. The police claimed that he was a wanted criminal and was killed in an encounter. Two days later, armed landlords went to Gonsa village and killed Inderdeo Mochi. While MKSS was busy preparing to hold the conference at Madua village, the local administration and police responded in the most undemocratic and repressive ways by not only banning the assembly of groups of people by clamping Sect. 144 of the Criminal Procedure Code (CRPC) but also beating up several activists mercilessly and arresting them (PUDR, 1983, pp. 1–18).

On December 31, 1984, evening, about a 1000 strong contingent of Central Reserve Police (CRP) and Bihar Military Police (BMP) attacked Mongar Bigha Tola, a Dalit hamlet of Kaithi Bigha village in Aurangabad district of Bihar and killed 10 Dalits. The contingent indulged in shooting, looting and arson for close to 36 h. The Tola was set on fire, and six Dalits were thrown into the fire. Dozens of heads of cattle were also burnt alive. After the operation was over, the police arrested eight persons and paraded them up to the Obera police station about a kilometre away. Five of them were believed to have been shot either on the way or in the police station. Ten days after the carnage, the Tola with burnt houses was still completely deserted. The whereabouts of its around 105 surviving inhabitants were still unknown. The police authorities in Patna acknowledged the incident after 6 days and described it as an encounter with Naxalites who had allegedly taken shelter in the Tola to attack the landlords in the village (Sinha, 1985, p. 343).

A national daily reporting about killing of ten Dalits at Kansara village thus observed: "It is astonishing that police headquarters neither at Patna nor at Gaya, which is close by the scene of the tragedy, was aware of it 40 hours after it had occurred. The Arwal carnage in April was a direct result of police firing on a peaceful assembly of scheduled castes in so brutal a manner that it proved a comparison with Jallianwala Bagh. While the police collusion with the landlords in the caste war is well known, the state government cannot wash away its responsibility. It has allowed the private armies like the Bhoomi Sena and the Lorik Sena to flourish. In 1984 Bhoomi Sena was declared illegal but nothing has been done since then to disarm its men. Unless measures are taken to disband the Senas and make the police at least impartial, if no more, Bihar could easily slide into anarchy" (The Times of India, 1986).

The Bihar police withdrew the criminal case against 9 of the 11 persons accused of killing seven Scheduled Castes of Koeria-Chatar village in Jehanabad district in September 1987. The police described one of the accused as a "sympathiser of the victims" while withdrawing the charges. The remaining two were chargesheeted as minor criminals and were expected to be let off in due course of time. The keenness of the police to exonerate the accused was apparent from the fact that chargesheet was filed in the case in a record 4 month of the incident. Moreover the police took the unusual recourse of informing the court that there was no evidence against the nine accused and pleaded that they be released from jail. All the nine Yadav desperados were said to have been patronized by the Bhumihar strongman Ramashray Prasad Singh, the Parliamentary Affairs and Power and Irrigation Minister in the outgoing Dubey Ministry (Telegraph, 1988).

On November 24, 1989, the polling day of the Lok Sabha election, a news of "Harijan killing" in a remote village of Bhojpur district figured in local newspapers in a casual way as if the happening was of a secondary importance. The kind of savage brutality that perpetrated in the village Danwar-Bihta of Bhojpur district, which involved massacre of 40 people, was a very serious matter. In cases of attacks and counter-attacks by the Indian Peoples Front (IPF) and dreaded gang of feudal elements like Jwala Singh, several lives were lost. The caste nexus between local officials and police with the landlords was directly responsible for such kind of massacre to have happened on that fateful day (Patnaik, 1990, pp. 1–25).

The state and its apparatus, especially the police, have always been found to be favourable to the rich, privileged and ruling caste/class combined. It is no surprise then that Bihar police has always been found wanting as far as the question of providing safety and security to the most disadvantaged sections of society is concerned. The political patronage received by various militias imparted to them the necessary leverage to obtain support from the administration. The kind of support extended to these elements by the executive laid bare, in a sense, their social power, for the oppression of the labouring poor was not possible unless the police, in particular, consciously acted in favour of the militias. On the other hand, by staging false encounters to eliminate political activists among the poor, the police have been found to be reinforcing the coercive power of the senas (PUDR, 1992, pp. 34–35).

On April 14, 1994, local newspapers reported the killing of 11 extremists in a fierce encounter with the police during the night of April 12, 1994, in Masaundha forest near Matgarha village under Mohanpur Block in Gaya district. This case of extrajudicial killing was closed without any proper investigation. In another incident of the same type, it was reported that four people were killed in an encounter between the police and the CPI (ML)-Party Unity squad at Gulzarbigha village under Haspura Block in Aurangabad district on July 3, 1995 (PUDR, 1996a, pp. 6–9). As a matter of fact, there were scores of such encounter killings reported from Bihar during this period.

The police and local administration in not being able to perform properly by carrying out their required mandate of being the protector and as agents of state testify to the fact that primordial loyalties of caste and community run quite deep in the society at large and even officials are also not immune from these. In response to the Ranveer Sena attack on the Dalit hamlet in Bathani Tola in July 1996, then Union Home Minister Indrajit Gupta expressed dissatisfaction with police protection in the affected region. Even though four police camps had been posted in the area, Gupta charged that they were "paralysed, impotent and did nothing" (The Times of India, 1996). Despite signs of rising tension in the area, police neglected to shift their booth to Bathani Tola. The officials had received written complaints about possible attack by the Ranveer Sena from the CPI (ML). According to press reports the superintendent of Police S. N. Pradhan dismissed the complaints from CPI (ML) as routine (Indian Express, 1996). The killings took place on July 11, 1996. During the attack itself, the police reportedly made no attempts to intervene despite being on duty a "stone's throw" away from the scene (The Hindu, 1996). Throughout this attack, the police in the camps situated within sight of Bathani Tola did not come to protect the victims but merely watched passively. The superintendent of police (SP) of Bhojpur took 7 h to reach the site of the massacre (PUDR, 1997, p. 6).

Thus, it was observed that massacre after massacre and other human rights abuses of Dalits in Bihar, the evil face of state and its agencies have been unmasked. In this connection it would not be wrong to say that the protector at times also became the perpetrators of crimes against humanity. The credibility of the state had been eroded. The prevailing lawlessness and jungle raj presented the picture of anarchy where the safety and security of the downtrodden always remained in danger. A news report further exposed the hypocrisy of the ruling party Rashtriya Janata Dal (RJD) on the question of caste killings in Bihar: "The recent selection of a Jehanabad strongman, Mahendra Prasad Singh, as an RJD nominee to the Rajya Sabha, has surprised one and all. This was done despite the fact Mahendra Prasad Singh was one of the alleged patron of caste militias like Ranveer Sena" (Times of India, 2000). It is also important to point out here that Congress Party had nominated the same Mahendra Prasad Singh as its Rajya Sabha member earlier.

There have been other evidences of the Ranveer Sena getting support from political parties in Bihar. Interestingly, the Ranveer Sena, the notorious upper caste militia which has been involved with the killings of Dalits, has been getting support from the Laloo Prasad Yadav's party (Janata Dal and then Rashtriya Janata Dal) and also the BJP in equal measure. Chandradeo Prasad Verma, a former Union Minister in H. D. Devegowda's regime and one of the co-accused in the fodder scam, had in 1996 put it on record that "the ban which the state administration sought to effect on the Ranveer Sena was wrong", while the BJP leader Sushil Kumar Modi also accepts that most of Ranveer Sena leaders were members of BJP. Even when the Ranveer Sena was banned by the government, it did not enforce this ban in a proper way as was done against Naxalites, and their leaders were free and continuing with their nefarious works (Mathew, 1997).

Kanti Singh, another RJD leader, reportedly presented a Maruti Gypsy to Sunil Pandey, a top leader of the Ranveer Sena for helping her out in the 1996 general election. Shakuni Chaudhary and Haridwar Singh, both member of Parliament (MP) belonging to Samata Party (Now Janata Dal United), and Anand Mohan Singh, MP and president of Bihar People's Party, also made no bones about their support to the Ranveer Sena. The political clout of the banned outfit was evident when it organized a public meeting attended by its top guns in Belaur, at its headquarters, on October 8, 1997. The police was fully aware of the meeting but did not take any action. "The Ranveer Sena men help us to flush out Naxalites", said a senior police officer. That perhaps explains the allegation that police have hand in glove with the Ranveer Sena activists (The Week, 1999). The state patronage and support from other political parties have been precisely the reason that even after being a banned organization, neither its leaders were arrested nor they were disarmed. And as a result of this, the Ranveer Sena struck at its own will, killing innocent Dalits with greater vengeance and sophisticated weapons.

The National Commission for Scheduled Castes and Scheduled Tribes (NCSCST) conducted on the spot enquiries in Haibaspur and Laxmanpur Bathe and made an observation. "These enquiries have revealed that the political situation in the state is responsible for creating 'Senas' and these senas owe allegiance to both the higher castes and lower castes. When sena of higher castes kills member of the Scheduled Castes and Scheduled Tribes, the sena of the lower castes takes revenge and thus fighting and killings go on periodically. The state police have been ineffective in dealing with such atrocities" (NCSCST, 1998–1999, p. 28).

3 The Role of Judiciary

The role the judiciary has been entrusted to dispensing justice. It was but essential that it should try to be neutral without taking side in any case that came before it for hearing. If the judiciary failed in its duty of being impartial, then the entire edifice of the judicial system may crumble. On many occasions it has been found that not only the judiciary continued to remain overburdened with a huge number of pending cases, but on a flip side it has also been found that caste/community interests easily influence the verdict. Article 17 of the Constitution abolished "untouchability" and forbade its practice in any form. To implement this policy effectively, the Protection of Civil Rights Act 1955 was enacted. Over 7000 cases registered under this Act were pending with the police and courts in several states at the beginning of 1993. In addition, nearly 1600 new cases were registered by the police in 1993. Of the 970 cases disposed of by the courts in 1993, only 158 resulted in convictions and the remaining 812 in acquittal (Godbole, 1997).

According to the Report of the SC and ST Commission, 12 cases were pending with the courts in Bihar at the end of the year 1977, 64 cases in 1978, 97 cases in

1979, 107 cases in 1980, 113 cases in 1981, 125 cases in 1982 and 135 cases in 1983 (SC and ST Commission, Government of India, 1982–1983 and 1983–1984). In the year 1984 in Bihar 205 cases were chargesheeted, out which 65 were convicted by the court, whereas 178 were acquitted. In 1985, 126 cases were reported, 760 were chargesheeted, 75 were convicted, and 225 were acquitted. In 1986, 217 cases were reported, 776 were chargesheeted, 62 were convicted, and 232 were acquitted. In 1988, 153 cases were reported, 967 were chargesheeted, 92 were convicted, and 262 were acquitted. In 1990, 175 cases were reported, 972 were chargesheeted, 96 were convicted, and 206 were acquitted. In 1991, 202 cases were reported, 1083 were chargesheeted, 78 were convicted, and 89 were acquitted. In 1992, 243 cases were reported, 1486 were chargesheeted, 102 were convicted, and 147 were acquitted. And in 1993, 206 cases were reported, 1302 were chargesheeted, 84 were convicted, and 99 were acquitted (Scheduled Caste Cell, Government of Bihar, 1994).

In the year 1996 a total of 72 cases under protection of Civil Rights Act 1955 were put up before the courts in Bihar. This included 48 cases from previous years and 24 new cases. The court disposed of with one case through conviction, and very surprisingly 71 cases were left pending by the courts at the close of the year. On the other hand, for the same time period a total of 1021 cases under Prevention of Atrocities Act 1989 were put up before the courts. This included 658 old cases from the previous year and 363 new cases. The courts disposed of with only 89 cases which included 76 acquittals and 13 convictions, and a large number of 940 cases were left pending at the close of the year (National Commission for Scheduled Castes and Scheduled Tribes, 1996b–1997). In the year 1997, the chargesheeting rate of crimes under PCR Act in Bihar was 88%, while under Prevention of Atrocities Act it was 92.06%. For the same time period the conviction rate of crimes under PCR Act was 58.82, whereas under Prevention of Atrocities Act it was only 26.88% (Crime in India, 1997).

The State Government of Bihar has so far established 15 Special Courts for speedy trial of cases of atrocities under the provision contained in section 14 of the Scheduled Castes and Scheduled Tribes (Prevention of Atrocities-PoA) Act 1989. In other districts the courts of the first Additional District and Session Judges have been entrusted with the additional powers to try cases vide notification No. 340/J dated February 10, 1995 of the Law Department, Government of Bihar. The position of the disposal of cases involving Scheduled Castes and Scheduled Tribes (SCs and STs) (PoA) Act 1989 in Bihar during the years 1995–1997 was as follows: In the year 1995 out of the 3138 cases challaned, only 160 cases were disposed of, and 2839 cases were left pending. In 1996 out of the total 4300 cases, only 535 cases were disposed of, and 3698 cases were left pending. Whereas in the year 1998 out of the total 5059 cases, only 428 cases were disposed of, and 4525 cases were left pending (NCSCST, 1998b-99 0p.cit: 28–29).

It transpired from the above facts that the disposal of cases by the Special Courts during the year 1995–1997 was not all satisfactory. The reasons for the poor disposal as reported by were as under non-appearance of accused persons, non-production of witnesses and non-execution of warrants of arrest.

Special judges also dispose of cases of session trials, criminal, appeal or revisions, title appeals, etc., besides the cases under SCs and STs (PoA) Act, and so do not have time to deal with more PoA cases of SCs and STs.

From the above figures it has been made very clear that the conviction rate continued to remain very low, whereas the acquittal rate was very high. It should remain a concern that the judiciary failed to deliver speedy justice to victims who were mainly Dalits. Lengthy and cumbersome procedures always complicate the matter, and moreover free legal aids were not easily available. In the meantime agony and frustration of Dalits remained as ever.

4 The Bathani Tola Massacre Case

Despite the barbarity and the brazenness with which the Ranveer Sena was operating while killing Dalits and other low caste people which also included at times lower caste Muslims as was evident in Bathani Tola and elsewhere in Bihar, the state and its agencies like police, and even the judiciary, failed to deliver justice. The credentials of the redressal mechanisms have come under cloud. The verdict of the Patna High Court acquitting all the accused once again laid bare open the casteist mindset that played its role even among the most enlightened sections of society, be it police, administration and even judiciary.

A national daily very aptly described the situation after the High Court judgement. Bathani Tola, an unsung hamlet in central Bihar, shot to fame as one of the many sites where the fearsome Ranveer Sena had left its bloody mark. Last week, the village was once more in the news, with the Patna High Court acquitting 23 men convicted of the gruesome murders. "We heard their howls of agony, but simply could not find the courage to come out", recounts Naimuddin Ansari, one of the prime witnesses who lost six family members in the carnage. "The Sena men encircled our hovels, drew out the victims and slaughtered them", recounts Sri Kishun Chaudhary, who lodged an FIR against 33 persons the day after the massacre. Fourteen years after the bloodbath in Bathani, the Ara sessions court sentenced three persons to death and awarded life sentence to another 20. The acquittal of the same men by the High Court has come as a shock to Bathani's residents. The court might have had its reasons—it cited "defective evidence"—for overturning the convictions, but the villagers are inconsolable and recollect every detail of the horror that visited them, including the fact that the Sena men killed women and children by design, not because they came in their way (The Hindu, 2012).

5 The Final Words of Judgement

The two judge benches of the Patna High Court, headed by Justice Navaniti Prasad Singh and Ashwani Kumar Singh, dated April 16, 2012, delivered its verdict in the Death Reference No. 7 of 2010. The final verdict is contained in last five paragraphs of the judgment, i.e. from paragraphs no. 68 up to 72. Considering the significance of the matter, these last five paragraphs are mentioned below (Judgment, 2012):

> 68. Thus, having considered the entire material, we regret that though such a ghastly incident took place where over 20 people, only one of them being a man, were brutally slaughtered, infant of three months not left alive, the investigation was not fair in respect of the persons who perpetuated this ghastly crime. Apparently, investigation was directed in a particular direction far from truth and not above suspicion. Witnesses who were examined were totally unreliable.
>
> 69. The result is that we are unable to confirm the death sentence and for the reasons noted above, we allow all the appeals as well and set aside the conviction of all the appellants.
>
> 70. As all appeals have been allowed and conviction set aside, we are required not to pass any order with regard to the three persons who were found to be juvenile in conflict with law.
>
> 71. All appeals are allowed as prosecution has failed to prove the involvement of the appellants in the crime beyond reasonable doubt and the death reference is rejected and discharged.
>
> 72 All appellants who are in custody shall be released forthwith, if not required in any other case. All bail bonds of all the appellants, who are on bail, stands discharged.

The High Court had overturned the lower court's convictions as it disbelieved the prosecution's story and picked holes in the evidence furnished. It cited a 12-h delay in the fardbayan and weighed this delay against the fact that there was definite information about the massacre from the afternoon of July 11. The court expressed regret over the fact that a false and misleading investigation had enabled those who "perpetrated the crime to" get "away with it" (PUDR, 2016, pp. 20–21). The questions are many and the answers few. For the survivors of Bathani Tola, the High Court judgement was not an act of "justice" but a travesty of it. If the court had found a deliberate attempt by the police to frame the accused, action should have been ordered against the police, and if the issue was of negligence on the part of the investigation and prosecution, it should have ordered a reinvestigation and a retrial. The net result is that no one has been held guilty for the killing of 21 people. The prosecution has filed an appeal in the apex court in 2012. What that will lead to is anybody's guess (Ibid: 23).

How to react to this kind of judicial pronouncements thereby overturning the session court's verdict and in the process acquitting all the accused is a question that must be answered if the faith in higher judiciary to dispense justice without any fear or favour is to be maintained. Bela Bhatia's comment is perhaps the most apt to describe the Patna High Court verdict in Bathani Tola massacre case. "Even in a generous mood, it would be difficult not to find the High Court judgment on the Bathani Tola case as anything but unconscionable. What the verdict does is to prepare the ground for the acquittal of the 23 found guilty by the sessions [lower] court.

It uses old tactics: overdrawing upon the weaknesses of the prosecution and discrepancies in witness accounts to discredit the investigation and garnered evidence as unreliable. Having effectively done away with the witnesses, it invokes case law to justify its decision. The High Court judgment reveals a clear leaning in the direction of the accused" (Bhatia, 2013, p. 49).

6 The Laxmanpur Bathe Case

In the Laxmanpur Bathe massacre case the FIR was filed at Mehandia PS on the basis of the statement of Binod Paswan on December 2, 1997, but reached the Chief Judicial Magistrate (CJM) Jehanabad only on December 4. This inexplicable delay was later to have tragic consequences. The case was committed to the sessions court on January 6, 1999, for the first time, 1 year and 4 months after the massacre took place. Since then things became stranger as the case never came up for hearing! Finally, the Patna High Court had to transfer the case to the court of the third Additional Sessions Judge in December 2008. It took as long as 11 years after the ghastly massacre for the trial to begin. Charges were finally framed in December 2008 against a total of 45 people. The court examined 91 witnesses of which 17 were eyewitnesses (PUDR, 2016, p. 23).

Based on this evidence, the Sessions Court III convicted 26 out of the 45 accused on April 7, 2010. A total of 16 of the 26 convicted were awarded the death sentence, while 10 were sentenced to rigorous imprisonment for life under various sections of the IPC, Arms Act and SC & ST (Prevention of Atrocities) Act and also slapped with a fine of Rs 31,000 each. The remaining accused individuals were acquitted. Those sentenced to death were Girija Singh, Surendra Singh, Ashok Singh, Gopal Sharan Singh, Baleshwar Singh, Dawarka Singh, Vijendra Singh, Nawal Singh, Baliram Singh, Nandu Singh, Sheomohan Sharma, Pramod Singh, Shatrughan Singh, Ramkeval Sharma, Dharma Singh and Nand Singh, all belonging to an upper caste community (Economic Times, 2010).

Those sentenced to life imprisonment were Babloo Sharma, Ashok Singh, Mithilesh Sharma, Dharikshan Choudhary, Navin Kumar, Ravindra Singh, Surendra Singh, Sunil Kumar, Pramod Kumar and Chandreshwar Singh. Two other accused Bhukhal Singh and Sudarshan Singh died in the course of the trial (Ibid).

The convicted persons appealed in the Patna High Court. The V.N. Sinha and A.K. Lal bench in a judgement passed on October 9, 2013, concurred with the defense view that the prosecution had failed to establish its case against the accused and that the massacre was carried out by unknown persons and acquitted all the accused persons (PUDR op.cit: 24–25).

7 The Final Words of Judgement

In the final judgement this is how one of judge remarked.

> "I would like to observe that there being no dispute about the factum of death, injury having been caused to 58, and 4 members of the weaker sections of the society in village Laxmanpur Bathe in the night of 01.12.1997, the State is obliged to pay compensation to the next of kin of the 58 deceased and 4 injured from its fund. The amount of compensation is to be calculated by the trial court taking into account the age, income of the deceased and the injured in the light of the provisions of Section 163-A and Second Schedule of the Motor Vehicles Act, 1988. In absence of any documentary proof of any of the victim, trial court will calculate the income of the victim on the basis of minimum wage payable on the date of occurrence. After calculating the amount of compensation, appropriate order for payment of compensation shall be passed by the trial court within twelve weeks of the receipt of this judgment directing the Collector, Arwal to make payment to the next of the kin of the 58 deceased and 4 injured, of course after adjusting ex gratia amount already paid to the next of the kin of the 58 deceased and the 4 injured. Payment in compliance of this judgment be made to the concerned by the Collector, Arwal within four weeks from the date of receipt of the order for payment of compensation from the trial court" (Judgment, Patna High Court, 2013, Paragraph 78).

The surviving family members of the massacre which took place at Laxmanpur Bathe in 1997 are still yearning for justice. A Special Leave Petition (SLP) filed in the Supreme Court is pending, and how much time it would take before judgement is delivered is still unknown. In other words the long and tortuous road to justice is still replete with uncertainty. But it would be good to analyse the High Court judgement. By finding fault with the prosecution, by disbelieving the witnesses who were mostly the victim's family members and by setting aside the trial court's verdict of 2010, thereby setting free/acquitting all the accused, leave a bad taste when one considers the brutality with which the carnage took place at Laxmanpur Bathe in 1997. The alleged perpetrators were convicted by the trial court at Patna and were accordingly awarded death sentence and life imprisonment and imposed monetary fines as well. But the manner in which the trial court verdict was set aside and the accused allowed to go scot-free is clearly an example of institutionalized impunity that afflicts the criminal justice system in the country. The order directed the trial court to calculate the amount of compensation by taking in to consideration the age, income of the deceased and the injured in the light of the provisions of Section 163-A and Second Schedule of the Motor Vehicles Act 1988. In absence of any documentary proof of any of the victim, trial court will calculate the income of the victim on the basis of minimum wage payable on the date of occurrence. This is highly unwarranted, and in any case which is filed under SC and ST (Prevention of Atrocities) Act, the judges should take in to account the provisions of the SC and ST (Prevention of Atrocities) Rules 1995. On the question of awarding compensation to the bereaved families, why did the two judge benches not invoke POA Rules 1995? PoA Act and PoA Rules are part of the legal system, and by not invoking them is a clear case of willful negligence. The Supreme Court must look in to this aspect as well whenever it hears the SLP.

On the question of prosecution not doing their job of investigation in a proper manner, why did the two judge benches not order for action against the police officials who were entrusted with the task of investigation of the Laxmanpur-Bathe massacre? It is quite strange also to note that nowhere in the judgement the High Court judges question whether proper investigation and awarding compensation to the bereaved families were carried out as per the provisions of the SC and ST (Prevention of Atrocities) Act 1989 and Rules 1995. The two judge benches also did not recommend another/new investigation in the case. This is quite baffling and remains unanswered till date. Whether Supreme Court would take a stand on these aspects remains unclear as of now.

8 Low Conviction and Large Number of Acquittals

It is but a fact that every year a good number of cases under Protection of Civil Rights (PCR) Act end in acquittal. On this score the report of the committee on untouchability, etc., which was set up in 1969, pointed out (Kshirsagar, 1989, pp. 249–50): "The complainants are compelled under duress to compromise with the case. The complainants fail to produce, sufficient cogent evidence to convince the judge. It is because of their socio-economic backwardness and apathy of caste Hindus towards them; which becomes hindrance in getting independent evidence for them".

Procedural lacuna comes in the way of social justice, and the police officers do not undertake expeditious and flawless investigation nor they have the interest to do so. The case ends in acquittal mainly because of the apathetic attitude of the judicial magistrates. They do not trust the evidence given by the Scheduled Castes saying that they are "interested witness" considering that vast majorities of Dalits are illiterate and live in rural areas without adequate means of communication, and it can hardly be taken for granted the requisite awareness and understanding on their part of the various constitutional provisions and legal measures which are meant for their benefit. Even if it is presumed that a Dalit is aware of the legal measures guaranteeing protection to him, the complainant and the witnesses needed to prove their cases are extremely vulnerable to intimidation and reprisal, as they are very often economically dependent upon higher caste for livelihood. Except in cases where outsiders are involved, witnesses other than their caste fellows are ordinarily not forthcoming. And if also a good case, he/she is in all likelihood to be subjected to pressure to compound it (Galanter, 1972, pp. 276–77).

Courts constitute the micro-level institutional arrangement which a Dalit is required to approach in order to secure protection or obtain the privileges guaranteed to him/her by legislations formulated at the macro-level. But our courts have become notoriously proverbial for the mess called interpretation. This is so because the Constitution, in its "practice in any form" or "a disability arising out of untouchability", has been guided by judicial interpretation (Jayaram, 1986, p. 17). And interpretations of laws relating to the Scheduled Castes seems to have made convictions more difficult to secure and thus enable the guilty to escape. Protracted delay substantially reduces the chances of conviction. Thus Marc Galanter very rightly noted: "the more the acquittals, the less the Act will be used; and the less it is used, the more difficult it will be for judges to make the extraordinary exertions required to carry out its original policy" (Galanter op.cit: 261).

9 The Role of Media

The media plays a significant role not only in moulding the public opinion but also at the same time in sensitizing and spreading awareness about various social evils. As far as reporting of Dalits and other vulnerable section of society is concerned, it is highly under-reported. The media in this country is owned and dominated by big industrial houses belonging to the upper strata of society. There is no representation of Dalits in the media world. This has been testified by a finding by a journalist in 1996. There is not even a single Dalit correspondent/journalist out of the total 686 Accreditation Index, 1996, of the Press Information Bureau, Government of India (Uniyal, 1996).

It can be said without any doubt that media always loves to sensationalize some of the major cases of human rights violation of Dalits and other equally vulnerable groups. But at the same time it has failed to sensitize the public at large about Dalits.

Portrayal of news in correct perspective has always been made a victim by the vested interests and also most of the times by the media men themselves in Bihar. It is no wonder then that violent outbursts by Dalits against continued socio-economic oppression in the countryside are quite often described as antisocial, anti-national Naxalite activities though the Dalits may not be directly attached with any Naxalite group. The media in Bihar has time and again lent credence to the official version of fake encounter killings in the name of countering Naxalite menace. Though it has also been a fact that innocent agricultural workers most of whom happen to be Dalits have been killed in these so-called encounters. The fake encounter killings of Dalit agricultural labourers by the police have been testified by the fact-finding teams of Peoples Union for Democratic Rights, Peoples Union for Civil Liberties (PUDR, PUCL) and other human rights organizations. But the local media in Bihar never bothers to expose the misdeeds of police in this connection. During 1977–1978 and 1982, it was observed many times that anti-reservation disturbances all over Bihar by the Hindu groups were propagated as a very big people's movement by the media in Bihar (Urmilesh, 1991, pp. 194–195).

As a matter of fact any progressive ideology, movement and government measures against the well-entrenched traditional socio-economic and political order have found very negligible and at times very reactionary response from the press in Bihar. And this has been an old practice which has continued even in the contemporary period. The reaction of "*Indian Nation*", a leading English Daily published from Patna, to the land reform measures of the Bihar government in the year 1948 is very illustrative: "The fire of power politics is consuming his whole being. The Revenue Minister is evidently insensible to the fact that the Zamindari Abolition

Bill when enacted will upset the rural economy. The Revenue Minister is either one-eyed or wilfully blind. Bihar is screeching under the stewardship of an aggressive politician who has no vision and faith but who is obstinate and petty" (Indian Nation, 1948).

News related to human rights violation of Dalits never finds the space it deserves. Large-scale massacres only seem to have a news value for the newspapers. Media has also failed to inform and educate people about various constitutional provisions meant for protection of human rights of the disadvantaged sections of Indian society. It is no wonder then that media has served the interest of the status quo of its caste Hindu forces. One may claim that a new breed of journalists has reported various gross violation of human rights through media from Bihar, but mere reporting may not be enough. The media must play a revolutionary role for social, cultural and economic transformation. This seems to be a near-impossible task in the time of make-believe world of status quoism, commercialization and consumerism. The caste Hindu-controlled media has thoroughly failed to give space and voice to the disadvantaged sections of Indian society. In this age of sensationalism, the media helps in creating spectacle on many occasions. The editorial may be quite rational, but the news reporting citing sources (undefined) has become a norm which is rigorously followed. The only newsworthy items are those events where a killing has happened, a gang rape is reported, houses have been burnt down, etc. Otherwise everyday human rights violation is never paid any attention to by the editors/reporters, and even awareness-raising activities are also not adhered to by them.

References

Appu, P. S. (1993). A Modest Performance for the Nineties. In B. N. Yugandhar & K. Gopal Aiyar (Eds.), *Land Reforms in India, 1: Bihar- Institutional Constraints* (p. 53). Sage Publication.

Bhagwati, P. N. (1984, January 21). Law, Justice and the Underprivileged, *Mainstream*, 20–24.

Bharti, I. (1990). Farce of Farm Wage Hike. *Economic and Political Weekly, 15*(8), 1512.

Bhatia, B. (2013). Justice Not Vengeance: The Bathani Tola Massacre and the Ranveer Sena in Bihar. *Economic and Political Weekly, XLVIII*(38), 49.

Chakravarti, A. (2001, April 28). Caste and Agrarian Class: A View from Bihar, *Economic and Political Weekly*, 1453.

Cited in Kshirsagar, R. K. (1989). *Untouchability in India: Implementation of the Law and Abolition* (pp. 249–250). Deep & Deep Publications.

Crime in India, National Crime Record Bureau. (1997). *Ministry of Home Affairs*. Government of India. 148–49 & 158–59.

Daftuar, A. K. (1986). *Harijan Thanas in Bihar: A Case Study* (pp. 9–20). A. N. Sinha Institute of Social Studies.

Dhar, H. (2000). Institutional Constraints to Land Reforms in Bihar. In B. K. Sinha & Pushpendra (Eds.), *Land Reforms in India, Vol. 5: An Unfinished Agenda* (pp. 124–138). Sage Publication.

Economic Times. (2010, April 08). 16 Gets Death in 1997 Dalit Carnage in Bihar.

Frankel, F. R. (1993). Caste, Land and Dominance in Bihar. In F. R. Frankel & M. S. A. Rao (Eds.), *Dominance and State Power in India* (p. 96). Oxford University Press.

Galanter, M. (1972). The Abolition of Disabilities: Untouchability and the Law. In J. M. Mahar (Ed.), *The Untouchability in the Contemporary India* (pp. 276–277). Arizona University Press.

Godbole, M. (1997, February 14). "Crime and Punishments", Times of India.
Indian Express. (1977, July 16). The Belchi Massacre.
Indian Express. (1996, July 26). Officials Ignored Pleas.
Indian Nation. (1948, April 6). *quoted in D. Thakur's, Politics of Land Reform in India, 1989*, Commonwealth Publishers, 43.
Jannuzi, F. T. (1974). *Agrarian Crisis in India: The Case of Bihar* (p. 33). Sangam Books.
Jayaram, N. (1986, May 17). "Can Law Save Scheduled Castes?" *Mainstream*, 17.
Judgment. (2012). Patna High Court, Death Reference No. 7 of 2010. Retrieved from https://patnahighcourt.gov.in/viewjudgment/MjgjNyMyMDEwIzEjTw==-uDyC5JSla0Y=
Judgment. (2013). Patna High Court, Death Reference No. 5 of 2010. Retrieved from https://patnahighcourt.gov.in/viewjudgment/MjgjNSMyMDEwIzEjTw==-Snu8Zq8w8S8=
Kohli, A. (1992). *Democracy and Discontent: India's Growing Crisis of Governability* (pp. 236–237). Cambridge University Press, Foundation Books.
Mathew, M. (1997, December 03). Bloodbath thy name is Bihar, Hindustan Times.
Mohsin, N. (1984). *Rural Development through Government Programmes* (p. 60). A. N. Sinha Institute of Social Studies.
National Herald. (1978, October 20). Tensions in Bihar.
New Age. (1978, December 24). Police Mute Spectator to Chopping of Harijan Heads, *XXVI*(52).
Ojha, G. (1977). *Land Problems and Land Reforms* (p. 122). New Delhi.
Pandey, M. P. (1979). *Land Records and Agrarian Situation in Bihar* (pp. 35–43). A.N.Sinha Institute of Social Studies.
Patnaik, B. N. (1990). *Harijan's Franchise- An Alibi of Class Conflict (A Case Study of Danwar-Bihta Massacre)* (pp. 1–25). A. N. Sinha Institute of Social Studies.
Prasad, A. (1986). *Impact of the Special Component Programme on the Harijans in Bihar* (p. 77). A.N. Sinha Institute of Social Studies. 87-89.
Report. (1981). *Agrarian Unrest in Patna* (p. 4). People's Union for Democratic Rights (PUDR). 21 & 28.
Report. (1983). *Jehanabad- Peasant Movement and Police Repression* (pp. 1–18). People's Union for Democratic Rights (PUDR) &People's Union for Civil Liberties (PUCL- Bihar).
Report. (1992). *Bitter Harvest: The Roots of Agrarian Massacres in Central Bihar* (p. 30 & 34-36). People's Union for Democratic Rights (PUDR).
Report. (1996a). *Encounters: A Report on Land Struggles in Bihar* (pp. 6–9). Peoples' Union for Democratic Rights (PUDR).
Report. (1997). *Agrarian Conflict in Bihar and the Ranveer Sena* (p. 6). Peoples' Union for Democratic Rights (PUDR).
Report. (1998a–99). National Commission for Scheduled Castes and Scheduled Tribes (NCSCST), Vol. 2, Chapter III, New Delhi, Government of India.
Report. (1998b-99), National Commission for Scheduled Castes and Scheduled Tribes (NCSCST), New Delhi, Government of India, 28–29.
Report. (2016). *Harvesting Death: Massacres in Bihar and the Question of Justice* (pp. 20–21). Peoples Union for Democratic Rights (PUDR). & 24-25.
Report. (1996b-97). National Commission for Scheduled Castes and Scheduled Tribes, New Delhi, Government of India, 241–42.
Report. (1980). National Police Commission, "Police and the Weaker Sections of Society", Chapter 19, New Delhi, Government of India, 4.
Report. (2021). *Government Compliance with Supreme Court Directives on Police Reforms* (p. 2). New Delhi.
Report. (1982–83 & 1983–84). SC and ST commission, New Delhi, Government of India.
Scheduled Caste Cell. (1994). *Crime Investigation Department*. Patna.
Sinha, K. K. (1987). *Antyodaya and Development, Patna*. A. N. Sinha Institute of Social Studies.
Sinha, U. (1985, March 2), Teaching the Landless a Lesson, *Economic and Political Weekly*. 343.
The Telegraph. (1988, February 23). Harijan Killers Go Scot Free in Jehanabad.
The Hindu. (2012, April 19). For Residents of Bathani, It is a Horror They Cannot Forget.

The Hindu. (1996, July 12). Laloo's Land or Lawless Land.

The Times of India. (2000, April 29). Govt Sleeps as Ranveer Sena Killings Peak.

The Times of India. (1986, July 12). Another Carnage in Bihar.

The Times of India. (1996, July 17). Bihar Carnage is a Socio-Political Problem.

The Week. (1999, May 14). Gandhi with a Gun, 19.

Umakant. (2012, December 28). *Violence against Women: Is Anyone Listening?, New Delhi, Hard News Magazine, Web Edition*. Retrieved from http://www.hardnewsmedia.com/2012/12/5750. Also available on: https://www.kractivist.org/india-violence-against-women-is-anyone-listening-vaw-womenrights/

Uniyal, B. N. (1996, November 16). In Search of a Dalit Journalist, Pioneer.

Urmilesh, Bihar Ka Sach. (Hindi- 1991). New Delhi, Prakashan Sansthan, 194–95.

Verma, R. (1987). *I.R.D.P. among the Harijans and Adivasis in Bihar* (p. 174). A.N. Sinha Institute.

Conclusion

Abstract The concluding chapter is an attempt for overall analysis of the situational analysis of the Dalit human rights violations at all levels in India with a special focus on Bihar. In this exercise the post-Laxmanpur Bathe caste of the caste carnage and other violations of Dalit human rights in Bihar have also been looked into. An attempt has been made to use the latest data available through "Caste Survey" undertaken by the government of Bihar along with other resource materials which have made the task easier to understand why the Indian state and society at large need to pay more attention to the issues related to Dalit human rights.

Keywords Untouchability Offence Act 1955 · Protection of Civil Rights Act 1976 · Scheduled Castes and Scheduled Tribes (Prevention of Atrocities) Act 1989 and 2016 · Caste-based militia in Bihar · Ranveer Sena · The National Commission for Scheduled Castes (NCSC) · Nagari Bazaar, Shankarbigha · Miyapur · Ranveer Sena chief shot dead · Dalits and right to development · Mahadalits in Bihar · Dalits and land reforms in Bihar

Dalit human rights are not something that could be done away with, but the state and society at large have been found wanting on this score. For human rights to become a reality, it is necessary that a country and its political system should be founded on a Constitution entrusted with the task of creating an egalitarian society based on the principles of liberty, equality and fraternity wherein justice, human rights and accountability of the state should be a paramount concern and also a duty to be performed. Why should Dalits be forced to live a life of misery, deprivation, untouchability, atrocities, exclusion and all kinds of violence perpetrated on them? And why have these issues remained unaddressed. The state and the society at large are to be squarely blamed for not granting equal status, dignity and justice to Dalits in every possible manner. The constitutional provisions and set of legislations along

UMAKANT, *Dalit Human Rights in India*, People, Cultures and Societies: Exploring and Documenting Diversities,
https://doi.org/10.1007/978-981-95-5751-6_6

with special programmes and policies by the government would not be able to perform in a judicious manner in the absence of due diligence and accountability mechanisms.

The Untouchability Offence Act 1955 which was rechristened as Protection of Civil Rights Act in 1976 failed to curb the growing cases of atrocities which were being committed on Dalits and Adivasis all across the country. That is why a new legislation in the form of Scheduled Castes and Scheduled Tribes (Prevention of Atrocities) Act 1989 was introduced. And that too has been replaced with an amended version in 2016 after notification in the Gazette of India Extraordinary on January 1, 2016, which came in to force with effect from January 26, 2016. The special legislations along with other laws like Indian Penal Code (IPC), etc., included in the Indian law book have either failed to check the growing crimes against Dalits and Adivasis, or perhaps it has not been possible for the government and law enforcing organs of the state to create an enabling atmosphere for due diligence and accountability mechanisms.

The Brahmanical caste system has an over-bearing influence on every aspect of human life in this part of the world. The duty bearers/officials who are entrusted with the task of implementing the legislations and special targeted programmes and policies of the government, majority of which belongs to non-Adivasi and non-Dalit background, are to be held responsible for poor track record on this question. Laws do not operate in isolation; on the contrary they operate in a socio-religious and cultural context which is highly discriminatory towards Dalits and Adivasis. Many a times it has also been observed that victims are blamed for their misery and violence inflicted on them by the society at large. The deprived community people from Dalit and Adivasi background do assert to be treated equally at par with everyone else, or in other words, any attempt to falsely implicate them in criminal/illegal activities put their life in danger. Caste privileges that are enjoyed by the upper echelons of Indian society have remained hereditary in every possible sense of the term. There is no attempt to make Indian society, economy and polity into an egalitarian system based on the principles of liberty, equality and fraternity. That has remained a goal enshrined in the Constitution of India. The ground realities to a large extent are completely different. There is antiquity and also continuity which rules the mindset of people which gets reflected in multiple ways in everyday life in this part of the world. Constitutional morality is completely absent from the public domain and discourse. This also poses a question: “How could the state be made liberal and progressive when society, religion, culture and people to a large extent are illiberal and conservative?”

Any and every attempt to present a rosy picture of India marching ahead with full glory is highly deceptive. The lived experiences of discrimination, exclusion and violence which happens on a regular basis in the life of average Dalits and Adivasis in the country expose the “Shining India” or “Incredible India” claim. India may send a mission to the Moon successfully, but why should manual scavengers be forced to get into the sewer/gutter to clean it with bare hands? Why should the millennia-old Brahmanical caste system still exist and operate in the most vehement ways? When would social and economic democracy along with political democracy become a reality? Why have social transformation and economic emancipation not happened for the wretched of the earth? These and many other similar questions have still remained unanswered.

There is a need to crack institutionalized impunity and also to hold the state and society at large accountable when we talk about human rights. For human rights of Dalits to be accorded a top priority, what is needed most importantly is to acknowledge that state and society at large have not been sincere enough in treating them at par with everyone else, and secondly all the symbols and practices which are against human rights should be abolished forever and for good. Until and unless that happens, all talk on human rights would remain meaningless. Human rights cannot be seen in bits and pieces. It has to be seen in its totality. Rights and privileges for some and duties and slavery for the other great mass of people can never pave the way for establishing an egalitarian society.

It would be instructive to quote Ambedkar to help us understand the ways through which the goal of egalitarianism could be achieved. On November 25, 1949, Dr. Ambedkar made a speech in the Constituent Assembly:

> From 26 January 1950, we are going to enter into a life of contradictions. In politics we will have equality i.e. one man one vote and one vote one value but in social and economic life we will still have inequality .....We must remove this contradiction at the earliest possible time or else those who suffer from inequality will blow up the structure of political democracy which we have so labouriously built-up (Ambedkar, cited in Gore 1993, p. 187).

As of now more than 75 years have passed since India attained independence from the British rule, and in this long journey, Dalits' lived experiences have been quite painful. More than 50,000 cases of cognizable crimes are being reported from across the country at police stations on a regular basis. The state, its different agencies and society at large have thoroughly failed to treat Dalits in general and Dalit human rights issues in particular in equal measures. On a varying degree untouchability is practised almost everywhere in the country. Even at the time of golden jubilee of India's independence, this is how the situation looked like. After 50 years of independence and democratic rule, the exploitation and atrocities on Dalits have increased manifold. It is clear that gains of development have reached the intended class and have been usurped by the better off in many cases. The very will to give priority to the upliftment of SCs/STs in the National Agenda is missing. Caste-based atrocities and untouchability practices are rampant and still growing over the years. The poor educational facilities, lack of representation in governance sector and services under central and state governments and no progress for economic emancipation coupled with inadequate budgetary allocation for development programmes related to SCs/STs have been the hallmark of ground situation (NCSCST, 1994–1995 & 1995–1996, pp. I–V).

The nation seems to have reneged on its promise of abolishing the practice of untouchability and establishment of an egalitarian society. As a matter of fact several centuries of uninterrupted and ritualistic adherence to the values of caste by the people and nurturing of these values by the social, religious, cultural and political systems have left the untouchables victims of oppressive inequalities. In other words, the caste system, through a series of orthogenetic modifications, created an environment in which the human cravings for freedom, equality, respect and dignity lay deeply buried under the weight of a tradition that sought to actively rob the human personality of its capacities departing of from that tradition (Khosla, 1987, pp. 6–7).

An important aspect of the current Indian social reality which powerfully illustrates the contradictions of Indian development and the need for the adoption of new approaches towards and understanding of them is the violence that is regularly and systematically inflicted against the Scheduled Castes by the more powerful caste Hindu groups and classes, especially in the rural areas. This is to further state that the violence against the Scheduled Castes is not a law and order or administrative problem. At the bottom, it is a socio-economic problem and arises out of the deeper process at work in the economic, social and political structures (Subramanian, 1987, p. 28).

The traditionally oppressed, the overwhelming majority of which are drawn from the lowest rungs of the traditional social hierarchy, continue to suffer on many counts. They are today the inequitable victims of the manifest professional inefficiency of the state apparatus as well as the social bias built within the democratic institutions. They are also the inequitable victims of its petty corruption and brutalized excesses, both in the urban areas and in the rural areas. They also find the process of legal redress against violation of their democratic rights or executives excesses too risky (often involving punitive terrorization by hired musclemen in league with corrupt police men). They find the fragmented party system and the middle class-led electoral process too weak to provide political defence against the social bias of the upper caste-dominated democratic institutions (Ray, 1986, p. 1203).

The Universal Declaration of Human Rights in 1948 found similar provisions in the Indian Constitution. But, as a matter of fact, the socio-economic base of the Indian political system has acted as a great barrier for establishment of an egalitarian society. Despite the constitutional mandate for uplift and against exploitation, the Dalits are still at the receiving end and also have been the victims of worst kind of crimes against humanity. The noble ideas in the form of rules and regulations for providing a better deal to the unfortunate social outcastes have remained only on paper. The crime against Dalits does not seem to disturb the nation's conscience. Occasionally, sympathies do come at times but have not been able to overpower the monster which strikes at its will at regular intervals against Dalits in various forms. In the Indian village republic, there is no place for democracy, equality, liberty and fraternity. In fact "the Indian village is a negation of republic. The republic is an empire of the Hindus over the untouchables. The untouchables have no rights because they are outside the village republic. For them there is no equal right and justice" (Ambedkar, 1989, p. 25).

Effective implementation of any legislation requires administrative rigours and more than that social and political will. In the absence of this, the real objectives of legislations are bound to be forsaken. Dr. B.R. Ambedkar had rightly emphasized, "rights are protected not merely by law, but also by the moral and social conscience of the society" (Ibid: 99).

The practice of untouchability, economic backwardness and non-implementation of land reforms have been the prime factors responsible for human rights violations of Dalits in erstwhile central Bihar and elsewhere. The post-independence abolition of zamindari and land reform has left the Dalits and agricultural labourers completely untouched. All the benefits of land reforms and green revolution production enhancement strategy have remained confined to the forward castes and upper sections of the backward castes such as the Yadavs, the Kurmis and the Koeris. Enforcement of the land ceiling act and the distribution of surplus land remained a non-starter in Bihar. In many cases, the ownership rights have been given to the Dalit families, but the land remained in possession of landlords. Attempts to recover "gairmazarua" land from the illegal possession of land lords remain a major source of discontent. Thus, the non-implementation of land reforms has left this vast section of labourers many of whom are Dalits, without even a small patch of land.

Disparities in the socio-economic hierarchy run alongside the caste hierarchy throughout Bihar although the degree of relationship may differ in some districts. Dalits invariably fall in the lowest category both socially and economically. The virtual dependence on others for survival has made the Dalits vulnerable to large-scale human rights violations. Wages for agricultural labourers have been abysmally low in Bihar. The Dalits and lower rung of backward castes, who constitute an overwhelming majority of agricultural labourers, have remained completely assetless. The economic divide has a caste pattern also. The agricultural workers not only face economic exploitation but also undergo the worst kind of discrimination. The attempts by Dalits and the landless labourers to organize themselves for their self-respect and other legitimate rights related to land and wages have always been viciously opposed by the landowning castes in several ways. Massacres have been rooted in the social reality of Bihar, and they fairly have a long history. Whether it was Belchi in 1977, Pipra in 1980, Arwal in 1986, Bathani Tola in 1996 or Laxmanpur Bathe in 1997, the Dalits have been victims of the sheer brutality of upper castes, middle castes and also at times the state itself.

However, from the late 1970s and onwards, the erstwhile central Bihar witnessed organized resistance by the oppressed people to which landowning castes responded by forming their so-called private armies. Bhoomi Sena, Lorik Sena, Brahmarshi Sena, Diamond Sena and Ranveer Sena have been involved in causing havoc in the lives of Dalits in central Bihar. The entire state machinery—right from the block level to the top—was and still remained tilted in favour of the landowning castes. Despite many incidents of massacres, there has not been a single instance of a police encounter with any of the private senas. The connivance of the local administration and the lack of political will as well as state patronage and support of various political formations have been responsible for the rise of different caste senas in Bihar.

On the other hand, the growing activism of Bihar rural poor, majority of whom were Dalits, must be understood in part as an attempt to resist the imposition of harsher patterns of domination. Absolute poverty may be debilitating, but even absolute poverty has limits. The steady pressure generated by nearly stagnant rural incomes and the simultaneous increase in agrarian militancy appeared to be logically connected. The absence of economic dynamism did provide the broad content for the increasing hostilities, but it was not a sufficient explanation. It may explain the caste class conflicts, but it certainly will not do as an explanation for the growing police brutality. Clearly other factors were also at work.

The fact cannot be denied that in the erstwhile central Bihar and elsewhere it was not exactly a class war, which was the main force behind the violent scene. It was both a caste and a status war: a war in which the origin of trouble in many cases may perhaps be economic, but in its actual occurrence, it became a caste war. Caste consciousness was as much real, perhaps more real than the class consciousness which simply did not play much significant role. The radical groups which have been operative in the region from 1970 onwards have no doubt raised the awareness level of the poor peasantry including Dalits regarding the exploitative economic relationship in the villages about the question of lands, minimum wages and other similar issues. On this score the radical groups have done a highly commendable job. But as a matter of fact in the caste-ridden society in the erstwhile central Bihar and elsewhere too, the class approach does not seem to have made much or rather any significant impact at all. This is also to say that radical groups failed to develop an anti-caste ideology/approach while dealing with the problems of Dalits in particular and other weaker sections in general. It has always been caste which determines the status of an individual in society which also has a wide ramification for economic and political fields. And this is precisely the reason that because of low status in social order which is based on the principles of graded inequality, the Dalits have been at the receiving end in every possible sense of the term. The practice of untouchability and other related exploitative systems have been responsible for human rights violation of Dalits in multiple forms. Poor Dalits and poor non-Dalits do not share equal status in society. The problems faced by Dalits are unique in the sense that social ostracism and humiliation which a Dalit faces are not faced by any other sections of society. The Dalit hamlets are always found to be located outside the main villages.

Any movement on behalf of the Dalits must develop an anti-caste ideology/approach. Moreover the patron-client approach has no relevance. Leadership must be in the hands of Dalits themselves. On these scores the radical groups have failed miserably. The leadership have always been in the hands of upper castes who claim to be radicals, whereas on the other hand the party workers are mainly Dalits. And invariably Dalits have been the victims of upper caste marauders in majority of caste-based attacks and not the upper caste leaders of these radical groups, though they claim to fight on behalf of Dalits. It will be very instructive once again to quote Dr. Ambedkar when he said:

> It is usual to hear all those who feel moved by the deplorable condition of the untouchables unburden themselves by uttering the cry 'we must do something for the untouchables'. One seldom hears any of the persons interested in the problems saying 'Let us do something to change the touchable Hindu'. It is invariably assumed that the object to be reclaimed is the untouchables. If there is to be a mission, it must be to the untouchables, and if the untouchables can be cured, untouchability will vanish. Nothing requires to be done to the touchables. He is sound in mind, manners and morals. He is whole; there is nothing wrong with

> him. Is this assumption correct? Whether correct or not, the Hindus like to cling to it. The assumption has the supreme merit of satisfying themselves that they are not responsible for the problem of the untouchables (Ambedkar op.cit: 3).

It is in the light of these observations that the radical groups and voluntary organizations, who sympathize with and fight for the Dalits, have failed to develop any genuine revolutionary movement of social transformation and economic emancipation. In other words, an anti-caste ideology and strategies for socio-economic democratization were never part of these left radical organizations. And that is why they failed to bring or even contribute in practising an emancipatory agenda which could have paved the way for social transformation and economic emancipation. Moreover, could the radical organizations like CPI (ML), IPF, BPKS, CPI (ML)-Party Unity and MKSS clarify why in their leadership ranks there was no space for Dalits and other lower caste persons?

Despite several protections as guaranteed by the Constitution of India, the Dalits are forced to live a life of misery and insecurity, and even children are not safe. A minor Dalit girl who was raped and found with nearly 20 knife wounds in Muzaffarpur died at the Patna Medical College and Hospital (PMCH) on June 1, 2025. The brutal assault took place on May 26, the police said. The 11-year-old was transferred to Patna on May 30 for better medical treatment but was allegedly left in pain inside the ambulance outside the Patna hospital for about 5 h and was admitted after intervention by Bihar Congress president Rajesh Kumar. The police said the girl was found with nearly 20 knife injuries on and around her neck in a pit at a brick kiln. A first information report (FIR) was lodged against a 30-year-old man on the complaint of the girl's uncle, and the accused was arrested in the same evening (The Hindu, 2025a). This is not an isolated incident as similar and other cases of atrocities are being reported almost on everyday basis.

In a bizarre yet sad incident a Dalit Member of Legislative Assembly (MLA) belonging to CPI (ML) was stopped from inaugurating a school building in Bihar on January 26, 2025. CPI (ML) legislator Gopal Ravidas lodged a complaint accusing locals of not allowing him to inaugurate a building of a government school because he belongs to a Scheduled Caste. The incident took place under Parsa Bazar police station limits in Patna district of Bihar. Based on the complaint, police have registered a first information report (FIR) and imposed several sections of Scheduled Castes and the Scheduled Tribes (Prevention of Atrocities) Act 1989. While speaking to *The Hindu*, Mr. Ravidas said: "I along with my supporters went to inaugurate the new building of the government school (higher secondary), which has been built on my recommendation. As soon as I reached there at 3 p.m., around 50 people from the dominant caste started protesting against me. In the crowd, some people said that *dome chamar and dusadh* (Scheduled Caste communities) will not inaugurate the school building and rather it would be inaugurated by the people from their caste" (The Hindu, 2025b). The question that needs to be asked is how long could/would Dalits be forced to live a life devoid of dignity, human rights and equal citizenship?

The nature of state is supposed to be geared up for bringing socio-economic revolution and the establishment of an egalitarian society. The experience so far has been such that seven and a half decades of free and democratic governance have belied this claim up to a great extent. Neither the initiatives for socio-economic transformation have been realized to a great extent nor any substantial work for establishing an egalitarian society has taken any shape. However, this is not to suggest that no change has taken place at all. But it would not be wrong to say that broad-based socio-economic transformation has not taken place. The country has witnessed tremendous growth in agriculture, science and technology and other sectors, but at the same time, a large majority of India's population has remained untouched. They are the most despised and most backward: the Dalits.

Despite constitutional mandate the practice of untouchability continues unabated in various forms and degrees. Various laws have been passed and put into use like the Untouchability Offence Act 1955, Rechristened as Protection of Civil Rights Act and then the Prevention of Atrocities Act 1989, but the plight of the Dalits remains as ever. In fact they have worsened in recent times. Dalits are still struggling/fighting for freedom, dignity and justice all over the country, and Bihar is not an exception. The state as an effective and powerful institution has undoubtedly failed in its duty of creating awareness and togetherness among various sections of society. The institution of Panchayati Raj and other similar democratic forums which were supposed to integrate the downtrodden into the social and national mainstream have remained the hegemonistic organ of dominant caste Hindu groups. The empowerment of Dalits and other weaker sections of society, however noble they may be, remains a pipe dream.

The lopsided development and various loopholes in the welfare programmes have not led to trickledown effect on vast majority of people. Crores are spent in the name of rural development and even Special Component Plans for Dalits, but ineffective implementation has proved to be a bane in this regard. Non-implementation of land reforms and subsequent land ceiling continue to remain a source of conflict among the landowning castes and agricultural labourers, who mostly happen to be Dalits. Successive political parties in power over the years have provided conscious support to various obscurantist upper caste groups and factions to maintain hegemony in society as well as control over the state machineries and also to browbeat any challenge to their supremacy from any quarter. The existence of the Ranveer Sena and its various previous avatars which also included some backward caste sena (militia) like Bhumi Sena and Lorik Sena is a classic example in this regard. Even police in connivance with local upper/middle caste landlords, letting loose a region of terror on Dalits in the erstwhile central Bihar and elsewhere, has become a fact of life.

1 Dalit Human Rights Violations Continues Unabated

The caste-based atrocities, killings and other violations did not stop with major massacre of Dalits at Laxmanpur Bathe in 1997. However, on a similar scale it has been continuing unabated on a regular basis. On seeing the pattern of caste-based violence that takes place, it is very clear that in a situation of more assertion by Dalits and other disadvantaged sections of society for better sociocultural and economic rights, there is bound to be more retaliation from the privileged sections/high caste people so as to maintain their stranglehold and status quo in society, economy and polity.

Bihar ranked second in the country in terms of crimes against SCs, chairman of the National Commission for Scheduled Castes (NCSC), Vijay Sampla, said on May 19, 2023, while expressing concern over the spurt in crimes against those from marginalized communities in Bihar. The NCSC chairman came down heavily on the state government for its alleged failure to protect the lives and interests of SCs. "Bihar ranks second in the dreaded list of states where murders of persons from SCs & STs were reported. The state government has not taken any concrete steps to check crimes against these communities," he said. The data provided by Bihar during meetings with NCSC members made it clear that the administration failed to provide benefits of the state and central governments' social, economic and welfare schemes to the SC community, he said after concluding a two-day state-level review meeting. Special drive to fill the vacant post belonging to SCs must be taken up on a priority basis, and the state government should also pay attention to the problem of almost 80% Dalit students dropping out of schools (India Today, 2023).

In the same press conference the NCSC Chairperson also raised some other concerns. While expressing disappointment over the fact that the state has only six hostels for the SC girl students, he ordered the state government to set up at least one hostel for SC girls in every district and ensure pre-matric scholarship to every SC child. Sampla, in a statement, further claimed that the status of disbursement of post-matric scholarship to the SC students in Bihar remained unsatisfactory. Data revealed that of the 3,51,730 SC students of Bihar in 2019–2020, only 61,489 students were able to apply for scholarship through the portal, while only 43,626 of them could receive the scholarship benefits. Similarly, in the 2020–2021, out of 4, 50,000 students, only 77,182 received scholarships. "It is also a matter of concern that the number of scheduled caste families getting benefits under MGNREGA is continuously decreasing in Bihar. In 2017-18, only 21.72% of the benefited families belonged to scheduled castes, while the number further decreased to only 11.56% in 2020-21", Sampla said and ordered the government to take effective steps immediately to ensure that employment is provided under MNREGA to the SC community (The Times of India, 2023a, 2023b).

As per Crime in India 2022, the total number of reported cases of cognizable crimes against Dalits in Bihar stood at 6509.

Case pending trial from the previous year: 53,387
Cases sent for trials during the year 2021: 5,135
Total cases for trials: 58,522
Total conviction: 146
Total acquittals: 193
Cases in which trials completed: 339
Cases pending investigation at the end of the year: 6,857

Cases disposed of by courts: 339
Cases pending trial at the end of the year 2022: 58183
Conviction rate: 43.1%
Pendency percentage in the courts: 99.4%

The figures mentioned above clearly mark the rising graph of cognizable crimes against Dalits over the years. What is also clear from the data mentioned above is the fact that Bihar had 20.51% of atrocities-related cases pending for trial at the end of year 2022. On the other hand, there were about 35.91% of atrocities-related cases pending police investigation in Bihar at the end of the year 2022. This places the state among the worst performers as far as criminal justice administration is concerned.

The total number of cases of cognizable crimes committed against Dalits from 1998 onwards up to the year 2021 remained a testimony to this unpleasant truth about Dalit human rights situation in the state. The number of caste-based atrocities and other crimes as compiled by the National Crime Record Bureau is mentioned here to further probe the precarious lives of Dalits in a state like Bihar (Table 1).

The other facts at the end of year 2021 were as follows (Crime in India, 2021):

Case pending trial from the previous year: 48,953
Cases sent for trials during the year 2021: 4,588
Total cases for trials: 53,541
Cases pending investigation at the end of the year: 6,087
Total conviction: 48
Total acquittals: 106
Cases in which trials completed: 154
Cases disposed of by courts: 154

Table 1 Reported cases of cognizable crimes against Dalits in Bihar (1998–2021)

Year	No. of cognizable crimes reported	Year	No. of cognizable crimes reported
1998	785	2010	3516
1999	820	2011	3623
2000	741	2012	4821
2001	1303	2013	6721
2002	1579	2014	7893
2003	1747	2015	6367
2004	2646	2016	5701
2005	1824	2017	6747
2006	2043	2018	7061
2007	2786	2019	6544
2008	3617	2020	7368
2009	3836	2021	5842
Grand total (from 1998 up to 2021): 95,931			

Source: Crime in India (1998–2021), National Crime Record Bureau (NCRB), New Delhi, Government of India

Cases pending trials at the end of year 2021: 53,387
Conviction rate: 31.2%
Pendency percentage: 99.7%

At the end of year 2021, the atrocities-related cases which were pending trial by the courts stood at 20.97%, and 32.78% of atrocities-related cases were pending police investigation in Bihar. Such high number/percentage of cases pending police investigation and trial by the courts clearly marks out the performance deficit by the government in power and the judiciary in the state.

* * *

As per the requirements under the PoA Act and Rules, several steps are to be taken by the central and respective state governments; accordingly, the Bihar government has also set up a State Level Vigilance and Monitoring Committee under the chairmanship of the Chief Minister. It met only once as per the Annual Report on the Implementation of the SC and ST (Prevention of Atrocities) Act and Rules by the Ministry of Social Justice and Empowerment, Government of India, for the year 2022. However, 145 meetings of the district level and 336 meetings of subdivision level Vigilance and Monitoring Committees were held during the year 2022 in the state of Bihar. Under Rule 12 (4) of the PoA Rules, the state government provided relief to 7551 persons who were victims of offences under the PoA Act in all the 38 districts. During the same year 372 persons were provided with travelling and maintenance expenses to attend the trial courts in all the 38 districts. No free legal aid was availed by any person. Of the 1173 cases that ended in acquittals, only in 4 cases appeals were made in superior courts (Report, Ministry of Social Justice and Empowerment, 2022, pp. 32–35).

The State Level Vigilance and Monitoring Committee in Bihar met only once in the year 2021. However, district level and subdivisional level Vigilance and Monitoring Committees had 155 and 227 meetings, respectively, in the year 2021. Bihar is among five states in the country which has set up special police station for Scheduled Castes. Currently there are 40 such police station in 38 districts, namely, Patna, Nalanda, Rohtas, Bhabhua, Bhojpur, Buxar, Gaya, Jehanabad, Arwal, Nawada, Aurangabad, Saran, Siwan, Gopalganj, Muzaffarpur, Sitamarhi, Sheohar, West Champaran (2), East Champaran, Vaishali, Darbhanga, Madhubani, Samastipur, Saharsa, Supaul, Madhepura, Purnia, Araria, Kishanganj, Katihar, Bhagalpur (2), Banka, Munger, Lakhisarai, Sheikhpura, Jamui, Khagaria and Begusarai (Report, Ministry of Social Justice & Empowerment, 2021, pp. 32–33).

Identification of Atrocity Prone Areas: 33 districts have been identified as sensitive from the point of view of atrocities against Scheduled Castes and Scheduled Tribes. They are Patna, Nalanda, Rohtas, Bhabhua, Bhojpur, Buxar, Gaya, Jehanabad, Nawada, Aurangabad, Saran, Siwan, Gopalganj, Muzaffarpur, Sitamarhi, West Champaran, East Champaran, Vaishali, Darbhanga, Madhubani, Samastipur, Saharsa, Madhepura, Purnia, Bhagalpur, Banka, Munger, Sheikhpura, Begusarai, Khagaria, Katihar, Jamui and Araria (Ibid, p. 33).

Special Courts: The Court of Additional District Session Judge has been specified as a special court under the PoA Act in the district of Bhabhua, Bhojpur, Buxar,

Jehanabad, Nawada, Aurangabad, Siwan, Sitamarhi, Sheohar, West Champaran, Madhubani, Saharsa, Supaul, Madhepura, Purnia, Araria, Kishanganj, Katihar, Banka, Munger, Lakhisarai, Sheikhpura, Jamui and Khagaria. In addition, 14 exclusive special courts also function at Patna, Gaya, Bhagalpur, Muzaffarpur, Begusarai, Nalanda, Rohtas, Nawada, Saran, Gopalganj, East Champaran (Motihari), Vaishali, Darbhanga and Samastipur districts (Ibid, p. 34).

In the year 2021 no free legal aid was provided to any person. During the same year there were 994 cases which ended in acquittal, but the state government did not file any appeal in the superior courts (Ibid, p. 35).

Some of the massacres which happened in the post-Laxmanpur Bathe massacre have been mentioned here so as to understand the situation of Dalit human rights in the larger context of lawlessness in the society at large and also the failure of state, its several agencies and also of judiciary.

2 Nagari Bazaar

Around 80–90 members of the Ranveer Sena, a banned private army of upper caste landlords, had raided Nagari Bazaar village under the jurisdiction of Charpokhri police station of Bhojpur in the evening of May 11, 1998. The members had opened fire, killing ten persons on the spot, while one person died in a nearby hospital, the prosecution said. On August 13, 2010, a civil court at Ara had convicted 11 accused in connection with the carnage while acquitting 4 others for lack of evidence. Another accused died during the trial. The court had handed down death sentence to three persons, while eight were given life imprisonment. The prosecution had filed chargesheet against 16 people in connection with the case. The local court at Ara acquitted four, and another accused died during the trial. Those awarded gallows by the local court were Chandra Bhushan Singh, Ravindra Singh and Sudarshan Pandey (The Telegraph, 2013a, 2013b).

The High Court acquitted all the 11 persons convicted in the Nagari Bazaar massacre of 1998. The court gave benefit of the doubt to the accused persons for want of evidence. The High Court said the involvement of these persons (accused) could not be proved beyond reasonable doubt. “Eyewitnesses could not be believed”, the court said (Ibid).

Trial in the sessions court in Ara against 15 accused was started in 1999. The sentence was delivered more than 10 years later in August 2010. Three persons were sentenced to death and eight to life imprisonment. The death reference case and the appeal against the conviction came before the two-member High Court bench of V.N. Sinha and A.K. Lal, which acquitted all 11 appellants on March 1, 2013 (Anil Kumar Singh vs State of Bihar, 2013). At the trial stage, a total of 15 witnesses were examined, of which 8 were eyewitnesses. Of these eyewitnesses, six supported their statement in court, but two were disbelieved by the trial court, and one never turned up for cross-examination. Yet another witness supported the prosecution story but could not identify the assailants. The evidence for the prosecution then rested on two witnesses. The High Court bench proceeded to demolish the credibility of the remaining two eyewitnesses (PUDR, 2016, p. 26).

The acquittal in this case means no one has been held responsible for the killing of ten people. The deaths of these people do not seem to be important enough for the High Court to order a retrial if it was not satisfied with the evidence or for the government to take the next logical step of moving the Supreme Court against the acquittals. While the Bihar government has abdicated its responsibility, an appeal has been filed by CPI (ML) Liberation. Currently, the pleadings in the petition number SLP (Crl) No. 5110/2013 are not complete, and the matter is yet to be listed for hearing (Ibid: 27).

3 Shankarbigha

The massacre took place at Shankarbigha village, 75 km from Patna, under the Mehandia police station area in the then undivided Jehanabad district (now Arwal) on the evening of January 25 in the year 1999. Fully armed with rifles, they entered Dalits' houses and fired indiscriminately. Nineteen people all belonging to Dalit and backward castes died on the spot. The 11 injured were rushed to Arwal Hospital, but 3 of them died on the way, thus bringing the number of dead to 22. On hearing the sound of firing, people from Dhawai, situated around half a kilometre away, rushed to Shankarbigha. They were also fired at, but their arrival forced the Ranveer Sena attackers to retreat. The police came 2 or 3 h later when villagers informed them about the incident. An FIR was filed under several IPC sections, Arms Act and also SC and ST (PoA) Act (PUDR, 1999, p. 6). According to the prosecution, Ranveer Sena activists raided a house in which Mahadalits had assembled for a religio-cultural function. The Sena activists rained bullets indiscriminately on the Mahadalits and later also set afire their huts. A Jehanabad court acquitted all the 24 accused named in the case pertaining to the infamous Shankarbigha massacre. While pronouncing the acquittals for lack of evidence, the court of additional district judge 1 Raghavendra Prasad Singh observed as many as 50 witnesses deposed in the court but none of them identified any of the accused (Times of India, 2015).

4 Narayanpur

Narayanpur village is situated in Makhdumpur block on the western side of the road joining Jehanabad and Gaya. Twelve Dalits, including five women, had been shot dead on February 10, 1999, by suspected members of the Ranveer Sena. The police arrived about 8 in the morning the next day (PUDR, 1999, pp. 7–8). The news report claimed that 12 Dalits were shot dead by the Ranveer Sena, a private army of Bhumihar landlords in this Bihar village in the night of February 10, 1999. Four of the victims were women and a 12-year-old girl. The attack lasted less than 15 min from around 9 pm. Those who saw the killers sneaking in ran for their lives; others were murdered in their sleep. Some of those who tried to escape were hunted down (The Hindu, 1999). Survivors of the attack alleged that the village head a week earlier had received by mail a pamphlet warning that the residents would be taught a lesson. The police was alerted, but no action was taken. On the other hand, the police pickets that were posted at Narayanpur following the massacre of Dalits at Laxmanpur-Bathe in December 1997 were withdrawn shortly before the February 10 attack (Frontline, 1999). A trial court acquitted all the ten accused in the Narayanpur massacre case for want of evidence. Additional district and session's judge, Jehanabad, Shambhu Nath Mishra, acquitted them as the prosecution failed to establish the charges against the accused beyond reasonable doubt (Times of India, 2009).

5 Miyapur

The Miyapur massacre was the last major carnage in which the Ranveer Sena killed 32 people, mostly Dalits, to avenge an earlier Naxal attack in Senari village of Jehanabad. Sources said that on June 16, 2000, 400–500 people entered the village and began firing at the villagers. The assailants allegedly shouted slogans seeking revenge for the Senari violence. The Aurangabad police filed chargesheets on September 4, 2000, and April 11, 2002, in two phases. The Aurangabad Scheduled Castes and Scheduled Tribes (SC and ST) special court judge had awarded life imprisonment to ten persons on September 20, 2007. The special court had also imposed a fine of Rs 5000 on each, failing which three more years would have been added. During trial in the lower court, 69 prosecution witnesses, including 9 doctors, 2 judicial magistrates and 4 police personnel were examined (The Telegraph, 2013a, 2013b).

The Patna High Court acquitted nine out of ten accused in the Miyapur massacre for lack of evidence, overturning a lower court's order. A division bench comprising Justice V.N. Sinha and Justice Amresh Kumar Lal directed the state government to give proper compensation to the families of those killed in the massacre. The bench also dismissed an appeal from the government seeking to enhance the punishment awarded by the lower court. The High Court upheld the life imprisonment of one Avinash Chandra Sharma of Senari village in Jehanabad while acquitting the others, namely, Pramod Sharma, Nand Kumar Sharma, Vijay, Gopal Sharma, Braj Mohan Sharma, Ram Janam Sharma, Laxmi Sharma, Ram Nath Sharma and Rajendra Sharma (Ibid).

Once again, no retrial or re-investigation was ordered. A statutory criminal appeal has been filed by the state against the acquittals in the Supreme Court in 2013. The matter is yet to be heard (PUDR op.cit: 29).

How could one react to such kind of verdicts delivered by the courts? The police and the judiciary are not blame-free while discharging their constitutional duties. The caste system and its pernicious influence through culturalization process get normalized, and it is reflected in human behaviour and actions in their everyday life. The learned judges of the High Court through their verdicts in caste atrocities cases did not bother to examine each case keeping under consideration the provisions of the Scheduled Castes and Scheduled Tribes (Prevention of Atrocities) Act 1989 and

Rules 1995. Section 4 of the PoA Act 1989, which deals with the willful negligence of the officials in carrying out their job in the atrocity cases, and which could penalize them, has never been invoked at all in the situations when they found that investigation by the prosecution was not proper. Even re-investigation is not favoured by the judges, and finally acquittals of the accused are granted. Members of the police and the judiciary in the conduct of their duties replicate the same caste structures and prejudices that characterize the society from which they come. The arc of history of people struggling for justice in India is long, but it bends in favour of injustice with a regularity which tends to make it a rule (PUDR Ibid: 36).

6 Ranveer Sena Chief Shot Dead

The chief of the Ranveer Sena, the banned private army of upper castes in Bihar, Brahmeshwar Singh alias Mukhiyaji, was shot dead as reported in the media on June 01, 2012. Singh was on a morning walk when he was accosted by gunmen who pumped several bullets into him, killing him on the spot at Katira Mohalla under Nawada police station, 71 km from Patna, police said. Singh, who was earlier facing life imprisonment in various carnage cases, was acquitted and recently released from jail. He assumed leadership of the then Ranveer Kisan Sangharsh Samiti in 1994. Brahmeshwar turned the samiti into a militant organization which finally became the Ranveer Sena. On July 25, 1995, the Ranveer Sena killed six people belonging to Musahar caste in Sarathua village, located near the Belaur village, the Sena headquarters. But Singh came into limelight after the infamous carnage at Bathani Tola under the Sahar block of Bhojpur district on July 10, 1996, in which the victims were mostly children and women. There were several other massacres which took place under his leadership. The Bihar government imposed a ban on the Ranveer Sena in 1995 (Times of India, 2012). The Ranveer Sena and its founders Brahmeshwar Sigh had been getting support from the political establishment and several other political parties in Bihar. On his murder, Giriraj Singh, a Bihar government Minister for Animal and Fish Resources, said that the slain Ranveer Sena founder "remained a true Gandhian all his life". Giriraj added that Mukhiya had dedicated his entire life to the betterment of the lives of the farmers and labourers. "He always worked for peace and harmony in society. Even after his release from the prison last year, he had floated an apolitical forum to champion their cause", he said (India Today, 2012).

7 Dalits Remain Vulnerable on Other Indicators of Development

The vulnerability of Dalits is reflected on several indexes of human and economic development. According to the poverty estimates for 2011–2012 prepared by the Planning Commission, Scheduled Tribes (47.4%) suffered the highest level of poverty among social groups in rural areas, followed by Scheduled Castes (42.3%) and other backward castes (31.9%) as against 33.8% for all classes. This indicated that even as compared to OBCs, the SCs and STs were poorer by more than 10% and 15% point, respectively. According to the Agricultural Census of 2005–2006, the concentration of marginal holdings in Bihar was very high in the case of Scheduled Castes (95%) and Scheduled Tribes (88%). Other sample studies conducted in Bihar confirmed this trend as well. As per a study of disparities in distribution of land in Bihar (Landlessness and Social Justice 2009), based on a land mapping project carried out in Bihar in 2009 in the districts of Gaya, Jamui, Nawada, Patna and West Champaran, the proportion of marginal landholders was highest among Scheduled Tribes and Scheduled Castes (95.1% and 92.6%, respectively) among all communities. Various studies undertaken by the National Sample Survey Organization also pointed at extremely limited degree of land ownership among Scheduled Castes and Scheduled Tribes in Bihar. The 61st round of National Sample Survey (Report No. 516, Employment and Unemployment Situation Among Social Groups in India 2004–2005) revealed the proportion of households possessing land of size 4.01 ha or more was the maximum for "others" category of households (6%), followed by the OBC (4%), ST (about 3%) and SC households at 1% only (Government of Bihar, 2012, pp. 17–18).

Economic empowerment measures that the government has been engaged with have failed to deliver the desired result. Lack of desired political will of the government in power, insincere administration and lack of accountability have been responsible for such a lacklustre performance of budgetary allocations for schemes and its poor implementation (Table 2).

The backwardness of SCs and STs in terms of their social and economic status reflects clearly in several vital indicators related to health. According to third edition of National Family Health Survey (NFHS-3) report on the relative levels of achievement of Millennium Development Goals in India, critical indicators reflecting on the early childhood mortality rates in India point at a much higher vulnerability of Scheduled Castes children compared to other social groups in the state of Bihar.

Table 2 Early childhood mortality rates by background characteristics (neonatal, postnatal, infant, child and under-5 mortality rates for the 10-year period preceding the survey, by background characteristics, Bihar 2005–2006)

Caste/tribe	Neonatal mortality	Postnatal mortality	Infant mortality	Child mortality	Under-5 mortality
Scheduled Caste	48.8	22.2	71	45.3	113.1
Other backward caste	36.6	20.6	57.2	29.2	84.7
Other	51.6	30.6	82.2	29	108.9

Source: National Family Health Survey (NFHS- 3), 2005–2006, Mumbai, IIPS, 59

The education scenario for Scheduled Caste students is abysmally low in the state of Bihar. There is certainly a higher trend seen for enrolment at primary level, but the problem of dropout seems to be much bigger a problem that has not been addressed adequately the government over the years (Table 3).

Even with regard to enrolment at primary and upper primary levels, the fact that merely 40–45% of Dalit children could be provided with school facilities bears a testimony of poor results of initiatives by the government (Table 4).

The data mentioned here reflects the sad realities of higher percentage of Dalit children dropping out from school education. Why the government has failed to take corrective measures on this aspect remains a puzzle for which no answer is provided by any government agency (Table 5).

Table 3 Total enrolment of SC students at primary and upper primary levels

Year	Primary	Upper primary	Total
2019–2020	27.82	12.22	40.04
2020–2021	29.26	12.95	42.20
2021–2022	30.62	13.79	44.41

Source: Report (2023b), Bihar Economic Survey 2022–2023, Finance Department, Patna, Government of Bihar, 522

Table 4 Dropout rates of SC students at primary, upper primary and secondary levels

Year	Primary	Upper primary	Secondary
2016–2017	23.8	42.9	56.7
2017–2018	16.8	48.3	58.1
2018–2019	19.9	51.9	61.6
2019–2020	19.2	13.0	65.1
2020–2021	1.5	1.7	58.6
2021–2022	0	0	49.8

Source: Report (2023b), Bihar Economic Survey 2022–2023, Finance Department, Patna, Government of Bihar, 462

Table 5 Dropout rates at primary, upper primary and secondary level for scheduled caste children in Bihar

Year	Primary (I–V)			Upper primary (I–VIII)			Secondary (I–X)		
	Girls	Boys	Total	Girls	Boys	Total	Girls	Boys	Total
2004–2005	56.1	54.6	55.2	82.7	80.2	81.1	90.8	89.1	89.5
2005–2006	59.4	56.2	57.4	79.9	78.2	78.8	92.7	89.1	90.4
2006–2007	51.2	51.6	51.5	77.8	72.8	72.8	86.7	85.4	85.9
2007–2008	51.0	53.3	52.4	70.3	71.8	71.2	86.0	83.0	84.1
2008–2009	49.5	50.5	50.1	69.4	70.5	70.1	83.2	82.8	83.0
2009–2010	49.7	50.9	50.4	69.8	72.7	71.6	80.7	81.4	81.1

Source: Department of Education, Patna, Government of Bihar, 2012, 22–23

Despite official claim, the problem of dropout rates among Dalit students remains a big concern even now. The situations have not much improved as it is seen in other reports in recent years.

8 Social Inclusion Scenario Reflects the Sad Reality of Deprivation and Destitution

The World Bank state brief for Bihar through "Bihar Social Inclusion Brief" highlighted the gloomy picture of uneven progress across social groups in Bihar. There are stark differences in education attainment and types of jobs across social groups. The poverty rate for Scheduled Castes in the state is highest in the country. Open defecation is high across social groups, particularly for the Scheduled Castes. And though households in Bihar have better access to drinking water than the rest of the country, the Scheduled Castes lag behind other social groups within the state (The World Bank, 2016).

9 High Poverty Rate Across Social Groups in Bihar

In the year 2005 the poverty rate for Scheduled Castes was highest at 77%, Scheduled Tribes and 59%, other backward castes at 52% and general at 34%.

Meanwhile, in the year 2012, the poverty rate for Scheduled Castes stood at 51%, Scheduled Tribes at 56%, other backward castes at 32% and general at 23%.

10 Educational Attainment Across Social Groups in Bihar: 2012

Among the illiterates, the Scheduled Castes accounted for 59%, followed by Scheduled Tribes at 58%, other backward castes at 44% and general at 20%.

Among the literate or primary school completed category, the Scheduled Castes stood at 21%, followed by Scheduled Tribes at 15%, other backward castes at 21% and general at 17%.

Only 8% of Scheduled Castes completed middle school. Among the Scheduled Tribes, this figure was 12%, other backward castes stood at 14% and the general accounted for 15%.

Only 12% of Scheduled Castes were able to complete secondary or higher education. Whereas for Scheduled Tribes, it was 15%; for other backward castes, it was 21%; and for general, it was 47%.

11 Employment/Jobs Status Across Social Groups in Bihar: 2012

Approximately 66% of Scheduled Castes were engaged in casual wage work. Whereas for Scheduled Tribes this figure stood at 61%, for other backward castes 40% and for general 18%.

Among the salaried jobs, the Scheduled Castes were at 5%, Scheduled Tribes 5%, other backward castes 4% and general 12%.

Among the self-employed, the figure of Scheduled Castes stood at 29% and Scheduled Tribes at 34%, other backward castes at 56% and general at 70%.

12 Open Defecation High Among All Social Groups in Bihar: 2012

Households practising open defecation were very high among Scheduled Castes at 85%, Scheduled Tribes at 73%, other backward castes at 71% and general at 35%.

13 Access to Drinking Water in Bihar: 2012

Among the households with drinking water on premises, the Scheduled Castes accounted for 56%, Scheduled Tribes for 65%, other backward castes for 76% and general for 85%.

14 Mahadalits in Bihar

In September 2007, the government of Bihar set up the Bihar State Mahadalit Commission and tasked it with identifying the most disadvantaged among the Scheduled Castes of the state. In addition, the Commission was asked to give suggestions for ways to improve the educational and social status of the Mahadalits. The Commission relied on demographic data, as well as data on educational attainment and occupational status from Census 2001, on its own visits to various parts of Bihar, as well as on letters and representations made to it by various civil society organizations to formulate its recommendations. In its first interim report submitted in November 2007, the Commission recommended that 18 of the Scheduled Castes of Bihar should be considered extremely oppressed and designated as "Mahadalit", thereby excluding four large castes, the Dusadhs, Chamars, Pasis and Dhobis. As per Census 2011, these 18 castes comprise just over 28% of the Scheduled Caste population of Bihar (Kumar & Somanathan, 2016, pp. 3–4).

In its next interim report submitted in April 2008, the Commission recommended including the Pasis and Dhobis in the list of Mahadalits, and in November 2009, on the basis of the third recommendation of the Commission, the government of Bihar also designated the Chamars as Mahadalits. Thus, at this time all Scheduled Castes (SC) except the Dusadhs (in other words, about 69% of the state's SC population) are designated as Mahadalit. By several measures, the Musahars, Bhuiyas and Doms fall at the lowest end of the hierarchy within the Scheduled Castes. As per Census 2011, while the average literacy rate for all Scheduled Castes in Bihar is just under 49%, the corresponding numbers for each of these castes are under 30%. While just under 70% of all Scheduled Caste main workers in Bihar are agricultural labourers, this is true of 80.4% of Bhuiyas and 87.2% of Musahars (Ibid).

How precarious Dalit life is continues to remain a matter of concern even now after 75 years of India's independence. This precariousness of Dalit life is nothing but an unsavoury reflection of deeply entrenched casteism in society. The problem of landlessness is far more acute among the Scheduled Castes, not just compared to non-SC/ST households but also in comparison to the Scheduled Tribes. Estimates based on the Land and Livestock Holdings Survey conducted as part of the 59th round of the National Sample Survey indicated that in India as a whole, over 56% of SCs do not own any land other than their homesteads, as compared to just under 38% for non-SC/STs and under 36% for STs. In Bihar, the severity of the problem among the SCs was much greater: over 72% of SCs were landless by this measure, as compared to 35% for non-SC/STs and only 22% for STs (Bakshi, 2008, p. 101).

The Mahadalit Commission set up by the government of Bihar in 2007 assigned the Revenue and Land Reforms Department the responsibility to identify Mahadalit families without house-sites in the entire state and provide them access to homestead land. As part of this programme, a survey of 10,380 villages was conducted during a span of one and a half years. The survey focused on (a) identifying Mahadalit families without house-sites and with house-sites of their own and (b) identifying suitable land, government or private *raiyati* land, which could be allotted to house-siteless Mahadalit families. About 17% of the Mahadalit families surveyed were found to be without house-sites of their own (Kumar & Singh, 2010, p. 37).

After the survey the government decided to impose a ceiling of three decimals per family for allotment of house-sites in order to maximize the benefit with available land and financial resources. For acquiring land, it also shifted its policy from land acquisition to land purchase with regard to *raiyati* land. Since land purchase from individual landowners has been envisaged as the major source for allocating house-sites, the government has also delineated the principles and modalities for acquiring land through purchase. The survey of Mahadalit families found numerous cases among them who had not got *parcha* or *parwana* (land papers) for their homestead land despite entitlement as per law. Hence, a drive was concurrently launched by the government to bring to surface such cases and grant settlement *parchas*, especially to Mahadalit families (Ibid: 38).

Till September 2009, 20,022 *parchas* for *raiyati* land involving an area of 423.36 acres had been issued to Mahadalit families. It was also ensured that along with the distribution of *parcha* for homestead land, the beneficiaries were also issued the current rent receipt against the *jamabandi* opened in their name to save them from the trouble of running to the Anchal office in this regard. Approximately 725.314 acres of *gair mazarua malik* land has also been settled with 14,540 Mahadalit families during the same period (Ibid).

But it remains to be seen how much time would be required before all Mahadalit families are provided with homestead land and start living in their houses constructed with support from Indira Awas Yojana. As experienced over the years what is clear on the ground is that due to administrative bottlenecks in the form of complicated procedures for land distribution among the landless and also due to lack of required political will, these welfare measures remain unimplemented to a large extent. The Mahadalit Awas Bhoomi Yojana quickly rose to become one of the most significant programmes managed by the Revenue and Land Reform department of the state. In its annual report for 2015–2016, the department reported having provided a total of 7284.8 acres of homestead land to 238,606 Mahadalit households all over Bihar, i.e. nearly 99% of the 241,745 targeted households. For the financial year 2016–2017, the budgetary provision for the programme stood at over Rs. 20 crore, making it the single largest programme under the charge of the department (Kumar & Somanathan, op.cit: 9). Actual possession of the land thus transferred to the most needy people, mainly targeting Mahadalit community, is a big challenge that Bihar has been witnessing since a long time.

15 Socio-economic and Educational Profile: The Plight of Dalits Continues

Even after seven and a half decades after independence, how difficult it is to explain that Dalits continue to live a life in misery and face all kinds of discrimination, exclusion and violence on a regular basis not only in Bihar but all across India in varying degrees. The government of Bihar conducted caste-based enumeration and also collected data through socio-economic survey which was released first on October 2, 2023, and then with larger details on November 07, 2023, in the Bihar State Assembly. The data thus collected are quite revealing and exposes the government's claim of whatever has been achieved as part of its developmental initiatives over the years. Yes, the date speaks for several open and not so open truths. Mentioned here is a snapshot of the caste-based enumeration/survey 2022–2023.

The government of Bihar issued gazette notifications on November 21, 2023, for raising the quota for deprived castes from 50% to 65% in state government jobs and educational institutions, after receiving assent from Governor Rajendra Vishwanath Arlekar. According to sources the governor had sent both the bills—The Bihar Reservation of Vacancies in Posts and Services Amendment Bill and the Bihar Reservation (Admission in Educational Institutions) Amendment Bill 2023—to the state government after giving his formal assent, paving the way for implementation of the new quota percentage in state government jobs and educational institutions. The Bihar Reservation of Vacancies in Posts and Services Amendment Bill and the Bihar Reservation (Admission in Educational Institutions) Amendment Bill 2023 were recently cleared by the state legislature during the winter session days after the government tabled the detailed analysis of the state's landmark caste survey report in the assembly. Both the bills sought a hike in the quota for Scheduled Castes (SC) from 16% to 20%, Scheduled Tribes (STs) from 1% to 2%, extremely backward castes (EBCs) from 18% to 25% and other backward castes (OBCs) from 15% to 18% to elevate the total quantum of caste-based reservations from 50% to 65%. The total quantum of reservation in jobs and educational institutions will now stand at 75% in the state, after taking into account the 10% already-existing quota for Economically Weaker Sections (Times of India, 2023a, 2023b).

In a setback to the Nitish Kumar government in Bihar, the Patna High Court on June 20, 2024, struck down its last year's decision to raise quotas for Dalits, backward classes and tribals from 50% to 65%. A division bench headed by Chief Justice K Vinod Chandran passed the order on a bunch of petitions which had opposed the legislation brought by the state government in November 2023. The quotas were increased following a comprehensive survey of castes which gave a fresh estimate of the population of SCs, STs, OBCs and extremely backward classes (EBCs) in Bihar (The Telegraph, June 20, 2024).

After hearing the counsels for the petitioners and the Advocate General of the Bihar government, the two judge benche of the Patna High Court averred that

> adequate representation is the core of both Articles 15(4) and 16(4); was reiterated and the rule of 50% limit in reservations was reaffirmed by the various decisions of the court. That, the exception provided, to exceed the 50% limit, was confined and restricted to extenuating circumstances and characteristically inherent aspects akin to far flung areas thus being kept away from the mainstream of National life, is undisputed. That, these conditions do not exist and was not demonstrated in the instant case is abundantly clear. That, the State attempted no in-depth study or analysis before providing for enhancement of the reservation percentage is established from the records. That, the State proceeded on the mere proportion of population of different categories as against their numerical representation in government services and educational institutions is the admitted position and is the pivotal argument of the State. That, this argument works against the core principles of Articles 15(4) & 16(4) is a given fact. In our judgment hence, the enhancement of reservations beyond the 50% limit is bad in law based on the principles of equality emanating from the Constitution, as laid down by the wealth of precedents discussed in this judgment; binding on us and the State equally. We, hence, set aside the Bihar Reservation of Vacancies in Posts

and Services (for Scheduled Caste, Scheduled Tribes and Other Backward Classes) Amendment Act, 2023 and the Bihar Reservation (in Admission to Educational Institutions) Amendment Act, 2023 as ultra vires of the Constitution and violation of the equality clause under Articles 14, 15 and 16. The Writ Petitions are allowed. (Judgment, Patna High Court, 2024, pp. 86–87)

In a further development regarding this, the Supreme Court on September 6, 2024, issued notice to the Centre and the Bihar government after hearing a petition filed by the Rashtriya Janata Dal (RJD) challenging the Patna High Court judgement in which it scrapped the 65% of caste-based reservation in jobs and admissions in Bihar. A three-judge bench headed by Chief Justice of India (CJI) DY Chandrachud issued the notice and tagged the case with a previous plea filed by the Bihar government against the June 20 judgement of the High Court. A hearing was on at the Supreme Court on a Bihar government plea that challenged the Patna High Court judgement that set aside the hike in the reservation quota for backward classes from 50% to 65% in public employment and admission into educational institutions in the state. During the brief hearing, senior advocate P. Wilson appearing for the RJD told the bench that Bihar had 85% of the population that fell in the other backward classes (OBC) category (India Today, 2024). The hearing for special leave petition against Patna High Court judgement has started, but it is not clear what shape it would take in future. Till the final verdict is out from the Supreme Court, it shall not be prudent to comment much on this matter due to it being sub-judice.

16 Economic Profile of People in Bihar

About 34.13% of the population in Bihar has a monthly income of Rs. 6000, Whereas 29.61% has income up to Rs. 10000, 18.06% has income up to Rs. 20000, 9.83% has income up to Rs. 50000, and only 3.90% of the population has income more than Rs. 50000 (Government of Bihar, 2023a, p. 43) (Table 6).

Table 6 Level of poverty caste-wise

Caste category	Poverty level in percentage
General category	25.09%
Other unlisted castes	23.72%
OBC	33.16%
EBC	33.58%
SC	42.93%
ST	42.70%

Source: Report (2023a), Bihar Caste Based Enumeration 2022–2023, General Administration Department, Patna, Government of Bihar, 44

Poverty level among Brahmins account for 25.31%, Bhumihar for 27.58%, Rajput for 24.89%, Kayastha for 13.83%, Sheikh for 25.84%, Saiyad for 17.61% and Pathan for 22–20% (Ibid: 45).

Among OBCs, the level of poverty among Yadav stands at 35.87%, Kushwaha at 34.32%, Kurmi at 29.90%, Bania at 24.62%, Sonar at 26.58%, Ghatwar at 44.17%, Gaddi at 38.72%, Sainthwar at 33.40% and Jogi at 34.05%.

Among the SCs, the level of poverty among Dusadh stood at 39.36%, Chamar at 42.06%, Musahar at 54.56%, Bhuiyan at 53.55%, Dom at 53.10%, Bhogta at 52.05%, Nat at 49.06%, Kanjar at 50.10%, Rajwar at 46.93% and Kurariar at 45.00% (Ibid: 64–66).

Such a large percentage (42.93%) of Dalits to be followed by Adivasis, EBC and OBCs as poor clearly reflects the faulty economic intervention programmes the government of Bihar has been following in last 75 years. In other words it is also an indicator of how big the role is played by the caste system in keeping a certain section of society in impoverished situation. At the same time it reflects the violation of economic rights of the disadvantaged section of society which cannot be justified on any ground (Table 7).

In the employment sector whether in the government jobs or in organized public sector along with private, both unorganized and organized, the situation for deprived sections continues to remain quite bleak. With such little chance of being employed and a regular source of monthly income, how difficult it becomes for Dalits, Adivasis and EBCs and OBCs even to subsist for a longer period of time, and it makes them more vulnerable for their exploitation and human rights violations (Table 8).

Table 7 Employment status in Bihar

	Caste category					
Job category	General	OBC	EBC	SC	ST	Unlisted castes
Government job	3.19%	1.75%	0.98%	1.13%	1.37%	2.04
Private job in organized sector	3.49%	1.13%	0.73%	0.51%	0.68%	3.07%
Private Job in unorganized sector	4.22%	2.15%	1.73%	1.30%	1.48%	2.79%
Self-employed	3.62%	3.34%	3.58%	1.32%	1.70%	9.67%
Agriculture	7.09%	9.97%	6.13%	7.70%	10.96%	3.89
Mason, labour, etc.	11.44%	13.74	18.62%	21.38%	18.51%	12.94%
Beggars	0.02%	0.02%	0.03%	0.03%	0.06%	0.10%
Ragpickers	0.01%	0.01%	0.02%	0.05%	0.02%	0.02%
Housewives, students, etc.	66.32%	67.89%	68.18%	66.58%	65.22%	65.48%

Source, Report (2023a), Bihar Caste Based Enumeration 2022–2023, General Administration Department, Patna, Government of Bihar, 92

Table 8 Housing status in Bihar

House by types	Caste category					
	General	OBC	EBC	SC	ST	Unlisted castes
Pucca (concrete) with two or more rooms	51.54%	43.47%	32.61%	24.26%	25.81%	52.98%
Pucca (concrete) with one room	22.95%	20.65%	22.96%	23.69%	16.87%	17.14%
Mud tile/tin roof	19.31%	25.68%	28.71%	28.34%	4.96%	19.67%
Huts	5.89%	10.04%	15.49%	23.45%	16.08%	9.06%
Homeless	0.31%	0.16%	0.23%	0.26%	0.28%	1.15%

Source: Report (2023a), Bihar Caste Based Enumeration 2022–2023, General Administration Department, Patna, Government of Bihar, 109

Table 9 Levels of education in Bihar

Levels of education	Caste category					
	General	OBC	EBC	SC	ST	Unlisted castes
Primary (1–5)	17.45%	21.67%	24.65%	24.31%	24.52%	18.32%
Middle (6–8)	13.11%	14.14%	15.30%	13.79%	14.31%	13.07%
Secondary (9–10)	18.77%	16.20%	13.89%	11.10%	13.01%	16.87%
Senior secondary (11–12)	13.99%	10.69%	7.95%	5.76%	7.48%	11.51%
Diploma/ITI	1.16%	0.67%	0.42%	0.28%	0.39%	1.10%
Graduate: engineering	0.96%	0.31%	0.14%	0.07%	0.11%	0.91%
Graduate: medicine	0.16%	0.06%	0.03%	0.02%	0.02%	0.17
Others: graduate	13.41%	6.77%	4.27%	3.05%	3.40%	13.45%
Postgraduate	2.50%	0.81%	0.43%	0.28%	0.27%	2.44%
Doctorate/CA	0.25%	0.07%	0.03%	0.02%	0.02%	0.40%
Others	18.24%	28.59%	32.89%	41.32%	36.47%	21.76%

Source: Report (2023b), Bihar Caste Based Enumeration 2022–2023, General Administration Department, Patna, Government of Bihar, 172

Housing status is such that access to decent housing remains out of reach for a large section of Dalits in the state of Bihar. The fact that such kinds of shortages with regard to housing exists even now, how could we explain the failure of state and society at large which remains unconcerned as a matter of fact? (Table 9).

Education, the light of enlightenment, which helps people to enjoy freedom and equality, remains out of reach of Dalits, Adivasis, EBCs and OBCs at different levels. Apart from lower percentage of Dalits acquiring education at different levels, the data mentioned above also highlights a growing number of dropouts as they move from primary to higher education. This also holds true for Adivasis, EBCs and OBCs.

Whatever is mentioned above is part of the latest data and that too from government sources which presents a dark picture of the current socio-economic and educational development of Dalits and other marginalized groups in the state. This kind of situation is not something new that is being reported now.

17 Suggestions

1. The National Human Rights Commission and the National Commission for Scheduled Castes and Scheduled Tribes should organize workshops/orientation programmes to sensitize the government officials, police personnel and even judges of the District Court, High Court and Supreme Court about the problems of the Dalits and other vulnerable groups/communities.
2. The National Commission for Scheduled Caste and Scheduled Tribes annual reports must be tabled in the parliament along with the action taken report by the central government at the earliest. The recommendations of the commission should be followed in the right earnest. The commission should be vested with the power to fix accountability for negligence on part of the state government and officials.
3. Widespread awareness and sensitization programmes should be launched by the central governments as well as the state governments in schools, colleges and universities and also through the print as well as visual media regarding the problems of Dalits and other vulnerable groups/communities to foster a harmonious relationship in civil society.
4. The government of Bihar should vigorously implement land reform and must ensure that Dalits get possession of the land as well. The government of Bihar should prepare a "White Paper" on the status of land in Bihar. Bihar Land Reforms Commission (2006–2008) headed by D. Bandyopadhyay submitted its report few years ago, which is lying unimplemented. Considering the seriousness of the matter, the government of Bihar should make necessary effort to accept recommendations of the Bandyopadhyay Commission and start its implementation without any further delay.
5. The additional district and Session Judges' courts which have now been ordered to function as special courts in Bihar should take up all the pending and present cases for speedy and fair trial in the right earnest. These courts should also pass strictures against the government and its officials for negligence of their duties.
6. Caste and communal violence should not be treated merely as a law-and-order problem. A comprehensive socio-economic restructuring should be given prime importance by the government of the day, as political democracy remains meaningless without social and economic democracy.
7. The government of Bihar should enforce with stringent measures the Bonded Labour System (Abolition) Act 1976 and ensure immediate release and sufficient rehabilitation package to victims to prevent their lapse into the system.

8. The government of Bihar should ensure the implementation of Minimum Wages Act and Equal Remuneration Act, without any grounds for caste-based discrimination.
9. The government of Bihar should immediately and urgently release and rehabilitate all members involved in the work of manual scavenging providing alternate and sustainable livelihoods and employment and development programmes for the victims as well as their families and prosecute all violators and perpetrators of the dehumanizing practice.
10. The government of Bihar should earnestly implement Scheduled Caste Sub-Plan (SCSP). No diversion of allocated fund should be allowed under any circumstance. The allocated fund must not be allowed to remain unspent and lapse.

References

Ambedkar, B. R. (1989). *Writings and Speeches, Education Department* (Vol. 5, p. 25). Government of Maharashtra.

Ambedkar, B. R. (1993). *Cited in M.S. Gore's, The social context of an ideology: Ambedkar's political and social thought* (Vol. 187). Sage Publications.

Bakshi, A. (2008). Social inequality in land ownership in India: A study with particular reference to West Bengal. *Social Scientist, 36*(9/10), 95–116.

Bihar Social Inclusion Brief. (2016). The World Bank Brief for Bihar, New Delhi, May 20. Retrieved from https://documents1.worldbank.org/curated/en/376521468185928955/pdf/105843-BRI-P157572-PUBLIC-Bihar-Social.pdf

Crime in India. (2022 and 2021). National Crime Record Bureau, New Delhi, Government of India.

Frontline. (1999). Carnage in Narayanpur, March 12, 28.

India Today. (2012). Bihar minister sparks controversy by calling slain Ranveer Sena chief a "true Gandhian", June 09. Retrieved from https://www.indiatoday.in/india/east/story/bihar-minister-sparks-controversy-by-calling-slain-ranvir-sena-chief-brahmeshwar-singh-a-true-gandhian-105067-2012-06-07

India Today. (2023). Bihar second in number of crimes against Scheduled Castes: National Panel, May 19. Retrieved from Bihar second in number of crimes against Scheduled Castes: National panel - India Today

India Today. (2024). Court Notice to Centre, Bihar on RJD's plea on 65% quota for backward classes, India Today, September 06. Retrieved from https://www.indiatoday.in/law/supreme-court/story/supreme-court-notice-centre-bihar-on-rjd-65-per-cent-quota-backward-classes-patna-high-court-2595114-2024-09-06

Judgment, Patna High Court. (2024). Civil Writ Jurisdiction Case No. 16760 of 2023, June 20. Retrieved from https://patnahighcourt.gov.in/viewjudgment/MTUjMTY3NjAjMjAyMyMxI04=-QTRWlRjIeAA=

Khosla, D. (1987). *Myth and reality of the protection of civil rights law* (pp. 6–7). Hindustan Publishing Corporation.

Kumar, H., & Somanathan, R. (2016). 'The Right to Shelter: An Evaluation of the Land Transfer Programme to Mahadalits in Bihar', Reference Number: 1-34107-1NB-1, Working Paper, International Growth Centre, 3–4.

Kumar, S., & Singh, P. D. (2010). *Right to housing and homestead land in rural Bihar: Status, issues and challenges* (p. 37). Deshkal Society.

Ray, A. K. (1986). Civil rights movements and social struggle in India, July 12. *Economic and Political Weekly*, 1203.

Report. (1994–1995 & 1995–1996). National Commission for Scheduled Castes and Scheduled Tribes (NCSCST), New Delhi, Government of India, pp. I–V.
Report. (1999). 'A Time to Kill: A Report on Massacres in Jehanabad', New Delhi, Peoples Union for Democratic Rights (PUDR), pp. 6, 7 & 8.
Report. (2012). 'Status of Backwardness of Scheduled Castes and Scheduled Tribes', SC and ST Welfare Department, Patna, Government of Bihar, pp. 16–18.
Report. (2016). Harvesting death: Massacres in Bihar and the Question of Justice, New Delhi, Peoples Union or Democratic Rights (PUDR), pp. 26–27, 29 &36.
Report. (2023a). Bihar Caste Based Enumeration 2022-23, Patna, Department of General Administration, Government of Bihar.
Report. (2023b). Bihar Economic Survey 2022-23, Finance Department, Patna, Government of Bihar.
Report, Annual. (2021). 'Implementation of Scheduled Caste and Scheduled Tribes (Prevention of Atrocities) Act', Ministry of Social Justice, New Delhi, Government of India.
Report, Annual. (2022). 'Implementation of the Scheduled Castes and Scheduled Tribes (Prevention of Atrocities) Act', Ministry of Social Justice and Empowerment, New Delhi, Government of India.
Subramanian, K. S. (1987). Violence against Scheduled Caste in India. *Man and Development, 1*(9), 28.
The Hindu. (1999). 12 Dalits Killed in Bihar Village, February 12.
The Hindu. (2025a). 11-year-old Dalit rape victim dies of injuries in Patna, June 01.
The Hindu. (2025b). FIR filed after Dalit MLA says he was not allowed to open building in Bihar, January 27.
The Telegraph. (2013a). HC Acquits 9 in the Massacre Case, July 4.
The Telegraph. (2013b). HC Acquits Massacre Convicts, March 02.
The Telegraph. (2024). Patna High Court strikes down Bihar govt's quota hike to 65% in jobs, education, June 20.
The Times of India. (2009). All 10 Narayanpur Massacre Case Accused Acquitted, March 09.
The Times of India. (2012). Ranveer Sena Founder Brahmeshwar Singh Shot Dead in Bihar, June 01.
The Times of India. (2015). 16 Years On, All Shankarbigha Carnage Accused Acquitted, January 15.
The Times of India. (2023a). Bihar Govt Issues Gazette Notifications for Raising Quota from 50 to 65 per cent, November 22.
The Times of India. (2023b). State Govt Indifferent towards Welfare of SCs: NCSC Chairman, May 20.

Appendix I: The Protection Of Civil Rights Act, 1955

(Act No. 22 of 1955)

[8th May, 1955]

An Act to prescribe punishment for the [preaching and practice of "untouchability"] for the enforcement of any disability arising there from and for matters connected therewith.

Be it enacted by Parliament in the Sixth Year of the Republic of India as follows:

1. *Short title, extent and commencement*:

    (1) This Act may be called [the Protection of Civil Rights Act] 1955.
    (2) It extends to the whole of India.
    (3) It shall come into force on such date, as the Central Government may, by notification in the official Gazette, appoint.

2. *Definitions*:

In this Act, unless the context otherwise requires, —

[(a) "Civil rights" means any right accruing to a person by reason of the abolition of "untouchability" by Art. 17 of the Constitutions]

[(aa)] "Hotel" includes a refreshment room, a boarding house, a lodging house, a coffee house and a cafe

[(b)] "place" includes a house, building and other structure and premises; and also includes a tent, vehicle and vessel

(c) "Place of public entertainment" includes any place to which the public are admitted and in which an entertainment is provided or held.

Explanation: "Entertainment" includes any exhibition, performance, game, sport and any other form of amusement.

(d) "place of public worship" means a place, by whatever name known, which is used as a place of public religious worship or which is dedicated generally to, or is

UMAKANT, *Dalit Human Rights in India*, People, Cultures and Societies: Exploring and Documenting Diversities,
https://doi.org/10.1007/978-981-95-5751-6

used generally by, persons professing any religion or belonging to any religious denomination or any section thereof, for the performance of any religious service, or offering prayers therein; [and includes—

(i) All lands subsidiary shrines appurtenant or attached to any such place;
(ii) A privately owned place of worship which is, in fact, allowed by the owner thereof to be used as place of public worship;
(iii) and such land or subsidiary shrine appurtenant to such privately owned place of worship as is allowed by the owner thereof to be used as a place of public religious worship;]

(da) ["Prescribed" means prescribed by rules made under this Act;

(db) "Scheduled Castes" has the meaning assigned to it in CI. 24 of Art. 366 of the Constitution;]

(e) "Shop" means any premises where goods are sold either wholesale or by retail or both wholesale and by retail [and includes:

1. Any place from where goods are sold by a hawker or vendor or from a mobile van or cart,
2. A laundry and a hair-cutting saloon,
3. Any other place where services are rendered to customers].

3. *Punishment for enforcing religious disabilities*:

Whoever on the ground of "untouchability" prevents any person—

(a) from entering any place of public worship which is open to other persons professing the same religion [***] of any sections thereof, as such person; or
(b) from worshipping or offering prayers or performing any religious service in any place of public worship, or bathing in or using the waters of, any sacred tank, well, spring or water-course [river or lake or bathing at any ghat of such tank, water-course, river or lake] in the same manner and to the same extent as is permissible to the other persons professing the same religion or any section thereof, as such person;

[Shall be punishable with imprisonment for a term of not less than one month and not more than six months and also with fine which shall be not less than hundred rupees and not more than five hundred rupees].

Explanation: For the purpose of this section and Sec. 4 persons professing the Buddhist, Sikh or Jaina religion or person professing the Hindu religion in any of its forms or developments including Virashaivas, Lingayats, Adivasis, followers of Brahmo, Prarthana, Arya Samaj and the Swaminarayan, Sampraday shall be deemed to be Hindus.

4. *Punishment for enforcing social disabilities*:

Whoever on the ground of "untouchability" enforces against any person any disability with regard to—

(i) access to any shop, public restaurant, hotel or place of public entertainment; or

(ii) the use of any utensils, and other articles kept in any public restaurant, hotel, dharmashala, sarai or musafirkhana for the use of the general public or of [any section thereof]; or
(iii) the practice of any profession or the carrying on of any occupation, trade or business [or employment in any job], or employment in any job]; or
(iv) the use of, or access to, any river stream, spring, well, tank, cistern, water tap or other watering place, or any bathing ghat, burial or cremation ground any sanitary convenience, any road, or passage, or any other place of public resort which other members of the public, or [any section thereof] have a right to use or have access to; or
(v) the use of, or access to any place used for a charitable or a public purpose maintained wholly or partly out of State funds or dedicated to the use of the general public or [any section thereof]; or
(vi) the employment of any benefit under a charitable trust created for the benefit to the general public or of [any section thereof]; or
(vii) the use of, or access to any public conveyance; or
(viii) the construction, acquisition, or occupation of any residential premises in any locality, whatsoever; or
(ix) the use of any dharmasala, sarai or musafirkhana, which is open to the general public, or
(x) to [any section thereof], or the observance of any social or religious custom, usage or ceremony or [taking part in, or taking out any religious, social or cultural procession]; or
(xi) the use of jewellery and finery;

[shall be punishable with imprisonment for a term of not less than one month and not more than six month and also with fine which shall be not less one hundred rupees and not more five hundred rupees].

[Explanation—For the purpose of this section, "enforcement of any disability" includes any discrimination on the ground of "untouchability"].

5. *Punishment for refusing to admit persons to hospital, etc*:

Whoever on the ground of "untouchability"—

(a) refuses admission to any persons to any hospital, dispensary, educational institution or any hostel, if such hospitals, dispensary, educational institutions or any hostel is established or maintained for the benefit of the general public or any section thereof; or
(b) does any act which discriminates against any such person after admission to any of the aforesaid institution;

[shall be punishable with imprisonment for a term of not less than one month and not more than six months and also with fine which shall be not less than one hundred rupees and not more than five hundred rupees].

6. *Punishment for refusing to sell goods or render services*:

Whoever on the ground of "untouchability" refuses to sell any goods or refuses to render any service to any person at the same time and place and on the on the same terms and conditions at or which such goods are sold or services are rendered to other persons in the ordinary course of business.

[Shall be punishable with imprisonment for a term of not less than one month and not more than six months and also with fine which shall be not less one hundred rupees and not more than five hundred rupees].

7. *Punishment for other offences arising out of "untouchability"*:

(1) Whoever prevents any person from exercising any right accruing to him by reason of the abolition of "untouchability" under Art. 17 of the Constitution; or molests, injures, annoys, obstructs or causes or attempts to cause obstruction to any person in the exercise of any such right or molests, injures, annoys or boycotts any person by reason of his having exercised any such right; or by words, either spoken or written, or by signs or by visible representations or otherwise, incites or encourages any person or class of persons or the public generally to practice "untouchability" in any form whatsoever; [or] [insults or attempts to insult, on the ground of "untouchability" a member of scheduled caste],

[shall be punishable with imprisonment for a term of not less than one month and more than six month, and also with fine which shall be not less than one hundred rupees and not more than five hundred rupees].

[Explanation I]—A person shall be deemed to boycott another person who refuse to let to such other person or refuses to permit such other person, to use or occupy any house or land or refuses to deal with, work for hire for, or do business with, such other person or to render to him or receive from him any customary service, or refuses to do any of the said things on the terms which such things would be commonly done in the ordinary course of business; or abstains from such social, professional or business relations as he would ordinarily maintain with such other person.

[Explanation II—For the purpose of CI. (c) a person shall be deemed to incite or encourage the practice or "untouchability" if he, directly or indirectly, preaches "untouchability" or its practice in any form; or if he justifies, whether on historical, philosophical or religious ground or on the ground of any tradition of the caste or any other ground, the practice of "untouchability" in any form].

[(1-A) Whoever commits any offence against the person or property of any individual as reprisal or revenge for his having exercised any right accruing to him by reason of the abolition of "untouchability" under Art. 17 of the Constitution shall, where the offence is punishable with imprisonment for a term exceeding two years, be punishable with imprisonment for term which shall not be less than two years and also with fine].

(2) Whoever denies to any person belonging to his community or and section thereof any right or privilege to, which person would be entitled as a member of such community or section, or takes any part in the ex-communication of such

person, on the ground that such person has refused to practice "untouchability" that such person has done any act in furtherance of the objects of this Act,

[shall be punishable with imprisonment for a term of not less than one month and not more than six months and also with fine which shall be not less than one hundred rupees and not more than five hundred rupees.]

[7-A. Unlawful compulsory labour when to be deemed to be practice of "untouchability":

(1) Whoever compels any person, on the ground of "untouchability", to do any scavenging or sweeping or to remove any carcass or to flay any animal, or to remove the umbilical cord or to do any other job of a similar nature shall be deemed to have enforced a disability arising out of a "untouchability".
(2) Whoever is deemed under sub-section (1) to have enforced a disability arising out of "untouchability" shall be punishable with imprisonment for a term which shall not be less than three months and not more than six months and also with fine which shall not be less than one hundred rupees and not more than five hundred rupees.

Explanation—For the purpose of this section, "compulsion" includes a threat of social or economic boycott]

8. *Cancellation or suspension of licenses in certain cases*:

When a person who is convicted of an offence under Sec. 6 holds any license under any law for the time being in force in respect of any profession, trade, calling or employment in relation to which the offence is committed, the Court trying the offence may, without prejudice to any other penalty to which such person may be liable under that section, direct that the license shall stand cancelled or be suspended for such period as the Court may deem fit, and every order of Court so cancelling or suspending a license shall have effect as if it had been passed by the authority competent to cancel or suspend the license under any such law.

Explanation—In this section, "license" includes a permit or permission.

9. *Resumption or suspension of grants made by Government*:

Where the manager or trustee of a place of public worship [or any educational institution or hostel] which is in receipt of a grant of land or money from the Government is convicted of an offence under this Act and such conviction is not reversed or quashed in any appeal or revision, the Government may, if in its opinion the circumstances of the case warrant such a course, direct the suspension of the whole or resumption of the whole or any part of such grant.

10. *Abetment of offence*:

Whoever abets any offence under this Act shall be punishable with the punishment provided for the offence.

[Explanation—A public servant who wilfully neglects the investigation of any offence punishable under this Act shall be deemed to have abetted an offence punishable under this Act.

10-A. Power of State Government to impose collective fine:

(1) If, after an inquiry in the prescribed manner, the State Government is satisfied that the inhabitants of an area concerned in, or abetting the commission of, any offence punishable under this Act, or harbouring persons concerned in the commission of such offence or failing to render all the assistance in their power to discover or apprehend the offenders or suppressing material evidence of the commission of such offence, the State Government may, by notification in the Official Gazette, impose a collective fine on such inhabitants and apportion such fine amongst the inhabitant who are liable collectively to pay it, and such apportionment shall be made according to the State Government's judgement of the respective means of such inhabitants and in making any such apportionment the State Government may assign a portion of such fine to a Hindu undivided family to be payable by it:

Provided that the fine apportioned to an inhabitant shall not be realised until the petition, if any, filed by him under sub-section (3), is disposed of.

(2) The notification made under sub-section (1) shall be proclaimed in the area by beat of drum or in such other manner as the State Government may think best in the circumstances to bring the imposition of the collective fine to the notice of the inhabitants of the said area.

(3) (a) Any person aggrieved by the imposition of the collective fine under sub-section (1) or by the order or apportionment, may, within the prescribed period, file a petition before the State Government or such other authority as that Government may specify in this behalf for being exempted from such fine or for modification of the order of apportionment:

Provided that no fees shall be charged for filing such petition.

(b) The State Government or the authority specified by it shall, after giving to the petitioner a reasonable opportunity of being heard, pass such order as it may think fit:

Provided that the amount of the fine exempted or reduced under this section shall not be realized from any person, and the total fine imposed on the inhabitants of an area under sub-section (1) shall be deemed to have been reduced to that extent.

(4) Notwithstanding anything contained in sub-section (3), the State Government may exempt the victims of any offence punishable under this Act or any person who does not, in its opinion, fall within the category of persons specified in sub-section (1), from the liability to pay the collective fine imposed under sub-section (1) or any portion thereof.

(5) The portion of collective fine payable by any person (including a Hindu undivided family) may be recovered in the manner provided by the Court of Criminal

Procedure, 1973 (2 of 1974), for the recovery of fines imposed by a court as if such portion were a fine imposed by a Magistrate.

11. *Enhanced penalty on subsequent conviction*:

Whoever having already been convicted of an offence under this Act or of an abatement of such offence is again convicted of any offence of abatement [shall, on conviction, be punishable—

(a) for the second offence, with imprisonment for a term of not less than six months and not more than one year, and also with fine which shall be not less than two hundred rupees and not more than five hundred rupees;
(b) for the third offence or any offence subsequent to the third offence with imprisonment for a term of not less than one year and not more than two years, and also with fine which shall be not less than five hundred rupees and not more than one thousand rupees.

12. *Presumption by courts in certain cases*:

Where any act constituting an offence under this Act is committed in relation to a member of a Scheduled Caste [***], the Court shall presume, unless the contrary is proved, that such act was committed on the ground of "untouchabilty".

13. *Limitation of jurisdiction of Civil Courts*:

(1) No Civil Courts shall entertain or continue any suit or proceeding or shall pass any decree or execute wholly or partially any decree or order or if the claim involved in such suit or proceeding or if the passing of such decree or order if such execution would in any way be contrary to the provisions of this Act.
(2) No Court shall, in adjudicating any matter or executing any decree or order, recognize any custom or usage imposing any disability on any person on the ground of "untouchability".

14. *Offences by companies*:

(1) If the person committing an offence under this Act is a company, every person who at the time the offence was committed was in charge of, and was responsible to the company for the conduct of the business of the company, shall be deemed to be guilty of the offence and shall be liable to be proceeded against and punished accordingly:

Provided that nothing contained in this sub-section shall render any such person liable to any punishment, if he proves that the offence was committed without his knowledge or that he exercised all due diligence to prevent the commission of such offence.

(2) Notwithstanding anything contained in sub-section (1), where an offence under this Act has been committed with the consent of any director or manager, secretary or other officer of the company, such director, manager, secretary or other

officer shall also be deemed to be guilty of that offence and shall be liable to be proceeded against and punished accordingly.

Explanation.—For the purposes of this section,—

"company" means anybody corporate and includes a firm or other association of individuals; and "director" in relation to a firm means a partner in the firm.

14-A. Protection of action taken in good faith

(1) No suit, prosecution or other legal proceeding shall lie against the Central Government or a State Government for anything which is in good faith done or intended to be done under this Act.
(2) No suit or other legal proceeding shall lie against the Central Government or a State Government for any damage caused or likely to be caused by anything which is in good faith done or intended to be done under this Act.

15. *Offences to be cognizable and triable summarily*

(1) Notwithstanding anything contained in the Code of Criminal Procedure, 1973 (2 of 1974), every offence punishable under this Act shall be cognizable and every such offence, except where it is punishable with imprisonment for a minimum term exceeding three months, may be tried summarily by a Judicial Magistrate of the first class or in a metropolitan area by a Metropolitan Magistrate in accordance with the procedure specified in the said Code.
(2) Notwithstanding anything contained in the Code of Criminal Procedure, 1973 (2 of 1974), when any public servant is alleged to have committed the offence of abatement of an offence punishable under this Act while acting of purporting to act in the discharge of his official duty, no Court shall take cognizance of such offence of abatement except with the previous sanction—

    (a) of the Central Government in the case of a person employed in connection with the affairs of the Union; and
    (b) of the State Government in the case of a person employed in connection with the affairs of a State.

15-A. Duty of State Government to ensure that the rights accruing from the abolition of "untouchability" may be availed of by the concerned person

(1) Subject to such rules as the Central Government may make in this behalf, the State Government shall take such measures as may be necessary for ensuring that the rights arising from the abolition of "untouchability" are made available to, and are availed of by, the person subject to any disability arising out of "untouchability".
(2) In particular, and without prejudice to the generally of the provisions of sub section (1), such measures may include—

    (i) the provision of adequate facilities, including legal aid to the persons subjected to any disability arising out of "untouchability" to enable them to avail themselves of such rights;

(ii) the appointment of officers for initiating or exercising supervision over prosecutions for the contravention of the provisions of this Act;
(iii) the setting up of Special Courts for the trial of offences under this Act;
(iv) the setting up of committees at such appropriate levels as the State Government may think fit to assist the State Government in formulating or implementing such measures;
(v) provision for a periodic survey of the working of the provisions of this Act with a view to suggesting measures for the better implementation of the provisions of this Act;
(vi) the identification of the area where persons are under any disability arising out of "untouchability" and adoption of such measures as would ensure the removal of such disability from such areas.

(3) The Central Government shall take such steps as may be necessary to coordinate the measures taken by the State Governments under sub-section (1).
(4) The Central Government shall, every year, place on the table of each House of Parliament, a report on the measures taken by itself and by the State Government in pursuance of the provisions of this section.

16. *Act to override other laws*

Save as otherwise expressly provided in this Act, the provisions of this Act shall have effect notwithstanding anything inconsistent therewith contained in any other law for the time being in force, or any custom or usage or any instrument having effect by virtue of any such law or any decree or order of any Court or other authority.

[16-A. Probation of Offenders Act, 1958, not to apply to person above the age of fourteen years

The provisions of the Probation of Offenders Act, 1958 (20 of 1958), shall not apply to any person above the age of fourteen years who is found guilty of having committed any offence punishable under this Act.

16-B. Power to make rules

(1) The Central Government may, by notification in the Official Gazette, make rules to carry out the provisions of this Act.
(2) Every rule made by the Central Government under this Act shall be laid, as soon as may be after it is made, before each House of Parliament while it is in session for a total period of thirty days which may be comprised in one session or in two or more successive sessions, and if before the expiry of the session immediately following the session or the successive session aforesaid, both House agree in making any modification in the rule or both Houses agree that the rule should not be made, the rule shall thereafter have effect only in such modified form or be of no effect, as the case may be; so, however, that any such modification or annulment shall be without prejudice to the validity of anything previously done under that rule.]

17. *Repeal*:

The enactments specified in the schedule are hereby repealed to the extent to which they or any of the provisions contained therein correspond or are repugnant to this Act or to any of the provisions contained therein.

The Schedule

[See. Sec. 17]

1. The Bihar Harijan (Removal of Civil Disabilities) Act 1949 (Bihar Act XIX of 1949).
2. The Bombay Harijan (Removal of Social Disabilities) Act, 1946 (Bombay Act X of 1947).
3. The Bombay Harijan Temple Entry Act, 1947 (Bombay Act XXXV of 1947).
4. The Central Provinces and Berar Scheduled Castes (Removal of Civil Disabilities) Act, 1947 (Central Provinces and Berar Act XXIV of 1947).
5. The Central Provinces and Berar Temple Entry Authorization Act, 1948 (Central Provinces and Berar Act XLI of 1947).
6. The East Punjab (Removal of Religious and Social Disabilities) Act, 1948 (East Punjab Act XVI of 1948)
7. The Madras Removal of Civil Disabilities Act, 1938 (Madras Act XXXI of 1938)
8. The Orissa Removal of Civil Disabilities Act, 1946 (Orissa Act XI of 1946).
9. The Orissa Temple Entry Authorization Act, 1948 (Orissa Act XI of 1948).
10. The United Provinces Removal of Social Disabilities Act, 1947 (U.P. Act XVI of 1947).
11. The West Bengal Hindu Social Disabilities Removal Act, 1948 (West Bengal Act XXXVII of 1948).
12. The Hyderabad Harijan Temple Entry Regulations, 1358-F (No. L V of 1358 Fasli)
13. The Hyderabad Harijan (Removal of Social Disabilities) Regulations, 1358-F (No. LV I of 1358 Fasli).
14. The Madhya Bharat Harijan Ayogta Nivaran Vidhan, Samvat 2005 (Madhya Bharat Act No. 15 of 1949)
15. The Removal of Civil Disabilities Act, 1943 (Mysore Act XLII of 1943).
16. The Mysore Temple Entry Authorization Act, 1948 (Mysore Act XIV of 1948)
17. The Saurashtra Harijan (Removal of Social Disabilities) Ordinance (No. XL of 1948)
18. The Travanvcore- Cochin Removal of Social Disabilities Act, 1125, (Travancore-Cochin Act VIII of 1125).
19. The Travancore- Cochin Temple Entry (Removal of Disabilities) Act, 1950 (Travancore- Cochin Act XXVII of 1950).
20. The Coorg Scheduled Castes (Removal of Civil and Social Disabilities) Act, (Coorg Act 1 of 1949).
21. The Coorg Temple Entry Authorization Act, 1949 (Coorg Act of 1949).

Protection of Civil Rights Rules, 1977

S.O. 3006, dated the 15th September, 1977.—In exercise of the powers conferred by Sec. 16-B of the Protection of Civil Rights Act, 1955 (22 of 1955), the Central Government hereby makes the following rules, namely:

1. Short title and commencement:

(1) These rules may be called the Protection of Civil Rights Rules, 1977.

(2) They shall come into force on the date of their publication in the Official Gazette.

2. *Definitions*: In these rules, unless the context otherwise requires,—

(a) "Act" means the Protection of Civil Rights Act, 1955 (22 of 1955);

(b) "Section" means a section of the Act.

3. *Manner of inquiry under sub-section (1) of sec.10A*:

(1) The State Government may appoint an officer not below the rank of a Sub-divisional Magistrate for the purpose of making an inquiry referred to in sub-section (1) of Sec.10-A.

(2) The officer appointed under sub-rule (1) (hereinafter in this rule referred to as the inquiry officer) shall issue a public notice specifying the date, time, place and the purpose of such inquiry and calling upon all residents of the area in respect of which the inquiry is to be held to furnish such information and materials including documents in their possession, as may be relevant for the purposes of the inquiry.

(3) The public notice referred to in sub-rule (2) shall be in the local language or languages of the area and the same shall be published on the notice board in the offices of the District Magistrate, the District Superintendent of police, the Village Panchayat or Municipal Committee of the area and such other places as the inquiry officer deems fit and at least in one daily newspaper circulating in the area; and proclaimed in the area by beat of drum or in such other manner as the inquiry officer may think best in the circumstance to bring the contents of the public notice to the notice of the inhabitants of the area.

(4) The inquiry officer, while making such inquiry, shall follow as nearly as practicable, the procedure for summary trials including the recording of evidence as laid down in Chapter XXI of the Code of Criminal Procedure, 1973 (2 of 1974).

(5) The inquiry officer shall complete the inquiry as expeditiously as possible and submit his report to the State Government within such period, not exceeding six weeks, as may be specified by the State Government in the order appointing the inquiry officer:

Provided that the State Government may with having regard to the nature of the inquiry extend the period of submission of the report by such period, not exceeding two months in total, as it may consider necessary.

4. *Period for filing a petition under sub-section (3) of Sec.10-A*:

Any person aggrieved by the imposition of a collective fine under sub-section (1) of Sec. 10-A or by the order of apportionment may within a period of thirty days from the date of proclamation of the notification and under Sub-Section (2) of that section file a petition before the State government or the authority specified by it:

Provided that where the State Government or the authority, as case may be, may entertain the petition after the expiry of the staid period if it is satisfied that the petitioner was prevented by sufficient cause from filing the petition in time.

The State Government or the authority before which the petition is filed shall dispose of the petition as expeditiously as possible.

5. *Reports by the State Government*:

Every State Government shall, for the purpose of enabling the Central Government to place the report referred to in sub-section (4) of Sec. 15-A, on the Table of each House of Parliament, furnish to that Government before the 15th day of February, each year, a summary of the measures taken by it under sub-sections (1) and (2) of that section during the proceeding calendar year and shall also furnish other information as may be required by the Central Government from time to time.

Appendix II: *The Scheduled Castes and the Scheduled Tribes (Prevention of Atrocities) Act, 1989*

NO. 33 OF 1989, (11th September, 1989)

An Act to prevent the commission of offences of atrocities against the members of the Scheduled Castes and the Scheduled Tribes, to provide for Special Courts for the trial of such offence and for relief and rehabilitation of the victims of such offences and for matters connected therewith or incidental thereto.

Be it enacted by Parliament in the Fortieth Year of the Republic of India as follows:—

Chapter I: Preliminary

1. Short title, extent and commencement

(1) This Act may be called the Scheduled Castes and Scheduled tribes (Prevention of Atrocities) Act, 1989.
(2) It extends to the whole of India except the State of Jammu and Kashmir.
(3) It shall come into force on such date as the Central Government may by notification in the Official Gazette, appoint.

2. Definitions

(1) In the Act, unless the context otherwise requires, "atrocity" means an offence punishable under section 3;

   (a) "Atrocity" is any of the offences punishable under section 3 of the Act.
   (b) "Code" means the code of Criminal Procedure, 1973 (2 of 1974);
   (c) "Scheduled Castes and Scheduled Tribes" shall have the meanings assigned to them respectively under clause (24) and clause (25) of Article 366 of the Constitution;

UMAKANT, *Dalit Human Rights in India*, People, Cultures and Societies: Exploring and Documenting Diversities,
https://doi.org/10.1007/978-981-95-5751-6

(d) "Special Court" means a Court of Session specified as a Special Court in section 14;
(e) "Special Public Prosecutor" means a Public Prosecutor specified as a Special Public Prosecutor or an advocate referred to in section 15;
(f) words and expressions used but not defined in this Act and defined in the Code or the Indian penal code (45 0f 1860) shall have the meanings assigned to them respectively in the Code, of as the case may be, in the Indian Penal Code.

(2) Any reference in this Act to any enactment or any provision thereof shall, in relation to an area in which such enactment of such provision is not in force, be construed as a reference to the corresponding law, if any, in force in that area.

Chapter II: Offences of Atrocities

3. *Punishments for offences of atrocities*

(1) Whoever, not being a member or a Scheduled Caste or a Scheduled Tribe,—

1. forces a member of a Scheduled Caste or a Scheduled Tribe to drink or eat any inedible or obnoxious substance;

(i) acts with intent to cause injury, insult or annoyance to any member of a Scheduled Caste or a Scheduled Tribe by dumping excreta, waste matter, carcasses or any other obnoxious substance in his premises or neighbourhood;
(ii) forcibly removes clothes from the person of a member of a Scheduled Caste or a Scheduled Tribe or parades him naked or with painted face or body or commits any similar act which is derogatory to human dignity;
(iii) wrongfully occupies or cultivates any land owned by or allotted to, or notified by any competent authority to be allotted to, a member of a Scheduled Caste or a Scheduled Tribe or gets the land allotted to him transferred;
(iv) wrongfully dispossesses a member of a Scheduled Caste or a Scheduled Tribe from his land or premises or interferes with the enjoyment of his rights over any land, premises or water;
(v) compels or entices a member of a Scheduled Caste or a Scheduled Tribe to do "begar" or other similar forms of forced or bonded labour other than any compulsory service for public purpose imposed by Government;
(vi) force or intimidates a member of a Scheduled Caste of a Scheduled Tribe not to vote or to vote to a particular candidate or to vote in a manner other than that provided by law;
(vii) institutes false, malicious or vexatious suit or criminal or other legal proceedings against a member of a Scheduled Caste or a Schedule Tribe;
(viii) gives any false or frivolous information to any public servant and thereby causes such public servant to use his lawful power to the injury or annoyance of a member of a Scheduled Caste or a Scheduled Tribe;

(ix) intentionally insults or intimidates with intent to humiliate a member of a Scheduled Caste or a Scheduled Tribe in any place within public view;
(x) assaults or uses force to any woman belonging to a Scheduled Caste or a Scheduled Tribe with intent to dishonour or outage her modesty;
(xi) being in a position to dominate the will of a woman belonging to a Scheduled Caste or a Scheduled Tribe and uses that position to exploit her sexually to which she would not have otherwise agreed;
(xii) corrupts or fouls the water of any spring, reservoir or any other source ordinarily used by members or the Scheduled Caste or the Schedule Tribes so as to render it less fit for the purpose for which it is ordinarily used;
(xiii) denies a member of a Scheduled Caste or a Scheduled Tribe any customary rite of passage to a place of public resort or obstructs such member so as to prevent him from using or having access to a place of public resort to which other members or public or any section thereof have a right to use or access to;
(xiv) forces or causes a member of scheduled Caste or a Scheduled Tribe to leave his house, village or other place of residence shall be punishable with imprisonment for a term which shall not be less than six months but which may extend to five years and with fine.

2. Whoever, not being a member of a Schedule Caste or a Scheduled Tribe,—

(i) gives or fabricates false evidence intending thereby to cause, or knowing it to be likely that he will thereby cause, any member of a Scheduled Caste or a Scheduled Tribe to be convicted of an offence which is capital by the law for the time being in force shall be punished with imprisonment for life and with fine; and if an innocent member of a Scheduled Caste or a Scheduled Tribe be convicted and executed in consequence of such false or fabricated evidence, the person who gives or fabricates such false evidence shall be punished with death;
(ii) gives or fabrics false evidence intending thereby to cause, or knowing it to be likely that he will thereby cause, any member of a Scheduled Cast or a Schedule Tribe to be convicted of an offence which is not capital but punishable with imprisonment for a term of seven years or upwards, shall be punishable with imprisonment for a term which shall not be less than six months but which may extend to seven years or upwards and with fine;
(iii) commits mischief by fire or any explosive substance intending to cause or knowing it to be likely that he will thereby cause damage to any property belonging to a member of a Scheduled Caste or a Scheduled Tribe, shall be punishable with imprisonment for a term which shall not be less than six months but which may extend to seven years and with fine;
(iv) commits mischief by fire or any explosive substance intending to cause or knowing it to be likely that he will thereby cause destruction of any building which is ordinarily used as a place of worship or as a place for human dwelling or as a place for custody of the property by a member of a Scheduled Caste or a scheduled Tribe, shall be punishable with imprisonment for life and with fine;

(v) commits any offence under the Indian Penal Code (45 of 1860) punishable with imprisonment for a term of ten years or more against a person or property on the ground that such property belongs to such member, shall be punishable with imprisonment for life and with fine;

(vi) knowing or having reason to believe that an offence has been committed under this Chapter, causes any evidence of the commission of that offence to disappear with the intention of screening the offender from legal punishment, or with that intention gives any information respecting the offence which he knows or believes to be false, shall be punishable with the punishment provided for that offence; or

(vii) being a public servant, commits any offence under this section, shall be punishable with imprisonment for a term which shall not be less than one year but which may extend to the punishment provided for that offence.

4. *Punishment for neglect of duties*

Whoever, being a public servant but not being a member of a Scheduled Caste or a Scheduled Tribe, wilfully neglects his duties required to be performed by him under this Act, shall be punishable with imprisonment for a term which shall not be less than six months but which may extend to one year.

5. Enhanced punishment for subsequent conviction

Whoever, having already been convicted of an offence under this chapter is convicted for the second offence or any offence subsequent to the second offence, shall be punishable with imprisonment for a term which shall not be less than one year but which may extend to the punishment provided for that offence.

6. Application of certain provisions of the Indian Penal Code

Subject to the other provisions of this Act, the provisions of section 34, Chapter III, Chapter IV, Chapter V, Chapter VA, section 149 and Chapter XXIII of the Indian Penal Code (45 of 1860), shall, so far as may be, apply for the purposes of this Act as they apply for the purposes of the Indian Penal Code.

7. Forfeiture of property of certain persons

(1) Where a person has been convicted of any offence punishable under this Chapter, the special Court may, in addition to awarding any punishment, by order in writing, declare that any property, movable or immovable or both, belonging to the person, which has been used for the commission of that offence, shall stand forfeited to Government.

(2) Where any person is accused of any offence under this Chapter, it shall be open to the Special Court trying him to pass an order that all or any of the properties, moveable or immovable or both, belonging to him, shall, during the period such trial, be attached, and where such trial ends in conviction, the property so attached shall be liable to forfeiture to the extent it is required for the purpose of realisation of any fine imposed under this Chapter.

8. *Presumption as to offences*

In a Prosecution for an offence under this Chapter, if it is proved that—

(a) the accused rendered any financial assistance to a person accused or, or reasonably suspected of, committing, an offence under this Chapter, the Special Court shall presume, unless the contrary is proved, that such person had abetted the offence;
(b) a group of persons committed an offence under this Chapter and if it is proved that the offence committed was a sequel to any existing dispute regarding land or any other matter, it shall be presumed that the offence was committed in furtherance of the common intention or in prosecution of the common object.

9. *Conferment of powers*

(1) Notwithstanding anything contained in the Code or in any other provision of this Act, the state Government may, if it considers it necessary or expedient so to do,—

    (a) for the prevention of and for coping with any offence under this Act, or
    (b) for any case or class or group of cases under this Act,

in any district or part thereof, confer, by notification in the Official Gazette, on any officer of the State Government, the powers exercisable by a police officer under the code in such district or part thereof or, as the case may be, for such case or class or group of cases, and in particular, the power of arrest, investigation and prosecution of persons before any Special Court.

(2) All officers of police and all other officers of Government shall assist the officer referred to in sub-section (1) in the execution of the provisions of this Act or any rule, scheme or order made thereunder.
(3) The provisions of the code shall, so far as may be, apply to the exercise of the powers by an officer under sub-section (1).

Chapter III: Externment

10. *Removal of person likely to commit offence*

(1) Where the special Court is satisfied, upon a complaint or a police report that a person is likely to commit an offence under Chapter II of this Act in any area included in 'Scheduled Areas' or 'Tribal areas' as referred to in article 244 of the Constitution, it may, by order in writing, direct such person to remove himself beyond the limits of such area, by such route and within such time as may be specified in the order, and not to return to that area from which he was directed to remove himself for such period, not exceeding two years, as may be specified in the order.
(2) The Special Court shall, along with the order under sub-section (1), communicate to the person directed under that sub-section the grounds on which such order has been made.

(3) The Special Court may revoke or modify the order made under sub-section (1) for the reasons to be recorded in writing, on the representation made by the person against whom such order has been made or by any other person on his behalf within thirty days from the date of the order.

11. Procedure on failure of person to remove himself from area and enter thereon after removal

(1) If a person to whom a direction has been issued under section 10 to remove himself from any area—

(a) fails to remove himself as directed; or
(b) having so removed himself enters such area within the period specified in the order, otherwise than with the permission in writing of the Special Court under sub-section (2), the Special Court may cause him to be arrested and removed in police custody to such place outside such area as the Special Court may specify.

(2) The Special Court may, by order in writing, permit any person on respect of whom an order under section 10 has been made, to return to the area from which he was directed to remove himself for such temporary period and subject to such conditions as may be specified in such order and may require him to execute a bond with or without surety for the due observation of the conditions imposed.
(3) The Special Court may at any time revoke any such permission.
(4) Any person who, with such permission, returns to the area from which he was directed to remove himself shall observe the conditions imposed, and at the expiry of the temporary period for which he was permitted to return, or on the revocation of such permission before the expiry of such temporary period, shall remove himself outside such area and shall not return thereto within the unexpired portion specified under section 10 without a fresh permission.
(5) If a person fails to observe any of the conditions imposed or to remove himself accordingly or having so removed himself enters or returns to such area without fresh permission, the Special Court may cause him to be arrested and removed in police outside such area as the Special Court may specify.

12. Talking measurements and photographs, etc., of persons against whom order under section 10 is made

(1) Every person against whom an order has been made under section 10 shall, if so required by the Special Court, allow his measurements and photographs to be taken by a police officer.
(2) If any person referred to in sub-section (1), when required to allow his measurements or photographs to be taken, resists or refuses to allow the taking of such measurements or photographs, it shall be lawful to use all necessary means to secure the taking thereof.
(3) Resistance to or refusal to allow the taking of measurements or photographs under sub-section (2) shall be deemed to be an offence under section 186 of the Indian Penal Code (45 of 1860).

(4) Where an order under section 10 is revoked, all measurements and photographs (including negatives) taken under sub-section (2) shall be destroyed or made over to the person against whom such order is made.

13. Penalty for non-compliance of order under section10

Any person contravening an order of the Special Court made under section 10 shall be punishable with imprisonment for a term which may extend to one year and with fine.

14. Special Court

For the purpose of providing for speedy trial, the State Government shall, with the concurrence of the Chief Justice of the High Court, by notification in the Official Gazette, specify for each district a Court of Session to be a Special Court to try the offences under this Act.

15. Special Public Prosecutor

For every Special court, the State Government shall, by notification in the Official Gazette, specify a Public Prosecutor or appoint an advocate who has been in practice as an advocate for not less than seven years, as a Special Public Prosecutor for the purpose of conducting cases in that Court.

Chapter V: Miscellaneous

16. Power of State Government to impose collective fine

The provisions of section 10A of the Protection of civil Right Act, 1955 (22 of 1955) shall, so far as may be, apply for the purposes of imposition and realisation of collective fine and for all other matters connected therewith under this Act.

17. Preventive action to be taken by the law and order machinery

(1) A District Magistrate or a Sub-divisional Magistrate or any other Executive Magistrate or any police office not below the rank of a Deputy Superintendent of Police may, on receiving information and after such inquiry as he may think necessary, has reason to believe that a person or a group of persons not belonging to the Scheduled Castes or the Scheduled Tribes, residing in or frequenting any place within the local limits of his jurisdiction is likely to commit an offence or has threatened to commit any offence under this Act and is of the opinion that there is sufficient ground for proceeding, declare such an area to be an area prone to atrocities and take necessary action for keeping the peace and good behaviour and maintenance of public order and tranquillity and may take preventive action.
(2) The provisions of Chapters VIII, X and XI of the Code shall, so far as may be, apply for the purposes of sub-section (1).

(3) The State Government may, by notification in the Official Gazette, make one or more schemes specifying the manner in which the officers referred to in sub-section (1) shall take appropriate action specified in such scheme or schemes to prevent atrocities and to restore the feeling of security amongst the members of the Scheduled Castes and Scheduled Tribes.

18. Section 438 of the Code not to apply to persons committing an offence under the Act

Nothing in section 438 of the Code shall apply in relation to any case involving the arrest of any person on an accusation of having committed an offence under this Act.

19. Section 360 of the Code or the Provisions of the Probation of offenders Act no to apply to persons guilty of an offence under the Act

The provisions of section 360 of the Code and the Provisions of the Probation of Offenders Act, 1958 (20 of 1958) shall not apply to any person above the age of eighteen years who is found guilty of having committed an offence under this Act.

20. Act to override other laws

Save as otherwise provided in this Act, the Provisions of this Act shall have effect notwithstanding anything inconsistent therewith contained in any other law for the time being in force or any custom or usage any instrument having by virtue of any such law.

21. Duty of Government to ensure effective implementation of the Act

(1) Subject to such rules as the Central Government may make in this behalf, the State Government shall take such measures as may be necessary for the effective implementation of this Act.
(2) In particular, and without prejudice to the generality of the foregoing provisions, such measures may include,—

(i) the provision for adequate facilities, including legal aid, to the persons subjected to atrocities to enable them to avail themselves of justice;
(ii) the provision for travelling and maintenance expenses to witnesses, including the victims of atrocities, during investigation and trial of offences under this Act;
(iii) the provision for the economic and social rehabilitation of the victims of the atrocities;
(iv) the appointment of officers for initiating or exercising supervision over prosecutions for the contravention of the provisions of this Act;
(v) the setting up of committees at such appropriate levels as the State Government may think fit to assist that Government in formulation or implementation of such measures;

(vi) provision for a periodic survey of the working of the provisions of this Act with a view to suggesting measures for the better implementation of the provisions of this Act;

(vii) the identification of the areas where the members of the Scheduled Castes and the Scheduled Tribes are likely to be subjected to atrocities and adoption of such measures so as to ensure safety for such members.

(3) The Central Government shall take such steps as may be necessary to co-ordinate the measures taken by the State Governments under sub-section (1).

(4) The Central Government shall, every year, place on the table of each House of Parliament a report on the measures taken by itself and by the State Governments in pursuance of the provisions of this section.

22. Protection of action taken in good faith

No suit, prosecution or other legal proceedings shall lie against the Central Government or against the State Government or any office or authority of Government or any other person for anything which is in good faith done or intended to be done under this Act.

23. Power to make rules

(1) The Central Government may, by notification in the Official Gazette, make rules for carrying out the purposes of this Act.

(2) Every rule made under this Act shall be laid, as soon as may be after it is made, before each House of Parliament, while it is in session for a total period of thirty days which may be comprised in one session or in two or more successive sessions, aforesaid, both Houses agree in making any modification in the rule or both Houses agree that the rule should not be made, the rule shall thereafter have effect only in such modified form or be of no effect, as the case may be; so, however, that any such modification or annulment shall be without prejudice to the validity of anything Previously done under that rule.

Appendix III: *The Scheduled Caste and Scheduled Tribes (Prevention of Atrocities) Rules, 1995*

(Prevention of Atrocities) Rules, 1995

G.S.R/ 316 (E), dated 31st March, 1995.—In exercise of the powers conferred by sub-section (1) of Sec. 23 of the Scheduled Caste and the Scheduled Tribes (Prevention of Atrocities) Act, 1989 (33 of 1989), the Central Government hereby makes the following rules, namely:

1. Short title and commencement.
   (1) These rules may be called the Scheduled Castes and the Scheduled Tribes (Prevention of Atrocities) Rules, 1995.
   (2) They shall come into force on the date of their publications in the Official Gazette.
2. Definition.

   In these rules, unless the context otherwise requires,

(a) "Act" means the Scheduled Castes and the Scheduled Tribes (Prevention of Atrocities) Act, 1989 (33 of 1989);
(b) "dependent", with its grammatical variations and cognate expressions, includes wife, children, whether married or unmarried, dependent parents, widows sister, widow and children of pre-deceased son of a victim of atrocity;
(c) "identified area" means such area where State Government has reason to believe that atrocity may take place or there is an apprehension of re-occurrence of an offence under the Act or an area prone to victim of atrocity;
(d) "Non-Government Organization" means a voluntary organization engaged in the welfare activities relating to the scheduled castes and the scheduled tribes and registered under the Societies Registration Act., 1860 (21 of 1860) or under any law for the registration of documents of such Organization for the time being in force;

UMAKANT, *Dalit Human Rights in India*, People, Cultures and Societies: Exploring and Documenting Diversities,
https://doi.org/10.1007/978-981-95-5751-6

(e) "Schedule" means the Schedule annexed to these rules;
(f) "Section" means Section of the Act;
(g) "State Government", in relation to a Union Territory, means the Administrator of that Union Territory appointed by the President under Art. 239 of the Constitution;
(h) Words and expression used herein and not defined but defined in the Act shall have the meanings respectively assigned to them in the Act.

3. *Precautionary and preventive measures*

With a view to prevent atrocities on the Scheduled Castes and the Scheduled Tribes, the State Government shall,—

(i) identity the area where it has reason to believe that atrocity may take place or there is an apprehension of reoccurrence of an offence under the Act;
(ii) order the District Magistrate and Superintendent of Police or any other officer to visit the identified area and review the law and order situation;
(iii) if deem necessary, in the identification area cancel the arm licenses of the persons, not being member of the Scheduled Castes or Scheduled Tribes, their near relations, servants or employees and family friends and get such arms deposited in the Government Armoury;
(iv) seize all illegal fire-arms and prohibit any illegal manufacture of fire-arms;
(v) with a view to ensure the safety of person and property, if deem necessary, provide arms licenses to the member of the Scheduled Castes and the Scheduled Tribes;
(vi) constitute a high power State-level committee, district and divisional level committees or such number of other committees as deem proper and necessary for assisting the Government in implementation of the provisions of the Act;
(vii) set up vigilance and monitoring committee to suggest effective measures to implement the provisions of the Act;
(viii) set up Awareness Centers and organize Workshops in the identified area or at some other place to educate the persons belonging to the Scheduled Caṣtes and the Scheduled Tribes about their rights and the protection available to them under the provisions of various Central and State enactment or rules, regulations and schemes framed there under;
(ix) encourage Non-Government Organizations for establishing and maintaining Awareness Centers and organizing workshops and provide them necessary financial and other sort of assistance;
(x) deploy special police force in the identified area;
(xi) by the end of every quarter, review the law and order situation, functioning of different committees, performance of Special Public Prosecutors, Investigating Officers and other Officers responsible for implementing the provisions of the Act and the cases registered under the Act.

4. *Supervision of prosecution and submission of report*

(1) The State Government on the recommendation of the District Magistrate shall prepare for each District a panel of such number of eminent senior advocate who has been in practice for not less than seven years, as it may deem necessary for conducting cases in the Special Courts. Similarly, in consultation with the Director Prosecution/in charge of the prosecution, a panel of such member of Public Prosecutors as it may deem necessary for conducting cases in the Special Courts, shall also be specified. Both these panels shall be notified in the Official Gazette of the State and shall remain in force for a period of three years.

(2) The District Magistrate and the Director of persecution in charge of the prosecution shall review at least twice in calendar year, in the month of January and July, the performance of Special Public Prosecutors so specified or appointed and submit a report to the State Government.

(3) If the State Government is satisfied or has reason to believe that a Special Public Prosecutor so appointed or specified has not conducted the case to the best of his ability and with due care and caution, his name may be, for reasons to be recorded in writing, de-notified.

(4) The District Magistrate and the Officer-in-charge of the prosecution at the District level shall review the position of cases registered under the Act and submit a monthly report on or before 20th day of each subsequent month to the Director of Prosecution and the State Government. This report shall specify the actions taken/proposed to be taken in respect of investigation and prosecution of each case.

(5) Notwithstanding anything contained in Sub-rule (1) the District Magistrate or the Sub-Divisional Magistrate may, if deem necessary or if so desired by the victim of atrocity engage an eminent Senior Advocate for conducting cases in the Special Courts on such payment of fees as he may consider appropriate.

(6) Payment of fee to the Special Public Prosecutor shall be fixed by the State Government on a scale higher than the other panel advocates in the State.

5. Information to Police Officers in-charge of a Police Station

   (1) Every information relating to the commission of an offence under the Act, if given orally to an officer in-charge of a police station shall be reduced to writing by him or under his direction and be read over to the informant, and every such information, whether given in writing or reduced to writing as aforesaid, shall be signed by the persons giving it, and the substance thereof shall be entered in a book to be maintained by that police station.

   (2) A copy of the information as so recorded under sub-rule (1) above shall be given forthwith, free of cost, to the informant.

   (3) Any person aggrieved by a refusal on the part of an officer in charge of a police station to record the information referred in sub-rule (1) may send the substance of such information, in writing and by post, to the Superintendent of Police concerned who after investigation either by himself or by a police officer not below the rank of Deputy Superintendent of Police, shall make an order in writing to the officer in charge of the concerned police station to enter the substance of that information to be entered in the book to be maintained by the police station.

6. Spot inspection by officers
   (1) Whenever the District Magistrate or the Sub-Divisional Magistrate or any other Executive Magistrate or any police officer not below the rank of Deputy Superintendent of Police receives an information from any person or upon his own knowledge that an atrocity has been committed on the members of the Scheduled Castes or the Scheduled Tribes within his jurisdiction he shall immediately himself visit the place of occurrence to assess the extent of atrocity, loss of life, loss and damage to the property and submit a report forthwith to the State Government.
   (2) The District Magistrate or the Sub-Divisional Magistrate or any other executive Magistrate and the Superintendent of Police, Deputy Superintendent of Police after inspecting the place or area on the spot,—

   (i) draw a list of victims, their family member and dependents entitled for relief;
   (ii) prepare a detailed report of the extent of atrocity, loss and damage to the property of the victims;
   (iii) order for intensive police patrolling in the area;
   (iv) take effective and necessary steps to provide protection to the witnesses and other sympathizers of the victims;
   (v) provide immediate relief to the victims.

7. *Investigating Officer*

   (1) An offence committed under the Act shall be investigated by a police officer not below the rank of a Deputy Superintendent of Police. The investigating officer shall be appointed by the State Government, Director General of Police, and Superintendent of Police after taking into account his past experience, sense of ability and justice to perceive the implications of the case and investigate it along with right lines within the shortest possible time.
   (2) The investigating officer so appointed under sub-rule (1) shall complete the investigation on top priority within thirty days and submit the report to the Superintendent of Police who in turn will immediately forward the report to the Director General of Police of the State Government.
   (3) The Home Secretary and the Social Welfare Secretary to the State Government, Director of Prosecution, the officer-in-charge of Prosecution and the Director General of Police shall review by the end of every quarter the position of all investigations done by the investigating officer.

8. Setting up of the Scheduled Castes and the Scheduled Tribes Protection Cell

The State Government shall set up a Scheduled Castes and the Scheduled Tribes Protection Cell at the State headquarters under the charge of Director of Police, Inspector General of Police. This Cell shall be responsible for—

(i) conducting survey of the identified area;
(ii) maintaining public order and tranquillity in the identified area;

(iii) recommending to the State Government for deployment of special police force or establishment of special police post in the identified area;
(iv) making investigations about the probable causes leading to an offence under the Act;
(v) restoring the feeling of security amongst the members of the Scheduled Castes and the Scheduled Tribes;
(vi) informing the nodal officer and special officer about the law and order situation in the identified area;
(vii) making enquiries about the investigation and spot inspections conducted by various officers;
(viii) making enquiries about the action taken by the Superintendent of Police in the cases where an officer-in-charge of the police station has refused to enter an information in a book to be maintained by that police station under sub-rule (3) of rule 5;
(ix) making enquiries about the wilful negligence by a public servant;
(x) reviewing the position of cases registered under the Act; and
(xi) submitting a monthly report on or before 20th day of each subsequent month to the State Government, nodal officer about the action taken proposed to be taken, in respect of the above.

9. *Nomination of Nodal Officer*

The State Government shall nominate a nodal officer of the level of a Secretary to the Government preferably belonging to the Scheduled Castes or the Scheduled Tribes, for coordinating the functioning of the Distinct Magistrate and Superintendent of Police or other officers authorized by them investigating officers and other officers responsible for implementing the provisions of the Act. By the end of the every quarter, the nodal officer shall review—

(i) the reports received by the State Government under Sub-rules (2) and (4) of rule 4, rule 6, CI. (xi) of rule 8;
(ii) the position of cases registered under the Act;
(iii) (III) law and order situation in the identified area;
(iv) various kinds of measures adopted for providing immediate relief in cash or kind or both to the victims of atrocity or his or her dependent;
(v) adequacy of immediate facilities like rationing, clothing, shelter, legal aid, travelling allowance, daily allowance and transport facilities provided to the victims of atrocity of his/her dependents;
(vi) performance of non-Governmental organizations, the Scheduled Castes and the Scheduled Tribes Protection Cell, various committees and the public servants responsible for implementing the provisions of the Act.

10. *Appointment of a Special Officer*

In the identified area a Special Officer not below the rank of an Additional District Magistrate shall be appointed to co-ordinate with the District Magistrate, Superintendent of Police or other officers responsible for implementing the provisions of the Act, various committees and the Scheduled Castes and the Scheduled Tribes Protection Cell.

The Special Officer shall be responsible for:

(i) providing immediate relief and other facilities to the victims of atrocity and initiate necessary measures to prevent or avoid re-occurrence of atrocity;
(ii) setting up an awareness center and organizing workshop in the identified area or at the District headquarters to educate the persons belonging to the Scheduled Castes and the Scheduled Tribes about their rights and the protection available to them under the provisions of various Central and State enactments or rules and schemes, etc. framed therein;
(iii) coordinating with the non-governmental organization and providing necessary facilities and financial and other type of assistance to non-governmental organizations for maintaining centers or organizing workshops.

11. *Travelling allowance, daily allowance, maintenance expense and transport facilities to the victim atrocity, his or her dependent and witness*

(1) Every victim of atrocity of his/her dependent and witness shall be paid to and fro rail fare by second class in express/mail/ passenger train or actual bus or taxi fare from his/her place of residence or place of stay to the place of investigation or hearing of trial of an office under the Act.
(2) The District Magistrate or the Sub-Divisional Magistrate or any other Executive Magistrate shall make necessary arrangements for providing transport facilities or reimbursement of full payment thereof to the victims of atrocity and witnesses for visiting the investigating officer, Superintendent of Police/Deputy Superintendent of Police, District Magistrate or any other Executive Magistrate.
(3) Every woman witness, the victims of atrocity or her dependent being a woman or a minor, a person more than sixty years of age and a person having 40% or more disability shall be entitled to be accompanied by an attendant of her/his choice. The attendant shall also be paid travelling and maintenance expenses as applicable to the witness or the victim of atrocity when called upon during hearing, investigation and trial of an offence under the Act.
(4) The witness, the victim of atrocity or his/her dependent and attendant shall be paid daily maintenance expenses for the days he/she is away from the place of his/her residence or stay during investigation, hearing and trial of an offence, at such rates but not less than the minimum wages, as may be fixed by the state government for the agricultural labourers.
(5) In additional to daily maintenance expenses the witness, the victim of atrocity (or his/her dependent) and the attendant shall also be paid diet expenses at such rates as may be fixed by the State Government from time to time
(6) The payment of travelling allowance, daily allowance, maintenance expenses and reimbursement of transport facilities shall be made immediately or not later than three days by the District Magistrate or the Sub-Divisional Magistrate or any other Executive Magistrate to the victims, their dependents/attendant and witnesses for the days they visit the investigating officer or in-charge police station or hospital authorities or Superintendent of Police, Deputy Superintendent

of Police or District Magistrate or any other officer concerned or the Special Court.

(7) When an offence has been committed under Sec. 3 of the Act, the District Magistrate or the Sub-Divisional Magistrate or any other Executive Magistrate shall reimburse the payment of medicines, special medical consultation, blood transfusion, replacement of essential clothing, meals and fruits provided to the victim(s) of atrocity.

12. Measure to be taken by the District Administration

(1) The District Magistrate and the Superintendent of Police shall visit the place or area where the atrocity has been committed to assess the loss of life and damage to the property and draw a list of victim, their family members and dependents entitled for relief.

(2) Superintendent of Police shall ensure that the First Information Report is registered in the book of the concerned police station and effective measures for apprehending the accused are taken.

(3) The Superintendent of Police, after spot inspection, shall immediately appoint an investigation officer and deploy such police force in the area and take such other preventive measures as he may deem proper and necessary.

(4) The District Magistrate or the Sub-Divisional Magistrate or any other Executive Magistrate shall make arrangement for providing immediate relief in cash or in kind or both to the victims of atrocity, their family members and dependents according to the scale as in the schedule annexed to these Rules (Annexure-1 read with Annexure-II). Such immediate relief also include food, water, clothing, shelter, medical aid, transport facilities and other essential items necessary for human beings.

(5) The relief provided to the victim of the atrocity or his/her dependent under sub-rule (4) in respect of death, or injury to, or damage to property shall be in addition to any other right to claim compensation in respect thereof under any other law for the time being in force.

(6) The relief and rehabilitation facilities mentioned in sub-rule (4) above shall be provided by the District Magistrate or the Sub-Divisional Magistrate or any other Executive Magistrate in accordance with the scales provided in the Schedule annexed to these rules.

(7) A report of the relief and rehabilitation facilities provided to the victims shall also be forwarded to the Special Court by the District Magistrate or the Sub-Divisional Magistrate or the Executive Magistrate or Superintendent of Police. In case the Special Court is satisfied that the payment of relief was not made to the victim or his/her dependent in time or the amount of relief or compensation was not sufficient or only a part of payment of relief or compensation was made, it may order for making in full or part the payment of relief or any other kind of assistance.

13. Selection of Officers and other State Members for completing the work relating to atrocity

(1) The State Government shall ensure that the administrative officers and other staff members to be appointed in an area prone to atrocity shall have the right aptitude and understanding of the problems of the Schedule Castes and posts and police station.
(2) It shall also be ensured by the State Government that persons from the Scheduled Castes and the Scheduled Tribes are adequately represented in the administration and in the police force at all levels, particularly at the level or police posts and police station.

14. Specific responsibility of the State Government

The State Government shall make necessary provisions in its annual budget for providing relief and rehabilitation facilities to the victims of atrocity. It shall review at least twice in a calendar year, in the month of January and July the performance of the Special Public Prosecutor Specified or appointed under Sec. 15 of the Act, various reports receives, investigation made and preventive steps taken by the District Magistrate, Sub-Divisional Magistrate and Superintendent of Police, relief and rehabilitation facilities provided to the victims and the reports in respect of lapses on behalf of the concerned officers.

15. Contingency Plan by the State Government
(1) The State Government shall prepare a model contingency plan for implementing the provisions of the Act and notify the same in the Official Gazette of the State Government. It should specify the role and responsibility of Rural/Urban Local Bodies and Non-Government Organisations. Inter alia this plan shall contain a package of relief measures including the following:

(a) scheme to provide immediate relief in cash or in kind or both;
(b) allotment of agricultural land and house sites;
(c) the rehabilitation packages;
(d) scheme for employment in Government or Government undertaking to the dependent or one of the family members of the victim;
(e) pension scheme for widows, dependent children of the deceased, handicapped or old age victims of atrocity;
(f) mandatory compensation for the victims;
(g) scheme for strengthening the socio-economic condition of the victim;
(h) provisions for providing brick/stone masonry house to the victims;
(i) such other elements as health care, supply of essential commodities, electrification, adequate drinking water facility, burial/cremation ground and link roads to the Scheduled Castes and the Scheduled Tribes.

(2) The State Government shall forward a copy of the contingency plan or a summary thereof and a copy of the scheme, as soon as may be, to the Central Government in the Ministry of Welfare and to all the District Magistrates, Sub-Divisional Magistrates, Inspectors-General of Police and Superintendents of Police.

16. Constitution of State-level Vigilance and Monitoring Committee

(1) The State Government shall constitute high power vigilance and monitoring committee of not more than 25 members consisting of the following:

(i) Chief Minister/Administrator—Chairman (in case of a State under President's Rule Governor-Chairman);
(ii) Home Minister, Finance Minister and Welfare Minister Members (in case of a State under the President's Rule, Advisors-Members);
(iii) all elected Members of Parliament and State Legislative Assembly and Legislative Council from the State belonging to the Scheduled Castes and the Scheduled Tribes-Members;
(iv) Chief Secretary, the Home Secretary, the Director-General of Police, Director/Deputy Director, National Commission for the Scheduled Castes and the Scheduled Tribes-Members;
(v) the Secretary in-charge of the welfare and development of the Scheduled Castes and the Scheduled Tribes-Convener.

(2) The high power vigilance and monitoring committee shall meet at least twice in a calendar year, in the month of January and July to review the implementation of the provisions of the Act, relief and rehabilitation facilities provided to the victims and other matters connected therewith, prosecution of case under the Act, rule of different officers/agencies responsible for implementing the provisions of the Act and various reports received by State Government.
17. Constitution of District Level Vigilance and Monitoring committee
(1) In each district within the State, the District Magistrate shall set up a vigilance and monitoring committee in his district to review the implementation of the provisions of the Act, relief and rehabilitation facilities provided to the victims and other matters connected therewith, prosecution of cases under the Act, role of different officers/agencies responsible for implementing the provision of the Act and various reports received by the District Administration.
(2) The district level vigilance and monitoring committee shall consist of the elected Members of the Parliament and Stage Legislative Assembly and legislative Council, Superintendent of Police, three-group 'A' Officers Gazetted Officers of the State Government belonging to the Scheduled Castes and the Scheduled Tribes, not more than 5 non-official members belonging to the Scheduled Castes and the Scheduled Tribes and not more than 3 members from the case categories other than the Scheduled Castes and the Scheduled Tribes having association with Non-Government Organizations. The District Magistrate and District Social Welfare Officer shall be Chairman and Member Secretary respectively.
(3) The district level committee shall meet at least once in three months.
18. Material for Annual Report

The State Government shall every year before the 31st March, forward the report to the Central Government about the measures taken for implementing provisions of the Act and various schemes/ plans framed by it during the previous calendar year.

Annexure 1: Schedule

[See rule 12 (4)]

Norms for Relief Amount

Name and section number of offense	Minimum amount of relief
1. Drink or eat inedible or obnoxious substance [Sec. 3 (1) (i)] 2. Causing injury insult or annoyance [Sec.3(1)(ii)] 3. Derogatory Act [Sec. 3 (1) (iii)]	Rs. 25,000 or more depending upon the nature and gravity of the offence to each victim and also commensurate with the indignity, insult and defamation suffered by the victim. Payment to be made as follows: 25% when the charge sheet is sent to the court; 75% when accused are convicted buy the lower court
4. Wrongful occupation or cultivation of land. Etc. [Sec.3 (1)(iv)] 5.Relating to land, premises and water [Sec.3 (1)(v)]	At least Rs. 25,000 or more depending upon the nature and gravity of the offense. The land/premises/water supply shall be restored where necessary at Government cost. Full payment to be made when charge sheet is sent to the Court
6. Begar or forced of bonded labour [Sec. 3 (1) (vi)]	At least Rs. 25,000 to each victim. Payment of 25% at first Information Report stage and 75% on conviction in the lower court
7. Relating to right to franchise [Sec. 3 (1) (vii)]	Up to Rs. 20.000 to each victim depending upon the nature and gravity of offense
8. False, malicious or vexatious legal proceedings [Sec.3 (1) (viii)] 9. False and frivolous information [Sec. 3(1)(ix)]	Rs. 25,000 or reimbursement of actual legal expenses and damages whichever is less after conclusion of the accused
10. Insult, intimidation and humiliation [Sec. 3(1)(x)]	Up to Rs. 25, 000 to each victim depending upon the nature of the offense. Payment of 25% when charge sheet is sent to the court and the rest on conviction.
11. Outraging the modesty of a woman [Sec. 3 (1)(xi)] 12. Sexual exploitation of a woman [Sec. 3 (1)(xii)]	Rs. 50,000 to each victim of the offense. 50% of the amount may be paid after medical examination and remaining 50% at the conclusion of the trial
13. Fouling of water [Sec. 3 (1) (xiii)]	Up to Rs. 1, 00,000 or full cost of restoration of normal facility, including cleaning when the water is fouled. Payment may be made at the state as deemed fit by District Administration
14. Denial of customary rites of passage [Sec.3 (1)(xiv)	Up to Rs. 1, 00,000 or full cost of restoration of rite of passage and full compensation of the loss suffered, if any. Payment of 50% when charge sheet is sent to the court and 50% on conviction in lower court
15. Deserting one from their place of residence [Sec.3 (1) (xv)]	Restoration of the site/right to stay and compensation of Rs. 25,000 to each victim and reconstruction of the house at Govt. cost, if destroyed. To be paid in full when charge sheet is sent to the lower court.

(*continued*)

(continued)

Name and section number of offense	Minimum amount of relief
16. Giving false evidence [Sec. 3(2)(i) and (ii)]	At least Rs. 1, 00,000 or full compensation of the loss or harm sustained. 50% to be paid when charge-sheet is sent to Court and 50% on conviction by the lower court
17. Committing offences under the Indian penal Code punishable with imprisonment for a term of 10 years or more [Sec.3(2)]	At least Rs. 50,000 depending upon the nature and gravity of the offense to each victim and or his dependents. The amount would vary if specifically provided for otherwise in the Schedule
18. Victimization at the hands of public servant [Sec.3(2)]	Full compensation on account of damages or loss or harm sustained. Fifty percent to be paid when charge sheet is sent to the Court and 50% on conviction by lower court
19. Disability (a) 100% incapacitation (i)Non-earning member of a family (ii) Earning member of a family (b) Where incapacitation is less than 100%	At least Rs. 1, 00,000 to each victim of offense. 50% on FIR and 25% at charge sheet and 25% on conviction by the lower court - At least Rs. 2, 00,000 to each victim of offense. Fifty percent to be paid on FIR/medical examination stage, 25% when charge sheet sent to court and 25% at conviction in lower - The rates are laid down in (i) and (ii) above shall be reduced in the same proportion, the stages of payment also being the same. However, not less than Rs. 15,000 to a non-earning member and not less than Rs. 30,000 to and earning member of the family
20. Murder/Death (a) Non-earning member of a family (b) Earning member of a family.	- At least Rs.1, 00,000 to each case. Payment of 75% after post-mortem and 25% on conviction by the lower court - At least Rs. 2, 00,000 to each case. Payment of 75% after post-mortem and 25% on conviction by the lower court
21. Victim of murder, death massacre, rape, mass rape and gang rape, permanent incapacitation and dacoity	In addition to relief amount paid under above items relief may be arranged within three months of date of atrocity as follows: (i) Pension to each widow and/or other dependents of deceased SC/ST at Rs. 1,000 per month, or employment to one member of the family of the deceased, or provision of agricultural land, a house, if necessary by outright purchase (ii) Full cost of the education and maintenance of the children of the victims. Children may be admitted to the Ashram Schools/residential schools (iii) Provision of utensils, rice, wheat, dals, pulses, etc. for a period of three months
22. Complete destruction/burnt houses	Brick/ stone masonry house to be constructed or provided at Government cost where it has been burnt or destroyed

The Scheduled Castes and Scheduled Tribes (Prevention of Atrocities) Act, 1989-With All Amendments https://ncsc.nic.in/files/review%20proforma/PoA%20 Act%201989%20with%20all%20ammendments.pdf

The Gazette Notification for The Scheduled Castes and Scheduled Tribes (Prevention of Atrocities) Amendment Act, 2018 https://ncsc.nic.in/files/Ammendment%202018.pdf

The Gazette Notification for The Scheduled Castes and Scheduled Tribes (Prevention of Atrocities), Rules, 2016 https://ncsc.nic.in/files/PoA%20Amendment%20Rules,%202016.pdf

Appendix IV: India and International Human Rights Treaties

India has signed and ratified eight human rights treaties and has also signed two other treaties but yet to ratify. The details are as follows:

Ratification Status for India

International human rights treaties	Signature date	Ratification date, accession (a), succession (d) date	Denunciation date
CAT: Convention against Torture and other Cruel and Inhuman or Degrading Treatment or Punishment	14 October 1997		
CAT-OP: Optional Protocol of the Convention against Torture			
CCPR: International Covenant on Civil and Political Rights		10 April 1979 (a)	
CCPR-OP2-DP: Second Optional Protocol to ICCPR aiming to the abolition of the death penalty			
CED: Convention for the Protection of All Persons from Enforced Disappearance	06 Feb 2007		
CED, Article 32: Interstate communication Procedure			
CEDAW: Convention on the Elimination of All Forms of Discrimination against Women	30 July 1980	09 July 1993	
CERD: International Convention on the Elimination of All Forms of Racial Discrimination	02 March 1967	03 Dec 1968	
CESCR: International Covenant on Economic, Social and Cultural Rights		10 April 1978 (a)	
CMW: International Convention on the Protection of the Rights of All Migrant Workers and Members of their Families			

(*continued*)

UMAKANT, *Dalit Human Rights in India*, People, Cultures and Societies: Exploring and Documenting Diversities,
https://doi.org/10.1007/978-981-95-5751-6

(continued)

International human rights treaties	Signature date	Ratification date, accession (a), succession (d) date	Denunciation date
CRC: Convention on the Rights of the Child		11 Dec 1992 (a)	
CR-OP-AC: Optional Protocol to Convention on the Rights of the Child on the Involvement of Children in Armed Conflict	15 Nov 2004	30 Nov 2005	
CRC-OP-SC: Optional Protocol to the Convention on the Rights of the Child on the Sale of Children for Prostitution and Child Pornography	15 Nov 2004	16 Aug 2005	
CRPD: Convention on the Rights of Person with Disabilities	30 March 2007	01 Oct 2007	

Source: UN Office of the High Commissioner for Human Rights, Geneva. tbinternet.ohchr.org/_layouts/15/TreatyBodyExternal/Treaty.aspx?CountryID=79&Lang=EN

Acceptance of the Inquiry Procedure for India

India has not expressed its view on any of the inquiry procedure under CAT, CED, CEDAW, CESCR, CRC and CRPD (Ibid)

Acceptance of the Interstate Communication Procedure

So far there is no response from India (Ibid).

Concluding Observations and Recommendations of Treaty Monitoring Bodies After Examining India's Periodic Reports

It is obligatory for the member states of the UN which has signed and ratified international human rights treaties to submit a periodic report to the treaty monitoring bodies. Five treaty monitoring bodies have so far given their concluding observations and recommendations on India's periodic reports. Starting from 1996 up to the year 2014, caste discrimination issues have been highlighted in these concluding observations and recommendations.

CERD Concluding Observations: India 2007

(CERD/C/IND/CO/19)

3. The Committee notes with appreciation the comprehensive constitutional provisions and other legislation of the State party to combat discrimination, including discrimination based on race and caste.

4. The Committee welcomes the special measures adopted by the State party to advance the equal enjoyment of rights by members of scheduled castes and schedules tribes, such as reservation of seats in Union and State legislatures and of posts in the public service.

5. The Committee welcomes the establishment of institutions responsible for the implementation of anti-discrimination legislation such as the Scheduled Castes and Scheduled tribes (Prevention of Atrocities) Act (1989) and for the monitoring of acts of discrimination and violence against members of scheduled castes and scheduled tribes, including the Ministry of Social Justice and Empowerment, the Union and State Parliamentary Committees on Social Justice, the Ministry of Tribal Affairs, and the National Commissions on Scheduled Castes and on Scheduled tribes.

6. The Committee notes with appreciation the declaration of the Indian Prime Minister before the Dalit- Minority International Conference in New Delhi on 27 December 2006 that the only parallel to the practice of Untouchability was Apartheid in South Africa. Such a declaration underlines the renewed commitment to address the discriminatory practice of Untouchability.

8. The Committee takes note of the State party's position that discrimination based on caste falls outside the scope of article 1 of the Convention. However, after an extensive exchange of views with the State party, the Committee maintains its position expressed in general recommendation No. 29—that discrimination based on descent includes discrimination against members of communities based on forms of social stratification such as caste and analogous systems of inherited status which nullify or impair their equal enjoyment of human rights. Therefore, the Committee reaffirms that discrimination based on the ground of caste is fully covered by article 1 of the Convention.

9. The Committee regrets the lack of information in the State party's report on concrete measures taken to implement existing anti-discrimination and affirmative action legislation, as well as on the de facto enjoyment by members of scheduled castes and scheduled and other tribes of the rights guaranteed by the Convention. (arts. 2 and 5)

Notwithstanding the above-mentioned legal position of the State party, the Committee invites it to include in its next periodic report detailed information on measures taken to implement anti-discrimination and affirmative action legislation, disaggregated by caste, tribe, gender, State/district and rural/urban population. The State party should also provide disaggregated data on the percentages of the Union, State and district budgets allocated for that purpose and on the effects of such measures on the enjoyment by members of scheduled castes and scheduled and other tribes of the rights guaranteed by the Convention.

13. The Committee notes with concern that, despite the formal abolition of Untouchability by article 17 of the Indian Constitution, de facto segregation of Dalits persists, in particular in rural areas, in access to places of worship, housing, hospitals, education, water sources, markets and other public places. (arts. 3 and 5)

The Committee urges the State party to intensify its efforts to enforce the Protection of Civil Rights Act (1955), especially in rural areas, including by effectively punishing acts of Untouchability, to take effective measures against segregation in public schools and residential segregation, and to ensure equal access for Dalits places of worship, hospitals, water sources and any other places or services intended for use by the general public.

14. The Committee is concerned about reports of arbitrary arrest, torture and extrajudicial killings of members of scheduled castes and scheduled tribes by the police, and about the frequent failure to protect these groups against acts of communal violence. (arts. 5 (b) and 6)

The Committee urges the State party to provide effective protection to members of scheduled castes and scheduled and other tribes against acts of discrimination and violence, introduce mandatory training on the application of the Scheduled Castes and Scheduled tribes (Prevention of Atrocities) Act (1989) for police, judges and prosecutors and take disciplinary or criminal law measures against police and other law enforcement officers who violate their duty of protection and/or investigation in relation to crimes against scheduled castes and scheduled and other tribes.

15. The Committee is concerned about the alarming number of allegations of acts of sexual violence against Dalit women primarily by men from dominant castes, in particular rape, and about the sexual exploitation of Dalit and tribal women who are being trafficked and forced into prostitution. (art. 5 (b))

The Committee urges the State party to effectively prosecute and punish perpetrators of acts of sexual violence and exploitation of Dalit and tribal women, sanction anyone preventing or discouraging victims from reporting such incidents, including police and other law enforcement officers, take preventive measures such as police training and public education campaigns on the criminal nature of such acts, and provide legal, medical and psychological assistance, as well as compensation, to victims. The State party should also consider adopting victim-sensitive rules of evidence similar to that of Section 12 of the Protection of Civil Rights Act (1955) and establishing special court chambers and task forces to address these problems.

17. The Committee notes with concern reports that Dalit candidates, especially women, are frequently forcibly prevented from standing for election or, if elected, forced to resign from village councils or other elected bodies or not to exercise their mandate, that many Dalits are not included in electoral rolls or otherwise denied the right to vote, and that public service posts reserved for scheduled castes and scheduled tribes are almost exclusively filled in the lowest category (e.g. sweepers). The Committee is also concerned that scheduled castes and scheduled and other tribes are underrepresented in the Union, State and local governments and legislatures, as well as in the public service. (arts. 5 (c) and 2 (2))

The Committee recommends to the State party to effectively enforce the reservation policy; to ensure the rights of members of scheduled castes and scheduled and other tribes to freely and safely vote and stand for election and to fully exercise their mandate if elected to their reserved seats; to apply the reservation policy to all categories of public service posts, including the highest, and to extend it to the judiciary; to ensure adequate representation of scheduled castes, scheduled and other tribes and ethnic minorities in Union, State and local governments and legislatures; and to provide updated statistical data on such representation in its next periodic report.

18. The Committee is concerned about the persistence of social norms of purity and pollution which de facto preclude marriages between Dalits and non-Dalits; it is also concerned about violence and social sanctions against inter-caste couples and the continuing practices of child marriage and dowry, and Devadasi whereby mostly Dalit girls are dedicated to temple deities and forced into ritualized prostitution. (art. 5 (d) (iv) and 5 (b))

The Committee urges the State party to effectively enforce the prohibition of child marriage, the Dowry Prohibition Act (1961) and State laws prohibiting the practice of Devadasi. The State party should punish such acts and acts of discrimination or violence against inter-caste couples and rehabilitate victims. Furthermore, it should conduct training and awareness-raising campaigns to sensitize police, prosecutors, judges, politicians, teachers and the general public as to the criminal nature of such acts.

20. The Committee is concerned about reports that Dalits are often denied access to and evicted from land by dominant castes, especially if it borders land belonging to such castes, and that tribal communities have been evicted from their land under the 1980 Forest Act or in order to allow private mining activities (art. 5 (d) (v) and 5 (e) (i) and (iii)).

The Committee recommends that the State party ensure that Dalits, including Dalit women, have access to adequate and affordable land and that acts of violence against Dalits due to land disputes are punished under the Scheduled Castes and Scheduled Tribes (Prevention of Atrocities) Act (1989). The State party should also ensure that tribal communities are not evicted from their lands without seeking their prior informed consent and provision of adequate alternative land and compensation, that bans on leasing tribal lands to third persons or companies are effectively enforced, and that adequate safeguards against the acquisition of tribal lands are included in the Recognition of Forest Rights Act (2006) and other relevant legislation.

21. The Committee notes with concern that Dalits who convert to Islam or to Christianity to escape caste discrimination reportedly lose their entitlement under affirmative action programmes, unlike converts who become Buddhists or Sikhs. (arts. 5 (d) (vii) and 2 (2))

The Committee recommends that the State party restore the eligibility for affirmative action benefits of all members of scheduled castes and scheduled tribes having converted to another religion.

22. The Committee is concerned about reports that Dalits were denied equal access to emergency assistance during the post-tsunami relief, while noting that, according to the State party, those allegations merely concern isolated cases. (arts. 5 (e) and 2 (1) (a))

The Committee recommends to the State party to investigate all alleged cases in which Dalits were denied assistance or benefits equal to that received by caste fishermen or cases in which they were otherwise discriminated against during the post-tsunami relief and rehabilitation process and to compensate or retroactively grant such benefits to the victims of such discrimination.

23. The Committee notes with concern that very large numbers of Dalits are forced to work as manual scavengers and child workers and are subject to extremely unhealthy working conditions and exploitative labour arrangements, including debt bondage. (art. 5 (e) (i) and (iv))

The Committee recommends that the State party effectively implement the Minimum Wages Act (1948), the Equal Remuneration Act (1976), the Bonded Labour (System) Abolition Act (1976), the Child Labour (Prohibition and Regulation) Act (1986) and the Employment of Manual Scavengers and Construction of Dry Latrines (Prohibition) Act (1993). The State party should also adopt measures to enhance Dalits access to the labour market, e.g. by extending the reservation policy to the private sector and issuing job cards under the National Rural Employment Guarantee Scheme to Dalit applicants, and report on the effects of the measures taken on the employment and working conditions of Dalits in its next periodic report.

24. The Committee is concerned about reports that members of scheduled castes and scheduled and other tribes are disproportionately affected by hunger and malnutrition, infant, child and maternal mortality, sexually transmitted diseases, including HIV/AIDS, tuberculosis, diarrhoea, malaria and other water borne diseases and that health care facilities are either unavailable in tribal areas or substantially worse than in non-tribal areas. (art. 5 (e) (iv))

The Committee recommends that the State party ensure equal access to ration shops, adequate health care facilities, reproductive health services, and safe drinking water for members of scheduled castes and scheduled and other tribes and to increase the number of doctors and of functioning and properly equipped primary health centres and health sub-centres in tribal and rural areas.

25. While noting the constitutional guarantee of free and compulsory education for all children up to the age of 14 and the rapid growth of the literacy rate among Dalits, in particular girls, the Committee remains concerned about the high dropout rate among Dalit pupils at the primary and secondary levels, reports of classroom segregation and discrimination against Dalit pupils, teachers and mid-day meal cooks, and the poor infrastructure, equipment, staffing and quality of teaching in public schools attended by Dalit and tribal children. (art. 5 (e) (v))

The Committee recommends that the State party take effective measures to reduce dropout and increase enrolment rates among Dalit children and adolescents at all levels of schooling, e.g. by providing scholarships or other financial subsidies and by sensitizing parents as to the importance of education, combat classroom segregation and discrimination against Dalit pupils and ensure non-discriminatory access to the Mid-Day Meal Scheme, adequate equipment, staffing and quality of teaching in public schools, as well as physical access by Dalit and tribal pupils to schools in dominant caste neighbourhoods and armed conflict areas.

26. The Committee notes with concern allegations that the police frequently fail to properly register and investigate complaints about acts of violence and discrimination against members of scheduled castes and scheduled tribes, the high

percentage of acquittals and the low conviction rate in cases registered under the Scheduled Castes and Scheduled tribes (Prevention of Atrocities) Act (1989), and the alarming backlog of atrocities cases pending in the courts. (art. 6)

The Committee urges the State party to ensure that members of scheduled castes and scheduled and other tribes who are victims of acts of violence and discrimination have access to effective remedies and, to that effect, encourage victims and witnesses to report such acts and protect them from acts of retaliation and discrimination; ensure that complaints under the Scheduled Castes and Scheduled tribes (Prevention of Atrocities) Act (1989) and other criminal law provisions are properly registered and investigated, perpetrators prosecuted and sentenced and victims compensated and rehabilitated; and establish and make operational special courts trying atrocity cases as well as committees monitoring the implementation of the Scheduled Castes and Scheduled tribes (Prevention of Atrocities) Act in all States and districts, as mandated by the Act. In this regard, the State party is invited to include in its next periodic report information on the number and nature of complaints registered, the convictions and sentences imposed on perpetrators, and the remedies and assistance provided to victims of such acts.

27. The Committee notes with concern that caste bias as well as racial and ethnic prejudice and stereotypes are still deeply entrenched in the minds of wide segments of Indian society, particularly in rural areas. (art. 7)

The Committee recommends that the State party strengthen its efforts to eradicate the social acceptance of caste-based discrimination and racial and ethnic prejudice, e.g. by intensifying public education and awareness-raising campaigns, incorporating educational objectives of inter-caste tolerance and respect for other ethnicities, as well as instruction on the culture of scheduled castes and scheduled and other tribes, in the National Curriculum Framework, and ensuring adequate media representation of issues concerning scheduled castes, tribes and ethnic minorities, with a view to achieving true social cohesion among all ethnic groups, castes and tribes of India.

The Government of India is requested to submit its next periodic reports to CERD before 4 January 2012.

* * *

CERD Concluding Observations: India 1996

Committee for the Elimination of All Forms of Racial Discrimination (CERD) after examining India's periodic report in 1996 made very prominent observations regarding the coverage of caste discrimination issues under article 1(1) of the International Convention for the Elimination of All Forms of Racial Discrimination (ICERD). It thus observed (CERD/C/304/Add.13)

2. The Committee expresses its appreciation for the opportunity to resume its dialogue with the State party on the basis of its tenth to fourteenth periodic reports. It regrets the brevity of the report, all the more so since 10 years have passed since

the previous report was submitted. It also regrets that the report does not provide concrete information on the implementation of the Convention in practice; it furthermore regrets that the report and the delegation claim that the situation of the scheduled castes and scheduled tribes does not fall within the scope of the Convention.

4. It is noted that India is a large multi-ethnic and multicultural society. It is also noted that the extreme poverty of certain groups in the population, the system of castes and the climate of violence in certain parts of the country are among the factors which impede the full implementation of the Convention by the State party.

5. The leading role played by India in the struggle against racial discrimination and apartheid at the international level is welcomed by the Committee. The Committee also acknowledges the far-reaching measures adopted by the Government to combat discrimination against members of scheduled castes and scheduled tribes.

10. Articles 15 (i) and 15 (ii) of the Constitution of India, prohibiting all forms of discrimination by the State and its agents, or between individuals, including discrimination based on race and castes, as well as article 153, paragraphs (a) and (b), and article 505 of the Penal Code, which prohibit actions that promote disharmony, hatred, feelings of enmity and ill-will on grounds of race or religion, are found to be mainly in conformity with article 2, paragraph 1, of the Convention.

14. Noting the declaration in paragraph 7 of the report, reiterated in the oral presentation, the Committee states that the term "descent" mentioned in article 1 of the Convention does not solely refer to race. The Committee affirms that the situation of the scheduled castes and scheduled tribes falls within the scope of the Convention. It emphasizes its great concern that within the discussion of the report, there was no inclination on the side of the State party to reconsider its position.

18. It is regretted that no information has been provided to the Committee on the effective implementation of the penal provisions referred to in paragraph 10 above. In this regard, concern is expressed at numerous reports of acts of discrimination based on race, colour, descent or national or ethnic origin, although it was stated that no such case has yet been brought before the courts; this leads the Committee to wonder whether individuals are sufficiently informed about their rights.

23. It is noted that although constitutional provisions and legal texts exist to abolish untouchability and to protect the members of the scheduled castes and tribes, and although social and educational policies have been adopted to improve the situation of members of scheduled castes and tribes and to protect them from abuses, widespread discrimination against them and the relative impunity of those who abuse them point to the limited effect of these measures. The Committee is particularly concerned at reports that people belonging to the scheduled castes and tribes are often prevented from using public wells or from entering cafés or restaurants and that their children are sometimes separated from other children in schools, in violation of article 5 (f) of the Convention.

25. Although it is noted that the Supreme Court and the high courts have the jurisdiction to award compensation to victims of human rights violations, including in the field of racial discrimination, concern is expressed that there exists no specific statute providing for the right of individuals to seek from the courts just and

adequate reparation or satisfaction for any damage suffered as a result of acts of racial discrimination, as required by article 6 of the Convention.

26. The Committee recommends that the State party continue and strengthen its efforts to improve the effectiveness of measures aimed at guaranteeing to all groups of the population, and especially to the members of the scheduled castes and scheduled tribes, the full enjoyment of their civil, cultural, economic, political and social rights, as mentioned in article 5 of the Convention. In this regard, the Committee recommends that the next report to be submitted by the State party contain full and detailed information on the legislative aspects and the concrete implementation of the Directive Principles of the State Policy of the Constitution.

27. The Committee recommends that special measures be taken by the authorities to prevent acts of discrimination towards persons belonging to the scheduled castes and scheduled tribes, and, in cases where such acts have been committed, to conduct thorough investigations, to punish those found responsible and to provide just and adequate reparation to the victims. In this regard, the Committee particularly stresses the importance of the equal enjoyment by members of these groups of the rights to access to health care, education, work and public places and services, including wells, cafés or restaurants.

29. The Committee recommends that the next periodic report of the State party include information on the powers and functions, as well as on their effective implementation, of the National Commission on Scheduled Castes and Scheduled tribes and of the National Commission on Minorities.

30. The Committee also recommends that the Government provide in its next periodic report information, including the number of complaints lodged and sentences passed, about the implementation in practice of the legal provisions prohibiting acts of racial discrimination and organizations which promote and incite racial discrimination, in accordance with articles 2 and 4 of the Convention.

31. The Committee recommends a continuing campaign to educate the Indian population on human rights, in line with the Constitution of India and with universal human rights instruments, including the International Convention on the Elimination of All Forms of Racial Discrimination. This should be aimed at eliminating the institutionalized thinking of the high-caste and low-caste mentality.

32. The Committee reaffirms that the provisions of article 6 of the Convention are mandatory and that the Government of India should adopt legal provisions making it easier for individuals to seek from the courts just and adequate reparation or satisfaction for any damage suffered as a result of acts of racial discrimination, including acts of discrimination based on belonging to a caste or a tribe.

The Committee recommends that the State party's next periodic report, due on 4 January1998, be a comprehensive report and that it address all the points raised in these concluding observations.

* * *

CESCR Concluding Observations: India 2008

E/C.12/IND/CO/5

13. The Committee is deeply concerned that in spite of the Constitutional guarantee of non-discrimination as well as the criminal law provisions punishing acts of discrimination, widespread and often socially accepted discrimination, harassment and/or violence persist against members of certain disadvantaged and marginalized groups, including women, scheduled castes and scheduled tribes, indigenous peoples, the urban poor, informal sector workers, internally displaced persons, religious minorities such as the Muslim population, persons with disabilities and persons living with HIV/AIDS. The Committee is also concerned about the obstacles faced by the victims in accessing justice, including the high costs of litigation, the long delays in court proceedings and the non-implementation of court decisions by government authorities.

14. The Committee notes with concern the lack of progress achieved by the State party in combating the persistent de facto caste-based discrimination that continues to prevail in spite of the legal prohibitions in place, most notably the 1989 Scheduled Castes and Scheduled Tribes (Prevention of Atrocities) Act. The Committee is particularly concerned at the low rate of prosecution of crimes against persons belonging to scheduled castes and scheduled tribes, and that discriminatory attitudes and prejudices in the enforcement of the law, especially by the police, is a serious obstacle in the victims' access to justice.

27. The Committee notes with concern that trafficking in persons remains a serious problem faced by the State party. The Committee is particularly concerned that women and children belonging to scheduled castes and scheduled tribes make up a large proportion of victims of trafficking and sexual exploitation. The Committee is also concerned that victims of trafficking and sexual exploitation, rather than being afforded protection and rehabilitation, are prosecuted under the Immoral Trafficking Prevention Act (ITPA), and that there is no legislation that specifically criminalizes trafficking in persons.

31. The Committee, while noting that the draft resettlement and rehabilitation bill is currently before Parliament, remains deeply concerned about the reports of displacement and forced evictions in the context of land acquisition by private and state actors for the purposes of development projects, including constructions of dams and mining, and that the members of disadvantaged and marginalized groups, in particular, the scheduled castes and scheduled tribes, are adversely affected by such displacement from their homes, lands and their sources of livelihood. The Committee is also concerned that urban renewal projects, sporting events, infrastructure expansion, environmental projects and more recently, the designation of large areas as tax-free special economic zones, have resulted in the displacement of millions of families, most of whom have not received adequate compensation and rehabilitation. Furthermore, the Committee is concerned about the lack of effective consultations and legal redress for persons affected by displacement and by forced evictions, and the inadequate measures to provide sufficient compensation or

alternative housing to those who have been removed from their homes and/or their ancestral lands.

40. The Committee is concerned that, despite the efforts made by the State party to achieve universal primary education, including the adoption of the Constitution (86th Amendment) Act in 2002 which makes the right to primary education a fundamental right, and the Sarva Shiksha Abhiyan (Education for All) programme, aimed at achieving 100 per cent primary enrolment, the wide disparity in enrolment and dropout rates in primary schools continue to persist, negatively affecting, in particular, girls, Muslim children and children belonging to scheduled castes and scheduled tribes.

51. The Committee requests the State party to submit, in its next periodic report, updated annually collected comparative data disaggregated by sex, age, caste, ethnicity, religion and by region, regarding all the provisions in the Covenant, paying particular attention to the disadvantaged and marginalized individuals and groups. The Committee also requests the State party to include, in its next periodic report, annual comparative data, disaggregated by sex, age, caste, ethnicity, religion and by region, the percentage of the gross domestic product allotted for education, health and housing programmes in the country.

53. The Committee stresses the need for a determined enforcement of the criminal justice system, and recommends that the State party strengthen procedures for prompt and impartial investigations and effective prosecutions of all allegations of violations under the 1989 Scheduled Castes and Scheduled tribes (Prevention of Atrocities) Act. The Committee also recommends that the State party improve awareness-raising and training programmes regarding the treatment of caste-based and other crimes related to discriminatory attitudes and prejudices, for professionals engaged in the administration of justice including judges, public prosecutors, lawyers and law enforcement officials, in particular members of the police, and remove any other existing obstacles faced by victims in accessing justice. The Committee further encourages the State party to expand throughout the State, preventive programmes to curb violence against persons belonging to scheduled castes and scheduled tribes, especially women.

68. The Committee recommends that the State party, in the context of the Eleventh Plan (2007-12), take urgent measures to address the issue of poverty and food insecurity. In this regard, the Committee recommends that the State party review its national poverty threshold, taking into account its Statement on Poverty and the International Covenant on Economic, Social and Cultural Rights, adopted on 4 May 2001 (E/2002/22- E/C.12/2001/17, annex VII) and establish specific mechanisms to monitor the implementation of poverty-reduction strategies and evaluate the progress achieved. The Committee requests the State party to provide, in its next periodic report, detailed annual data on the incidence and depth of poverty, disaggregated by gender, caste, ethnicity and by region.

70. The Committee urges the State party to address the acute shortage of affordable housing by adopting a national strategy and a plan of action on adequate housing and by building or providing low-cost rental housing units, especially for the disadvantaged and low income groups, including those living in slums. In this

connection, the Committee reminds the State party of its obligations under article 11 of the Covenant and refers to its general comment No. 4 (1991) on the right to adequate housing to guide the Government's housing policies. The Committee also requests the State party to provide, in its next periodic report, detailed information on homelessness in the State party and the extent of inadequate housing, disaggregated by, inter alia, sex, caste, ethnicity and religion.

The State party is requested to submit its sixth periodic report by 30 June 2011.

* * *

CEDAW Concluding Observations: 2014 India

CEDAW/C/IND/4-5

10. The Committee notes the State party's efforts to enact a legal framework to prevent and respond to violence against women, including women from the marginalized castes and communities, such as Dalit and Adivasi women, and the establishment in 2013 of the Justice Verma Committee on Amendments to Criminal Law to review existing normative gaps. The Committee is concerned, however, about the:

(a) Stark increase in violent crimes against women, especially rape and abduction, and the high number of cases of rape reported by the National Crime Records Bureau in 2012, indicating an increase by 902.1 per cent since 1971, and continuing impunity for such acts;

(b) Retention in the Penal Code of an exemption from punishment when a rape is committed by the victim's husband if the wife is above 15 years of age;

(c) Escalation of caste-based violence, including rape, against women and girls and the downplaying by key State officials of the grave criminal nature of sexual violence against women and girls;

(d) Poor implementation of the Scheduled Castes and the Scheduled Tribes (Prevention of Atrocities) Act and the impunity of perpetrators of serious crimes against women;

(e) High number of dowry-related deaths since 2008;

(f) Persistence of so-called "honour crimes" perpetrated by family members against women and girls;

(g) Declining girl child sex ratio from 962 per 1,000 in 1981 to 914 per 1,000 in 2011;

(h) Criminalization of same-sex relationships, as referred to in the ruling of the Supreme Court (*Suresh Kumar Koushal and another v. NAZ Foundation, 2013*);

(i) Increasing number of acid attacks against women since 2002, the underreporting of such crimes notwithstanding.

18. The Committee is concerned that the State party may not have full understanding of the purpose of temporary special measures in accordance with article 4 (1) of the Convention and the Committee's general recommendation No. 25 on the subject. It is also concerned that no temporary special measures have been or are

being applied as part of a necessary strategy to accelerate the achievement of substantive equality of women and men in areas in which women are disadvantaged, such as education or in the judiciary, and for promoting the participation of women from religious minorities and scheduled castes and scheduled tribes in various areas under the Convention.

20. The Committee notes with concern that the State party has maintained its declarations regarding articles 5 (a) and 16 (1) and (2) of the Convention and reiterates its view that this is incompatible with the State party's constitutional guarantees of equality and non-discrimination. It is also concerned at the persistence of patriarchal attitudes and deep-rooted stereotypes entrenched in the social, cultural, economic and political institutions and structures of Indian society and in the media that discriminate against women. It is further concerned about the persistence of harmful traditional practices in the State party, such as child marriage, the dowry system, so-called "honour killings", sex-selective abortion, sati, Devadasi and accusing women of witchcraft. The Committee is particularly concerned that the State party has not taken sufficient sustained and systematic action to modify or eliminate stereotypes and harmful practices.

Women from Scheduled Castes and Scheduled Tribes

34. The Committee is concerned that Dalit women and women from scheduled tribes face multiple barriers in gaining access to justice, owing to legal illiteracy, lack of awareness of their rights and limited accessibility of legal aid. It notes with concern the financial, cultural and physical barriers faced by Dalit women and women from scheduled tribes in gaining access to gynaecological and maternal health services, their limited knowledge of birth registration procedures and the existence of bureaucratic obstacles and financial barriers that prevent them from registering births and obtaining birth certificates for their children.

35. *The Committee recommends that the State party:*

(a) Monitor the availability and efficiency of the legal services authorities, implement legal literacy programmes, raise the awareness of Dalit women and women and girls from scheduled tribes of all legal remedies available to them and monitor the results of such efforts;

(b) Strengthen public awareness-raising campaigns and take specific measures to ensure that Dalit women and women from scheduled tribes are aware of the procedures for registering births and obtaining birth certificates and ensure their access to those facilities;

(c) Provide training to medical and health professionals in order to ensure that Dalit women and women from scheduled tribes are attended by trained health-care personnel.

49. The Committee invites the State party to submit its sixth periodic report in July 2018.

CEDAW Concluding Comments: India 2007

CEDAW/C/IND/CO/3

8. The Committee is concerned that the State party has not taken adequate steps to implement the recommendations in regard to some concerns raised in the Committee's previous concluding comments adopted in 2000. In particular, the Committee finds that its recommendations in paragraphs 67 (to introduce a sex discrimination act in order to make the standards of the Convention applicable to non-State action and inaction), 70 (to develop a national plan of action to address the issue of gender-based violence in a holistic manner), 75 (to enforce laws preventing discrimination against Dalit women) and 81 (to take affirmative action to increase women's participation in the judiciary) have been insufficiently addressed. The Committee is also concerned that it has not been provided with any information on the report of the committee established to review the Armed Forces Special Powers Act in response to its previous concluding comments.

14. The Committee regrets that the report does not provide sufficient statistical data, disaggregated by sex, caste, minority status and ethnicity, on the practical realization of equality between women and men in all areas covered by the Convention and does not provide information on the impact of, and results achieved by, various legal and policy measures described in the report.

15. The Committee requests the State party to set benchmarks and to include adequate, appropriate and comparative statistical data and analysis, disaggregated by sex, caste, minority status and ethnicity, in its next report so as to provide a full picture of the implementation of all the provisions of the Convention and trends over time in the practical realization of equality between women and men. In particular, it calls upon the State party to review and monitor the fulfilment of the provisions of the Convention in respect of scheduled caste, scheduled tribe, backward class and minority women in all sectors. It also recommends that the State party regularly conduct impact assessments of its legislative reforms, policies and programmes to ensure that measures taken lead to the desired goals and that it inform the Committee about the results of these assessments in its next periodic report.

19. The Committee urges the State party to provide free legal services to poor and marginalized women in rural and tribal areas in addition to urban areas and to monitor the quality and impact of such services in regard to ensuring women's access to justice. It requests the State party to provide information about access of women, including scheduled caste, scheduled tribe, backward class and minority women, to free legal services and the scope and effectiveness of such services in its next periodic report.

21. The Committee calls upon the State party to develop, in consultation with women's groups, a coordinated and comprehensive plan to combat all forms of violence against women taking a life cycle approach. It urges the State party to take steps in partnership with states and union territories to fully and consistently implement and enforce the Domestic Violence Act and to ensure that all women victims of domestic violence, including scheduled caste, scheduled tribe, backward class

and minority women, are able to benefit from the legislative framework and support systems in place and that perpetrators are effectively prosecuted under the Penal Code and adequately punished. It recommends that public officials, especially law enforcement officials, the judiciary, health-care providers and social workers, are fully sensitized to all forms of violence against women, including domestic violence. It requests that adequate statistics on all forms of violence against women be collected in a consistent manner. In particular, it requests the State party to provide information, disaggregated by caste, minority status and ethnicity, in its next periodic report, on the number of cases of domestic violence reported to the police and other relevant authorities, the number of protection and other orders granted under the Domestic Violence Act and the number of convictions of perpetrators of domestic violence under the Penal Code.

28. The Committee is concerned about the ongoing atrocities committed against Dalit women and the culture of impunity for perpetrators of such atrocities. The Committee is concerned that, despite a law banning manual scavenging, this degrading practice continues with grave implications for the dignity and health of the Dalit women who are engaged in this activity.

29. The Committee recommends that the State party put in place a mechanism to monitor effective enforcement of the Scheduled Castes and Scheduled Tribes Prevention of Atrocities Act in order to ensure accountability and end impunity for crimes committed against Dalit women. It calls upon the State party to increase Dalit women's legal literacy and improve their access to justice in bringing claims of discrimination and violation of rights. It requests the State party to report specifically on the impact of such initiatives in its next periodic report. The Committee also urges the State party to study the health implications of manual scavenging on Dalits engaged in this profession and on the community as a whole, and to address all the impediments to eradicating this practice, including by putting in place modern sanitation facilities and providing the Dalit women engaged in this practice with vocational training and alternative means of livelihood.

32. While appreciating the additional data provided by the State party during its dialogue with the Committee, which indicates improvements in enrolment rates of women in primary education, and while commending the State party's future plans of focusing efforts on education of marginalized sections of the population, the Committee is concerned about the continuing disparities in the educational status of scheduled caste, scheduled tribe and Muslim women and the limited access of these groups of women to higher education. It is also concerned about the educational performance disparities among regions and states, the continuing gap in literacy rates between men and women and the lack of information on the budgetary allocation to adult literacy programmes.

33. The Committee recommends that the State party provide, in its next periodic report, comparable data disaggregated by sex, caste, minority status and ethnicity, on the enrolment and retention rates of girls and women at all levels of education and trends over time. Given the particularly disadvantaged situation of Muslim women and girls, the Committee requests the State party to provide information in its next periodic report about the action taken on the recommendations of the Sachar

Committee with regard to the education of Muslim women and girls. It urges the State party to increase efforts to enable scheduled caste, scheduled tribe and Muslim women to access higher education. The Committee calls upon the State party to strengthen its efforts, at the national, state and union territory levels, to close the gap in literacy rates between men and women, establish benchmarks in this regard and create mechanisms to monitor the achievement of such benchmarks. It also urges the State party to provide, in its next periodic report, information on the budgetary allocation to adult education programmes and the impact, and trends over time, of such programmes. Moreover, it calls upon the State party to meet its commitment of allocating 6 per cent of its gross domestic product to education in its eleventh five-year plan.

37. The Committee calls upon the State party to ensure that rural women benefit de facto from the National Rural Employment Guarantee Act, 2005. It requests the State party to provide data disaggregated by sex, caste, minority status and ethnicity of the beneficiaries under this Act. The Committee recommends that the State party take proactive measures to bring financial institutions on board with the agenda of development and empowerment of women through issuance of microcredit. It urges the State party to establish, after consultation with women's groups, appropriate mechanisms to regulate the functioning of microcredit finance institutions that protect interests of poor women. The Committee also urges the State party to establish programmes, with goals and timelines, to issue credit to poor women who are not able to participate in the self-help groups and do not otherwise have access to credit.

75. The Committee urges the Government to enforce laws preventing discrimination against Dalit women and prohibiting the Devadasi system. It urges the Government to introduce affirmative action programmes in such areas as education, employment and health so as to provide life chances to Dalit women and girls and create an environment conducive to their progress. The Committee calls upon the Government to set a time-frame for those interventions and provide information on the progress made in the next report.

The Committee requests the State party to respond to the concerns expressed in the present concluding comments in its next periodic report under article 18 of the Convention. It invites the State party to submit its fourth periodic report, which was due in August 2006, and its fifth periodic report, which is due in August 2010, in a combined report in 2010.

* * *

CEDAW Concluding Comments: India 2000

A/55/38

74. The Committee is concerned with the continuing discrimination, including violence, suffered by women of the Dalit community, despite the passage of the Scheduled Castes and Scheduled Tribes (prevention of atrocities) Act of 1989.

75. The Committee urges the Government to enforce laws preventing discrimination against Dalit women and prohibiting the Devadasi system. It urges the Government to introduce affirmative action programmes in such areas as education, employment and health so as to provide life chances to Dalit women and girls and create an environment conducive to their progress. The Committee calls upon the Government to set a time-frame for those interventions and provide information on the progress made in the next report.

* * *

CRC Concluding Observations: 2014 India

CRC/C/IND/CO/3-4

31. The Committee is concerned at the disparity among different groups of children in access to education, health care, safe water and sanitation and other social services and to the enjoyment of the rights enshrined in the Convention. It is also concerned at the persisting discrimination against children from scheduled castes and scheduled tribes, children with disabilities, children with HIV/AIDS, as well as asylum-seeking and refugee children.

32. *The Committee recommends that the State party:*

(a) Adopt and implement a comprehensive strategy to address all forms of discrimination, including multiple forms of discrimination, against all categories of children in marginalized and disadvantaged situations and ensure adequate human, financial and technical resources to implement it in collaboration with a wide range of stakeholders and involving all sectors of society, with a view to facilitating social and cultural change;

(b) Ensure that children in marginalized or disadvantaged situations, such as children from scheduled castes and scheduled tribes, children with disabilities, children with HIV/AIDS, and asylum-seeking and refugee children, have access to basic services and enjoy their rights under the Convention, and to that end, adopt adequate programmes and assess their results.

71. The Committee welcomes the adoption of the Right of Children to Free and Compulsory Education Act, 2009, and the almost-universal enrolment rate of children in Grade 1. However, it is concerned at the high drop-out rates, in particular among children from the scheduled castes and scheduled tribes and girls. The Committee is also concerned about the large number of children who are not in school, the high drop-out rates at Grade 5, poor numeracy and literacy skills, the low quality of education, as well as the shortage of qualified teachers and classrooms.

72. *The Committee recommends that the State party:*

(a) Strengthen its efforts to fully implement the Right of Children to Free and Compulsory Education Act, 2009, at the federal and state levels, including by, inter alia, drawing up development plans for schools, in compliance with the Act;

(b) Take the necessary measures to improve the quality of education and provide adequate training for teachers, in particular at the state level and in rural areas;
(c) Introduce child rights education in the school curricula nationwide;
(d) Address various discriminatory practices in the education setting, such as forcing children in marginalized situations to sit at the back of the classroom;
(e) Improve preparedness for schooling and expansion of programmes on early childhood education;
(f) Further adopt specific programmes aimed at decreasing the high dropout rates and ensure that out-of-school children, child labourers, children in disadvantaged and marginalized situations, as well as girls, are supported and assisted in exercising their right to education;
(g) Improve data and information systems to track out-of-school children, measure quality and learning outcomes and correlate education and child protection data for effective planning and response;
(h) Take measures to increase access by adolescents to secondary education, and develop and promote quality vocational training for children who have dropped out of school to enhance the skills of children.

Children Belonging to Religious Minorities, Scheduled Castes and Scheduled Tribes

79. The Committee is seriously concerned that, despite the State party's initiatives aimed at addressing inequalities and improving living conditions and access to education, health and social services of religious minorities, scheduled castes and scheduled tribes, many children belonging to these groups continue to be deprived of a number of their rights under the Convention.

80. The Committee urges the State party to strengthen its efforts to ensure that all children, irrespective of their religious background or whether they are from a scheduled caste or scheduled tribe, enjoy the entire range of rights enshrined in the Convention.

92. The Committee invites the State party to submit its combined fifth and sixth periodic reports by 15 July 2020 and to include therein information on the follow-up to the present concluding observations.

* * *

CRC Concluding Observations: India 2004

CRC/C/15/ADD.228

22. The Committee recommends that the State party develop a system of data collection and indicators consistent with the Convention and disaggregated by

gender, age, social status (Scheduled Castes and Tribes, or religious community), and urban and rural area and make it publicly available. This system should cover all children up to the age of 18 with specific emphasis on those who are particularly vulnerable. It further encourages the State party to use these indicators and data for the formulation of policies and programmes for the effective implementation of the Convention. The Committee recommends that the State party seek technical assistance from UNICEF, UNDP and UNFPA, among others.

25. In light of article 2 of the Convention, the Committee is deeply concerned at the widely disparate levels of enjoyment of the rights in the Convention by girls, children living in certain states, rural areas and slums, and children belonging to certain castes and tribal and indigenous groups.

27. The Committee is deeply concerned at persistent and significant social discrimination against children belonging to Scheduled Castes and Tribes and other tribal groups, reflected, inter alia, by the many violations of the 1989 Scheduled Castes and Scheduled Tribes (Prevention of Atrocities) Act, the low number of such violations dealt with by the courts, and the fact that a majority of the states have failed to set up the special courts provided for under this Act.

28. The Committee recommends that the State party, in accordance with article 17 of its Constitution and article 2 of the Convention, take all necessary steps to abolish the discriminatory practice of untouchability, prevent caste- and tribe-motivated abuse, and prosecute State and private actors who are responsible for such practices or abuses. Moreover, in compliance with article 46 of the Constitution, the State party is encouraged to implement, inter alia, special measures to advance and protect these groups. The Committee recommends the full implementation of the 1989 Scheduled Castes and Scheduled Tribes (Prevention of Atrocities) Act, the 1995 Scheduled Castes and Scheduled tribes Rules (Prevention of Atrocities) and the Employment of Manual Scavengers and Construction of Dry Latrines (Prohibition) Act, 1993. The Committee encourages the State party to continue its efforts to carry out comprehensive public education campaigns to prevent and combat caste-based discrimination with a view to changing social attitudes, by involving, inter alia, religious leaders.

32. The Committee recommends that all existing and future special temporary programmes be provided with specified goals and timetables, in order to evaluate their success and justify their continuation, expansion and dissemination. The Committee further recommends that the State party start to develop special programmes for the allocation of educational and other benefits that are based on the child's needs and rights rather than on the basis of sex, caste or tribe, or any other characteristic that may result in unjustifiable discrimination.

65. The Committee recommends that the State party:

(a) Improve the education system with a view to achieving the aims mentioned in article 29, paragraph 1 of the Convention and the Committee's general comment No. 1 on the aims of education, and introduce human rights, including children's rights, into the school curricula;

(b) Strengthen its efforts to progressively ensure that that all girls and boys, in urban, rural and least developed areas and children belonging to Scheduled Castes and Tribes, have equal access to educational opportunities;
(c) Raise awareness of the importance of early childhood education and introduce it into the general framework of education;
(d) Encourage the participation of children at all levels of school life;
(e) Take the necessary measures to improve the quality of education and to ensure better efficiency in the management of education, including by decreasing the dropout rate;
(f) Hire more qualified teachers and provide them with more opportunities for training;
(g) Take all necessary measures to curb teachers' absenteeism;
(h) Build better infrastructure for schools; and
(i) Seek assistance from UNICEF and UNESCO.

The State party should submit its next 3rd and 4th periodic reports on 10 July 2008. The dates for the examination of India before the CRC has not yet been scheduled, but is expected to take place in 2010 or 2011.

* * *

CRC Concluding Observations: India 2000

CRC/C/15/ADD.115

28. In the light of article 2 of the Convention, the Committee is deeply concerned at the widely disparate levels of enjoyment of the rights in the Convention by children living in different states, living in rural areas, living in slums and belonging to different castes, tribal and indigenous groups.

30. In the light of article 2 of the Convention, the Committee is concerned at the existence of caste-based discrimination and discrimination against tribal groups, despite these practices being prohibited under the law.

31. In accordance with article 17 of the Constitution and article 2 of the Convention, the Committee recommends that the State party take steps to ensure states abolish the discriminatory practice of untouchability, prevent caste- and tribe-motivated abuse, and prosecute State and private actors who are responsible for such practices or abuses. Moreover, in compliance with article 46 of the Constitution, the State party is encouraged to implement, inter alia, affirmative measures to advance and protect these groups. The Committee recommends the full implementation of the 1989 Scheduled Castes and Scheduled Tribes (Prevention of Atrocities) Act, the 1995 Scheduled Castes and Scheduled tribes Rules (Prevention of Atrocities) and the 1993 Employment of Manual Scavengers Act. The Committee encourages the State party to continue its efforts to carry out comprehensive public education campaigns to prevent and combat caste-based discrimination. In line with the Committee on the Elimination of Racial Discrimination (CERD/C/304/Add.13),

the Committee stresses the importance of the equal enjoyment by members of these groups of the rights in the Convention, including access to health care, education, work, and public places and services, such as wells.

56. Welcoming the 83rd Constitutional Amendment Bill concerning the fundamental right to education, the Committee, however, expresses its concern at the prevailing poor situation in the State party with respect to education, which is characterized by a general lack of infrastructure, facilities and equipment, insufficient numbers of qualified teachers and a drastic shortage of text books and other relevant learning materials. There is serious concern regarding the striking disparities in terms of access to education, attendance at primary and secondary levels and dropout rates between: different states, rural and urban areas, boys and girls, the affluent and poor, and children belonging to scheduled castes and tribes. The Committee emphasizes the importance of focusing attention on improving the provision and quality of education, especially in view of its potential benefit for addressing various concerns, including the situation of girls and reducing the incidence of child labour.

66. The Committee encourages the State party to withdraw its declaration with respect to article 32 of the Convention, as it is unnecessary in the light of the efforts the State party is making to address child labour. The Committee recommends that the State party ensure the full implementation of the 1986 Child Labour (Prohibition and Regulation) Act, the 1976 Bonded labour (System Abolition) Act and the 1993 Employment of Manual Scavengers Act.

74. The Committee notes the Plan of Action to Combat Trafficking and Commercial Sexual Exploitation of Women and Children. However, in view of the scale of the problem, the Committee is concerned about the sexual abuse and exploitation of children especially those belonging to the lower castes and from poor urban and rural areas, in the contexts of: religious and traditional culture; child domestic workers; children living and/or working on the streets; communal violence and ethnic conflict; abuse by the security forces in areas of conflict, such as Jammu and Kashmir, and the north-eastern states; and trafficking and commercial exploitation, especially girls from neighbouring countries, particularly Nepal. It is also concerned about the absence of adequate measures to combat this phenomenon and the lack of adequate rehabilitation measures.

75. The Committee recommends that the State party ensure that legislation criminalizes the sexual exploitation of children and penalizes all the offenders involved, whether local or foreign, while ensuring that the child victims of this practice are not penalized. While noting that Devadasi, or ritual prostitution, is prohibited under the law, the Committee recommends that the State party takes all necessary measures to eradicate this practice. In order to combat trafficking in children, including for commercial sexual purposes, the Penal Code should contain provisions against kidnapping and abduction. The Committee recommends that the State party ensure that laws concerning the sexual exploitation of children are gender neutral; provide civil remedies in the event of violations; ensure that procedures are simplified so that responses are appropriate, timely, child-friendly and sensitive to victims;

include provisions to protect from discrimination and reprisals those who expose violations; and vigorously pursue enforcement.

* * *

CCPR Concluding Observation: India 2024

CCPR/C/IND/CO/4

The Committee considered the fourth periodic report of India at its 4134th and 4135th meetings held on July 15 and 16, 2024. At its 4144th meeting held on July 22, 2024, it adopted the Concluding Observations for India.

15. While the Committee appreciates the constitutional and legal measures adopted to prevent, protect and address discrimination and violence against "Scheduled Castes" and "Scheduled Tribes", such as the Scheduled Castes and Scheduled Tribes (Prevention of Atrocities) Act, 1989, it is concerned by reports indicting systemic challenges to the implementation of these measures, such as delayed registration of "first information report" (FIRs), inadequate police investigations, lengthy trials and non-compliance with the mandate of 60 day case disposal requirement. The Committee remains concerned by multiple reports about widespread discrimination and violence against these groups, including lynching, mob violence, displacement, as well as attacks on Adivasis for practicing Christianity and vigilante lynching of Muslims. The Committee is further concerned by non-extension of scheduled caste status and reservation benefits for Dalits who converted to Islam and Christianity. The Committee acknowledges the State Party's efforts to prevent manual scavenging, including through the Prohibition of Employment as Manual Scavengers and their Rehabilitation Act, 2013, however, the Committee has information that this is not effectively enforced, and the practice continues in several regions, including by local governments (arts. 2 and 26).

16. The State Party should ensure that everyone can enjoy the human rights enshrined in the Covenant without discrimination, in particular, it should:

a. Strengthen the implementation, monitoring and enforcement of its legal and policy framework to prevent and address discrimination and violence against "Scheduled Castes" and "Scheduled Tribes", as well as the Dalits and the other so-called backward classes and national minorities, in particular by timely registration of first information reports, effective police investigations, reducing delay in judicial proceedings and complying with 60-day case disposal requirement.
b. Ensure that all allegations of discrimination and violence against "Scheduled Castes" and "Scheduled Tribes", Dalits and the other so-called backward classes and other ethnic and national minorities and Dalits converted to Islam or Christianity are promptly, impartially and effectively investigated, that perpetrators are prosecuted, and, if convicted, punished with penalties commensurate with the gravity of the offences and victims are provided with full reparation and means of protection;

c. Consider amending legislation to ensure that Dalits, Muslims and Christians enjoy adequate protection against discrimination and violence;
d. Effectively implement and enforce existing legal and policy framework on addressing manual scavenging, in particular regarding local governments and municipalities, and provide adequate financial resources for rehabilitation.

CCPR Concluding Observations: India 2000

CCPR/C/79/Add.81

5. It notes, moreover, that the size of the country, its huge population, the massive poverty and the great disparities in the distribution of wealth among various social groups affect the advancement of rights. The persistence of traditional practices and customs, leading to women and girls being deprived of their rights, their human dignity and their lives, and to discrimination against members of the underprivileged classes and castes and other minorities, and ethnic, cultural and religious tensions constitute impediments to the implementation of the Covenant.

8. The Committee also welcomes the establishment of the National Commission for Scheduled Castes and Scheduled Tribes and the National Commission for Women in 1992, and the National Commission for Minorities in 1993. These commissions have initiated some improvements, in particular in the levels of education and in the representation of the various groups concerned within elected bodies and other authorities.

10. The Committee has noted that positions in elected bodies are reserved for members of scheduled castes and tribes and that a constitutional amendment has reserved one third of the seats in elected local bodies (Panchayati Raj) for women. The Committee also notes the introduction of a bill to reserve one third of the seats for women in the Federal Parliament and in state legislatures.

15. The Committee notes with concern that, despite measures taken by the Government, members of scheduled castes and scheduled tribes, as well as the so-called backward classes and ethnic and national minorities continue to endure severe social discrimination and to suffer disproportionately from many violations of their rights under the Covenant, inter alia, inter-caste violence, bonded labour and discrimination of all kinds. It regrets that the de facto perpetuation of the caste system entrenches social differences and contributes to these violations. While the Committee notes the efforts made by the State party to eradicate discrimination: it recommends that further measures be adopted, including education programmes at national and state levels, to combat all forms of discrimination against these vulnerable groups, in accordance with articles 2, paragraph 1, and 26 of the Covenant.

Index

UMAKANT, *Dalit Human Rights in India*, People, Cultures and Societies: Exploring and Documenting Diversities,
https://doi.org/10.1007/978-981-95-5751-6

L

M

N

MIX
Papier aus verantwortungsvollen Quellen
Paper from responsible sources
FSC® C105338

If you have any concerns about our products,
you can contact us on
ProductSafety@springernature.com

In case Publisher is established outside the EU,
the EU authorized representative is:
Springer Nature Customer Service Center GmbH
Europaplatz 3, 69115 Heidelberg, Germany

Printed by Libri Plureos GmbH
in Hamburg, Germany